AMERICANS AND EUROPEANS
DANCING IN THE DARK

AMERICANS AND EUROPEANS

DANCING IN THE DARK

*On Our
Differences and Affinities,
Our Interests, and
Our Habits of Life*

DENNIS L. BARK

HOOVER INSTITUTION PRESS
STANFORD UNIVERSITY
STANFORD, CALIFORNIA

FOR

France Marie Catherine Pauline
&
Dwight, Matthew, Samuel

Whichever way they cross
the Atlantic
they are going home

www.hoover.org

Hoover Institution Press Publication No. 554

First printing, 2007
14   13   12   11   10   09   08   07   9   8   7   6   5   4   3   2   1

Manufactured in the United States of America

The paper used in this publication meets the minimum requirements
of the American National Standard for Information Sciences—
Permanence of Paper for Printed Library Materials, ANSI Z39.48–1992.♾

Library of Congress Cataloging-in-Publication Data

Bark, Dennis L.
    Americans and Europeans dancing in the dark : on our differences and affinities,
our interests, and our habits of life / Dennis L. Bark.
       p.   cm.— (Hoover Institution Press publication ; no. 554)
    Includes bibliographical references and index.
    ISBN-13: 978-0-8179-4801-6 (cloth : alk. paper)
    ISBN-13: 978-0-8179-4802-3 (alk. paper)
1. National characteristics, European.   2. National characteristics, American.
3. Europe—Relations—United States.   4. United States—Relations—Europe.
I. Title.
D1055.B266   2007
303.48′24073—dc22   2007003568

Contents

Foreword   ix

Acknowledgments   xv

About the Author   xix

Introduction   1

PART ONE
Continental Contrasts

Preface   9

Chapter I: Differences   11
  The Essential Difference   11
  From the Top Down   12
  Aristocrats, Old and New   14
  From the Bottom Up   27
  The Essential Difference, Again   32

Chapter II: On History, Heritage, and Habits of Life   45
  Geography, Distance, and Space   45
  Art and Music, Language, Manners, and Habits of Life   58
  Views from the Backyard   79

PART TWO
Qualities of Life

Preface   91

Chapter III: Equality, Opportunity, Stability   93
  The European Socio-Economic Model, The American Model   93
  Socialism in Europe and America   98
  The post-1945 Political and Economic Order   109

Chapter IV: Uncommon Marketplaces   123
  The Concept of the Union   123
  When Realities Are Trump   136
  Great Expectations   149
  Competition   153

PART THREE
Freedom and Order

Preface   165

Chapter V: Legacies, Ancient and Modern   167
  The Idea and the Tree   167
  History Lessons   181

Chapter VI: The Fly in the Soup   193
  Changing Relationships   193
  Interpreting September 11, 2001   202

Chapter VII: The Force of Things   211
  Aspects of Leadership   211
  New Crossroads   219
  Obligations Written in the Heart   223

Appendix 1: A Comparative Chart of European Countries   227

Appendix 2: "An American is . . ."   231

Appendix 3: "The International"   233

Notes   235

A Selected Bibliography for Further Reading   253

Index   261

Foreword

ENNIS BARK is an unabashed Atlanticist who believes that
what Americans and Europeans have in common is far more
important than what divides them, and that as allies they have
a responsibility to provide clear and strong leadership in a world badly in
need of it.

The collapse of communist regimes in 1989–1990 gave Americans and
Europeans an unprecedented chance to do so. But during the decade of
the 1990s, while this opportunity was open to them, they ignored the
logical consequence of the end of the Cold War; namely, the obligation
to set new economic, political, and diplomatic goals to replace the common front they had maintained while the Iron Curtain divided Europe.
Instead, they remained within the comfortable confines of their respective
backyards, from which, in the wake of the terrorist attack on the World
Trade Center, they safely hurled insults at each other, thus demonstrating
aspects of leadership that were unworthy of the word.

If the twentieth century was marked by an American-European partnership of unprecedented mutual interests, and by an appreciation of
common values, and for some by a friendship made of trust, affection
and respect, this book's title suggests that the once-storied relationship is
coming apart. For many the Atlantic Divide has widened. Indeed, a great
many things have changed since the first quarter of the twentieth century
when Theodore Roosevelt invited his good friend, French ambassador
Jean-Jules Jusserand—married to an American from a New England family—to attend cabinet meetings in Washington.

These changes are the subject of the author's reflections on differences between Europeans and Americans. Bark focuses on our varied habits of life about which widespread ignorance exists in both America and in Europe. His observations are neither pro-American nor anti-European, but they are astute, and they warrant careful reading as he sets out what our differences are, where they come from, and how they affect our judgments of each other. He points out as well that Europeans think they know a great deal more about America than they really do, and conversely that Americans are blithely unaware of how little they know about Europe.

In a series of essays that describe significant differences between America and Europe, Bark sends his readers a clear and powerful message; namely, that we Europeans should pay greater attention to the values we share with America, as we did following World War II and during the first decades of European unification, until the fall of the Berlin Wall in 1989.

Europeans should cast aside our prejudices and jealousies, and especially our absurd sense of superiority that is sometimes conducive to hatred. At the same time, Americans need not inflame these tendencies by needlessly dealing with their European counterparts in an overbearing or dismissive manner, such as drawing a gratuitous distinction between "Old Europe" and "New Europe." A more respectful and nuanced approach, the norm when European elites conduct business among themselves, is very much in order and much more effective.

These latter considerations, far from new, as Bark is well aware, also concerned Jean-Jules Jusserand. He knew America well, and, in fact, served as president of the American Historical Association in 1921, and received the first Pulitzer Prize in American History in 1923. Jusserand was unusually prescient in his final letter to his American friends; a letter, virtually unknown today, that Bark cites with effect. Written late in his life and after his retirement from the French diplomatic service, he called his message, "farewell forever:"

> The sands in the hour-glass are running low; I must take leave, probably forever. May peace, prosperity, happy homes be the meed of your energy, good sense and kind hearts. When we judge each other we are not bound to applaud all that the other does, nor even to avoid expressing our blame

when there is cause; but blame must not be peppered with sarcasm and
irony; the tone should be that of the affectionate reproach to a loved
brother. . . . Remember this also, and be well persuaded of its truth: the
future is not in the hands of Fate, but in ours.

Europeans should also develop greater respect and tolerance for the history, heritage and habits of life of our oldest and most important ally,
because as Bark accurately concludes, many Americans and Europeans
who still seek a harmonious relationship, strongly endorse Edmund
Burke's conclusion drawn more than two centuries ago: "Nothing is so
strong a tie of amity between nation and nation as correspondence in law,
customs, manners and habits of life. They have more than the force of
treaties in themselves. They are obligations written in the heart."

From my Parisian perspective, much misunderstanding between
America and Europe (and especially between America and France) comes
from a decline of confidence in who we are and where we are going, but
it comes also from our failure to recognize that the idea of Europe has
little in common with the American idea of freedom. Our misjudgment
of what defines the American character also, and too often, takes the form
of unwarranted criticism such as, for example, castigation of globalization,
as though this term defines a grand American conspiracy. This approach
sometimes verges on anti-Americanism as many European leaders attack
the straw man that they derisively call the American economic model.
Americans, of course, tend to contribute, albeit inadvertently, to the shrill
temper of differences of opinion because, as a people, they are much more
direct than we are and prefer to analyze issues in terms that are often black
and white. Europeans generally take exception to this analytical approach
and are more prone to view the world's complexities in different shades
of gray.

Bark points out that the issue is not whether one American or European view of the world is better than the other. His concern is that they
are different, and that without understanding the reasons why, Americans
and Europeans lose their way in the dark, with a predictable result. In the
darkness we continue to hold one another in a fond embrace, while stepping on each other's toes and trying to lead at the same time.

Ignorance is also present on the American side (of the Atlantic), however, especially as it concerns the reasons why so much of European life is structured by rule and governance from the top down. So Bark describes the essential difference between America and Europe, one of rule from the bottom up, and rule from the top down, respectively. In particular, in an essay intended primarily for an American readership, he provides a useful historical sketch of the reasons underlying the lure of socialism in Europe—a concept of rule from the top down that traces its practice to a feudal and aristocratic past. This essay, however, is enlightening for European elites, too, many of whom consider rule from the top down— whether from the left or from the right—as the twenty-first-century incarnation of eighteenth-century enlightenment.

Here the author pointedly draws our attention to the major debate that raged during the enlargement of the European Union that continued unabated during the decade of the 1990s. It was the struggle over the proper role, size, and power of government. Initially, Americans interpreted as convergence the European adoption of what America already had: an internal market for goods, services and capital flows, a common market, a single currency (the euro) and the expansion of Europe to the east (just as the United States, much earlier, had gone west).

In the vacuum left by the end of the Cold War, however, birth of unexpected progeny has taken place. Today, we are experiencing growing disagreement among Europeans and Americans on the value of individual liberty and free marketplaces, versus the asserted safety of state control and government-mandated equality.

The fly in the soup is that there exists in Europe a contradiction between the Anglo-Saxon "ultraliberal" free-market model of the United Kingdom and America on the one hand and the centralized state and welfare dependence practiced by France and Germany on the other. Because of the economic policies followed in Ireland, that country is becoming a model of freedom and free-market forces at work, just as the governments of France and Germany maintain allegiance to an aged and statist social model that is out of step with the demands and challenges presented by globalization and rapid technological innovation.

The case of Germany is noteworthy. West Germany was reconstructed with the principles of a free-market economy long before Margaret Thatcher came to power in the U.K. in 1980, at a time when the Anglo-Saxon "ultraliberals" were socialists. The Germans, indeed, have departed completely from the Fribourg school of economic and social thought and hence, from the classically liberal economic and social model they promoted under the leadership of Konrad Adenauer and Ludwig Erhard.

Bark's judgment, as pro-American as it is pro-European, is simple and straightforward: the health of our transatlantic relationship, despite our differences and because of the values we share, is vital to us both. On both sides of the Atlantic Divide there is agreement that the world is without strong leadership. America and Europe have an obligation to provide it and we can do so much more effectively together than we can separately.

In the best of times or in the worst, we enjoy a relationship made of many things—of differences and disagreements, but also of rich histories and proud heritage. That does not mean we always admire each other, or that we always like each other, but it does mean that we have a joint and persuasive interest in the success of each other's undertakings. In principle these are not contradictory, but complementary, as Austrian Nobel laureate Friedrich Hayek defines the principle ingredients of classical liberalism: "the sacredness of truth . . . the ordinary rules of moral decency . . . a common belief in the value of human freedom . . . an affirmative action towards democracy . . . opposition to all forms of totalitarianism."

It should be self-evident that the Europeans, and especially the French and Germans, must build on their own strengths, with their own efforts. But we Europeans cannot leave it at that and bask in the glow of self-righteousness from within the European Union. America cannot act as the police of the world on its own, nor should it be expected to do so. Europe must show that it possesses the political will, the military power, and the economic strength to take an active role in preserving peace and order in a world tragically lacking in both. Without this resolve, Europe cannot play a role on the world's stage as a dependable and respected partner, and America, at risk to itself and to Europe, will become the de facto gendarme of the world without a mandate to do so.

That Europe is without leaders of real stature and conviction, and that Europe as a "union" is in disorder, cannot be denied, which is why Bark concludes his book with three essays on freedom and order. What Americans and Europeans both need is strong leaders, with the courage to define clearly where we want to go and how we want to get there. What is today especially depressing to partisans of European unity is the inability of Europe's leaders to recognize and support the strengths of free markets at a time when the state is becoming increasingly incapable of meeting the needs of a world in social, economic and political turmoil. To illustrate, Bark cites French president Jacques Chirac's simplistic assessment of free-market philosophy: "Le libéralisme, ce serait aussi désastreux que le communisme" (*Le Figaro*, March 16, 2005): "liberalism would be as disastrous as communism." What is especially telling in this assertion is the central concern underlying it: that the freedom to choose offered by free markets represents a threat to the monopoly on state power held by those European political leaders who rule from the top down, irrespective of their political persuasion.

As we are fond of saying in France, however, "the worst is not always a certainty"—*Le pire n'est pas toujours sûr*. Looking to the future many argue, on both sides of the Atlantic, that Europe should be able to make a fresh start once the present generation of leaders has retired from the political stage; that is to say, when a new generation of statesmen and -women take the reins of political and economic life in 2007 and thereafter.

Few Americans, and even fewer Europeans, have the knowledge, background and ability to write a book like this one. Dennis Bark does, and has. He identifies the differences that separate us, and provides us with reasons that should compel us to narrow the divide. In doing so he presents us with a *tour de force*. This book will delight many, and anger some, but it cannot be ignored.

Bertrand Jacquillat
Professor, Institut d'Etudes Politiques de Paris
Paris, in February 2007

Acknowledgments

THE IDEA FOR THIS BOOK comes from a series of conversations between Kurt Leube, a longtime friend from Salzburg, and me. The first one was impromptu. With the assistance of a bottle of German Gesindelsfingen Assmannshäuserrosenfahrt Spätlese 1997, it took place in front of the fireplace in the kitchen of an old Spanish-style house in which my wife and I live on the Stanford campus. Over the next year and a half Kurt and I continued to talk about America and Europe at regular intervals, usually in the afternoon over coffee at the Hoover Institution. Our conversations were never recorded, but I always took notes and later on we often referred to them.

By 2004 I had a complete manuscript in the form of eleven conversations. I also had one enthusiastic critic, who loved them. But I had a dozen more who didn't like them at all. They were too polite to say so then, but I later learned that they either became bored and didn't finish the manuscript, or they fell asleep. In all cases they said, politely, "the conversations are very interesting."

But, finally, another reader whose judgment I trusted and whom I had known for more than thirty years, called me in December 2004 and told me the truth. Hisako Matsubara, a novelist who writes in English, German and Japanese, explained, candidly, that the conversations just didn't work. She said they were heavy, stilted, and difficult to follow. She also found them tired and forced, because she couldn't tell the difference between Kurt's "voice" and my own. But she also thought the content was unusual, so she suggested that I present the conversations in a more conventional manner. I did so in the course of 2005.

The relationship between America and Europe is so intimate that it is, in fact, a kind of conversation. This is why I wanted to construct the book along those lines. I hope the current format better suits my purposes in illuminating this important topic.

The foregoing is the genesis of this book. Much of what is in it does come from my discussions with Kurt, but a good deal also comes from conversations with acquaintances carried on over a long period of time, from the moment I began my studies as a graduate student at the Freie Universität Berlin in 1966. Among them, and there are many more than those whose names are written below, are some who have traveled widely and some who have never left the country in which they were born, some who speak several languages and some who speak only their own, some who hold Ph.D. degrees and some who completed their formal educations in country schoolhouses.

Their viewpoints are as diverse as their backgrounds. Many of the observations in this book are theirs, but the focus, accents, and conclusions are all my own.

In addition to university scholars and political leaders, their professions paint a fascinating picture full of contrast, to wit: schoolteacher, novelist, shop keeper, human resources director, farmer, retirement home director, psychiatrist, investment manager, ex-communist, banker, newspaper publisher, chairman of the board of a tire company, car dealer, stock analyst, rare book expert, forester, housekeeper, photographer, book editor, real estate salesman, estate manager, picture framer, mathematician, attorney, foundation executive, automobile executive, wine maker, priest, geologist, student, minister, physician, sculptor, cabaret entertainer.

Their names appear here because they have all offered their time, in one way or another, to give me their views about the differences and affinities, the interests, and the habits of life described in this book. As individuals they are grouped together here as Americans, and as Europeans.

From America:

James W. Hodgen, William Carter, Alvin Rabushka, Deborah M.

Skelly, Robert G. Van Dine, Charles G. Schott, Allan E. Goodman, Henry N. Kuechler, Hisako Matsubara, Doyen P. McIntosh, Becky Andersen, David R. Gress, Dean A. Cortopassi, William Carter, Kirsten Buehler, Peter E. Thieriot, Hansi Rigney, Jared C. Bark, Ingrid A. Gregg, Earl I. Heenan III, Thomas A. Barclay †,[1] David B. Kennedy, Reginald and Helle Dale, Bill and Barbara Geisler,

From Europe:

Christian and Christel Hacke, Bertrand Jacquillat, Roselyn de Caudrelier-Bénac, Diemut Koestlin, Marina Eloy Jacquillat, Stephane de Chambarlhac, Hans† and Marie† Herzfeld, Charles-Antoine and Christine de Meaux, Peter and Marie-Caroline Hammerer, David Charters, Hubert Jousset, Olivier† and Thérèse† de Sugny, Burkhard and Erika Koch, Markus Kerber, Klaus and Christiane Wagner, Eric Bourdais de Charbonnière, Charles† and Eveline Jurien de la Gravière, Marie-Pierre Bouligaud, Felix and Theodora de Marez Oyens, Elisabeth Burgess, Yolande Poirier, Ghislain and Marie-Thérèse de Maigret, Margarita Mathiopoulos, Kaisa de Tristan, Georges Liebert, La famille Béal—Maurice, Noémie, Jean-Luc, Gilles et Séverine, Pauline and Louis, Daniel and Françoise Bartholoni, Roland Denis, Dolores Figueras de Wakonigg, Petr, Jája and Ondřej Čepek, Jean de Sugny†, Eberhard Hoene, Michael and Bärbel Zöller, Corneilia and Victoria Hoene, Bruno and Marie-Pierre Thiollier, Xavier de Marqueissac, Horst† and Marlene† Rühland, Henning Köhler, Jens Hacke, Jacques and Lily de Vieville, Bim and Eva Borgh, Amaury et Hélène de Chaunac, André† and Claude Bary, Peter-Carl Rühland†, Guillermo Wakonigg†, Myriam de Mandat-Grancey, Alain de Maigret, Aubert and Pamela de Villaine, Jean-Lou Nicolas†, Pater Heinz Wanke, S.J.†, Horst and Brigitte Rühland, Patrick Chamorel, Peter Bauer†, Robert Stewart Fothringham, Dietrich Mende†, Milorad Drachkovitch†, Klaus Ritter, Herbert Giersch, Gerlinde Kempendorff, Anna von Bayern, Benoît and Marie-France de Soultrait, René de Chambrun†, Kurt and Nini Leube.

A debt of thanks is owed each of them that I gladly pay with gratitude made of friendship, affection, and respect.

---

1. This symbol, †, denotes deceased.

The last two words go to the staff of the Hoover Institution Press whose expertise has played an essential role in the making of this book and to my research assistant of many years. The first goes to Jen Navarrette, Marshall Blanchard, Ann Wood, and Jennifer Presley of the Press. Each of them is an exemplary professional. The second belongs to Ulla Morris Carter, the most talented researcher I know. She can find anything; that is high and well-deserved praise. With enormous respect and gratitude to you, all.

Dennis L. Bark
St. Romain d'Urfé, France
November 2006

About the Author

WHEN I THINK ABOUT Europe and America I call often upon memories. They come from the experiences of growing up in America followed by living in Europe.

I am the eldest son of a professor of medieval history who taught at Stanford University, whose own father had come to America from Sweden in the 1870s. Like many American families in the middle of the twentieth century, my own had close ties to Europe both in the present and in the past. My parents were proud of those ties and kept them alive; they were a constant and normal part of my life.

I was twenty in June 1962 when my brother and I traveled to Europe for the first time. Although I had never been there, I had met many Europeans in America and thought I already knew the Old World. But of course I didn't, as I learned very quickly during that summer. Preoccupied with the excitement of going, I hadn't thought about the consequence of being unable to speak any European language. I was able to say *danke schön* when we arrived in Stuttgart, but I quickly realized that others didn't speak English. As we traveled throughout Germany, I recognized, finally, the importance of foreign languages, because all I could do was observe. As I think about it today it reminds me of Christopher Isherwood's Berlin diary of 1930 in which he wrote, "I am a camera with its shutter open, quite passive, recording . . ."

Wherever I looked I saw something I had never seen before, and for some unknown reason I still remember the odd shapes of doorknobs. There were also new smells, not only of food, but of wax and wood in the inns where we stayed. It was a mustiness that I was convinced smelled like

time. The rooms themselves were often oddly shaped, with uneven floors
and crooked staircases which creaked. As we walked in the villages of
southern Germany the houses, like the inns, had the dates of when they
were built chiseled into the wood above their doorways. Many of the
houses and the inns weren't quite straight either, but leaned and looked
down into the narrow, cobble-stoned streets that had been built for people, not for cars. Present, everywhere, was age. I was captivated by it, and
made mental comparisons with what I had seen in California. It wasn't
that I liked American architecture less; I didn't. But in California the
houses I was familiar with were modern, and I hadn't yet seen the picturesque towns of New England or the colonial architecture of the South.

In Germany we visited cities my parents already knew, like Dinkels-
bühl, Rothenburg ob der Tauber, and Nürnberg. I remember walking
through them in the late afternoon, in and out of the hazy shadows cast
by the golden sunlight on the stones of ancient buildings. I saw the spires
of country churches and heard their bells, and marveled at the grace and
elegance of gothic cathedrals.

On village squares there were flowers, everywhere. They were beautiful
and welcoming, but in many of those same squares I also saw a darker
side of European history. I was familiar, of course, with our cemeteries for
American veterans of foreign wars; but they were wars fought by Americans on foreign soil, and I had never thought much about it. I was unaware that in the squares of hundreds of European towns stood
monuments to the memory of those who had died in World War I and
in World War II. The Europeans, I thought, didn't seem to pay much
attention to them. But I was wrong. The monuments served as daily reminders of death and destruction, and I noticed that flags and flowers
were often placed in front of them.

By the beginning of August I had been traveling for almost two months
in what I was now calling the "Old World." I thought the phrase had a
romantic touch to it, because this old world, completely new to me, was
an adventure that gave me a sense of independence I had never felt before.
No one knew me, and wherever I went I could be whomever I wanted to
be. But, of course, it was really the euphoria of that summer's vacation of
freedom without responsibilities.

My brother and I made the most of it when we successfully persuaded our parents to let us hitchhike from Florence to Berlin. It was there, in Berlin, that my romantic image of Europe received a rude jolt, of a kind I had never anticipated.

We knew that West Berlin was protected by American, British, and French soldiers, because the three western sectors had been cut off from communist East Germany the previous year, by the Berlin Wall built in August 1961. But we had no idea what was on the other side of it. So we decided to go to East Berlin. This meant, as Americans, that we had to pass through the Allied border control point in the American Sector of West Berlin, called Checkpoint Charlie. Once on the other side, after the East German soldiers had stamped our passports and let us continue, we decided the best way to see the Soviet Sector was to get on a bus and ride it to the end of the line. So we got on the first bus we found. By the time we reached the last stop we were the only people still on it.

When we got off there wasn't a lot to see except decaying, gray apartment buildings. They had obviously been built before the war, and their facades were crumbling. We began walking across a big empty lot, when suddenly a soldier stood straight up, right in front of us, like a puppet coming out of the ground. He had been in some kind of hole and we hadn't seen him. He pointed his machine gun at us and said, *Halt*. He asked why we were there, and my brother, who spoke German, told him we were American students. The soldier told us it was forbidden to be there. He ordered us to leave, and we agreed that it was a really good idea.

It seemed to us that we waited a long, long time for the next bus to take us back on that Friday afternoon of August 17. When we got to the East Berlin side of the Wall we could hardly wait to get out of what we now knew was a dangerous place. We went into the border control office, and were told to give a soldier our passports. They disappeared through a narrow opening in the wall and we waited. The soldier told us to put our East German coins into a tin can covered in white paper with a red cross on it (we still wonder if that money really went to the Red Cross). After about fifteen minutes our passports reappeared, with no explanation, but with an exit visa stamp that took up an entire page. We were then allowed to leave, and walked out of the other end of the wooden barrack, to find ourselves looking at Checkpoint Charlie about one hundred yards away. To get there we had to walk through "No Man's Land"—a huge, empty square covered with asphalt—toward the white line on the pavement that separated east from west.

We were about half way across when, to our left, we heard what sounded like gunshots, and saw people running. A Vopo (the slang term for Volkspolizist; German for "People's Policeman") appeared out of nowhere, pointed his machine gun at us, and told us to stop. He kept us standing there for probably a quarter of an hour, then told us to keep on going toward the border. When I put my foot over the white line, I had a feeling of overwhelming relief in my stomach. I still remember it. I was free.

Now on the western side we asked the American soldiers what had happened. They told us that the *Vopos* had fired shots at someone trying to climb over the Wall, and they pointed toward Zimmerstrasse where, about a hundred yards away, a crowd was gathering. So we went there, too. The Wall was so high we couldn't see over it, and no one dared climb up on top of it. But on the other side we could hear a man's voice screaming "Hilf mir doch!" (Help me !). No one came to help him, and after about an hour he didn't scream any more.

The crowd on the West Berlin side, however, had continued to grow and that night thousands of West Berliners marched in protest down the city's main street, the Kurfürstendamm. The killing at the Berlin Wall that afternoon turned out to be the most callous of what was to be its twenty-eight-year history, from 1961 to 1989. The Vopos had shot an 18-year-old boy, Peter Fechter, because he wanted to flee from one part of Berlin to another, from dictatorship to freedom. They let him bleed to death at the foot of the Wall.

My brother and I stayed in Berlin for several more days to sightsee; that after all was why we had come in the first place. But neither of us could forget that moment in "No Man's Land." We started talking about things that had never occurred to us before: Why did people want to get out of East Germany? Why had the East German government built a wall to keep their citizens in? Why was it necessary for American, British and French troops to defend West Berlin? But neither one of us really knew very much about the history of Berlin and Germany, or even why Europe was divided. The only thing we both recognized was that Peter Fechter knew something about freedom that we didn't, and that he had been murdered trying to get it.

In Berlin I had seen a face of Europe no one had prepared me for. It had nothing to do with the bucolic scenes of the German countryside. But it had everything to do with education, and it had a dramatic impact on mine. That September, when I returned to Stanford University to begin my junior year, I changed my major from drama to European history. The last quarter of my senior year, in the spring of 1964, a course was offered on the postwar history of Berlin by a visiting professor from Germany, Hans Herzfeld, of whom I had never heard. But I took it, and as I listened to Herzfeld talk about Berlin in a heavy German accent I thought, again and again, about Peter Fechter. In January 1966, a year and a half following my graduation, I was offered a fellowship to take my Ph.D. degree at a university of my choice. So I wrote to Professor Herzfeld, and asked him if he would consider taking on a student who hadn't yet learned German, but who did know why he wanted to study at the Freie Universität Berlin. He agreed.

In the early autumn of 1966 I went to the Freie Universität Berlin to earn my doctorate in modern European history under Professor Herzfeld's direction. He was of "the old school," both in terms of erudition and reputation. He was born at the end of the nineteenth century, in 1892, in the town of Halle, in Saxony. Although I had met him two years earlier in California, I didn't yet know that he was one of Germany's most distinguished living historians, together with Hans Rothfels and Percy Schramm. Nor was I familiar enough, then, with the hierarchy of German universities to appreciate fully the compliment of Herzfeld's agreement at the age of 74 to take me on as his student. I was to be, as it turned out, his last.

The first time I called on him it was late afternoon in mid-September, at his home at number 5, Buchsweiler Strasse in the suburb of Dahlem, in the American Sector. On the advice of a new German friend, Peter Rühland, I had brought with me flowers for Professor Herzfeld's wife, hopeful that this would demonstrate a young American's sensitivity to

German customs. Peter had suggested that I memorize something in German, so I could greet Frau Herzfeld properly, and proposed "Diese Blumen habe ich in meinem Garten gepflückt" (I picked these flowers in my garden). I found this just as amusing as he did, and I rehearsed it during the forty-five-minute bus ride to the Herzfeld's house.

I was nervous and not really confident when I rang the doorbell, but I was ready to greet Frau Herzfeld. It didn't happen that way, of course, because such things seldom do. When the door opened I found myself, holding my bouquet of roses, facing Professor Herzfeld, and I wasn't about to tell him that I had picked the flowers in my garden. To make matters worse I was embarrassed, because Professor Herzfeld seemed very amused about something and I didn't know why. I had never brought flowers to a European lady before, and I thought I had made some sort of disastrous mistake. He turned slightly, and speaking over his shoulder into the house, he said, "Marie! I think Herr Bark has something for you." It was only later I learned that the red roses I had brought Frau Herzfeld meant a declaration of great affection. And, in fact, we became great friends, and we enjoyed that friendship until her death in 2002.

Marie Herzfeld was a lady of dry wit and sophistication, with a highly refined sense of style. She loved to laugh, and she had tremendous admiration and respect for America. While her husband directed my doctoral work, she presided over my introduction to Germany and to German culture. She taught me that German food is not just sausage, sauerkraut and beer, but is also filet of wild hare with red cabbage and chanterelle mushrooms; and she introduced me to Germany's rich white wines—when Frau Herzfeld drank red wine it came from Burgundy!—and I taught her that America's national drink was not Coca-Cola, but ice water found on every restaurant table in America, without charge. I became not only the beneficiary of her love of music and the theater, but she and her husband made me a part of their rich life of art and letters, which included chamber music in their garden and dinners at their home with scholars, journalists, businesspeople, and political figures from throughout Germany. Their kindness was nothing less than a unique and extraordinary education in all manner of things German and European. And so began with my arrival at the Herzfeld's doorstep, holding a bouquet of red roses, my European education. From it emerged my friendship with Germany and the Germans, and with Europe and the Europeans. It changed my life, permanently.

As a graduate student at the Freie Univesität I lived in Berlin for four years, in a suburb called Der Grünewald (the Green Forest). During that time I never returned to the United States. My father had explained to me, before I left, that I was going to Germany to earn my Ph.D. degree and to learn about Europe. So he made clear, in no uncertain terms, that if I wanted to return to the United States I would do so at my expense. But he also proposed that if I wanted to further my education by traveling on the continent he would gladly finance it. The result was that I went all over Germany and Europe, and met Europeans. With many of them, over the next three decades, I developed professional and private friendships that continue to this day. And later I became the godfather to the children of four of them, to Victoria Sophie in Berlin, to Liliom Alexander in Bonn, to Sophie Charlotte in Braunschweig, and to Matthew Thomas in Copenhagen.

These travels also had another consequence, which I am sure my father had considered when he made his proposal. I began to learn how Europeans see America and judge Americans. I learned about the other side of the coin, too—about the cultural and historical differences between Europeans and Americans, and why they exist. The differences, likes, and dislikes, weren't nearly as disturbing as they were fascinating. So I listened a lot, and also tried to answer the never ending questions about American democracy, about our culture, about our economic life, about our racial problems, and about a subject of never-ending curiosity, "cowboys, Indians, and the Wild West."

We also talked about our holidays. When I think of all those I spent in Europe I always remember my first Christmas in Westphalia, walking through the snow on the way to church in a little village on Christmas Eve, then singing carols in German, and finally hearing the church bells on the way home. It was the holidays, more than any other thing, that made a lasting impression on me, because how the Europeans celebrated them taught me so much about how they live. They were private gatherings of family and good friends, but I was included in them all. It was a compliment that I valued enormously, and it was also an opportunity to talk about our different customs, traditions, and habits of life. So we often had long conversations about Halloween and Thanksgiving, Valentine's Day and the Fourth of July, the birthdays of George Washington and Abraham Lincoln, and of course how we celebrated Christmas and Easter in America.

When I came from the New World to study in the Old World, I had not yet thought that I might become part of them both. But that's what had happened by the time I received my Ph.D., and I intended to keep it that way. I also intended to keep my new European friendships, because many Europeans had told me why they considered themselves to be old friends of America, long before I had made their acquaintance of Europe. In West Berlin they explained that it was the Americans, together with the English and French, who had saved the city from communist dictatorship. In Paris they explained that it was the American GI who had come to liberate France from German occupation. And whether they were French or Germans, they all said to me, "We will never forget what America did for us." They shared an appreciation of liberty with Americans that I had just begun to understand. But in fact it was much more than that, and I now know it. They looked at America and saw something of themselves in a distant land, across the ocean, either because they had met American soldiers at the end of the war, or because they had relatives and friends living in America, and had affection for them. And I, just as thousands of other Americans before me, now felt the same way toward them.

Those four years in Germany and in Europe made me think a lot more about America than I ever had before. It wasn't that America was newer or Europe older, or Americans faster and Europeans slower, nor was it a question of who or what was better, richer, or poorer. The differences between life in Europe and America just made both that much more interesting, and invariably prompted me to think about why the differences existed. But something else was also accomplished during those four years. I had discovered that Europeans and Americans had an enormous amount in common, and that both worlds, equally full of life and culture, complemented each other.

When I left Berlin in the early autumn of 1970,[1] the Europeans had a new friend in me, and I had many friends among them. Today it is more than forty years ago that I first arrived in Germany, and since that time my life has been both a European and an American one. From it I have learned that the European-American relationship is much more than that. It is a friendship, built on common interests, shared values, trust, affection, and respect. It is unique, and it is irreplaceable. To let it unravel is unthinkable, and to let it come apart would have disastrous consequences for all of us.

---

1. The author was granted a Ph.D. degree by the Freie Universität Berlin in January 1970, summa cum laude. His major field of study was Neuere Geschichte and his twin minor was in Mittelalterliche Geschichte und Politische Wissenschaft.

Introduction

THE CROWNING transatlantic achievement of the twentieth century was the preservation of freedom on the European continent. Europeans and Americans, united in a common cause, did it together. Ours was, initially, a partnership of mutual interests, but it became a relationship based on common values, and for some also a friendship made of trust, affection, and respect.

At the beginning of the twenty-first century, like the disappearing smile of Lewis Carroll's Cheshire cat, the vision of our once grand relationship is fading away. It is being replaced with criticism and dissension. We have become quick to interpret our contrary opinions as signs of weakness or arrogance, rather than to consider the differences between us and how they affect our regard for each other.

One of the few things that Europeans and Americans do agree on is that we are drifting apart. Does it matter, some of us wonder? Well, that depends on whom you ask, but I believe it does matter, enormously. If our current estrangement continues, and worsens, our relationship will eventually dissolve.

The dissolution will not happen overnight, and its progress will not capture our undivided attention. In that event, however, Americans and Europeans would no longer be allied in the defense of the principles we have protected in the past. The former union would consist, instead, of fragmented coalitions of expediency between America and individual European countries. Rivalry and strife would replace constructive competition and healthy cooperation.

If this occurs there will be unhappy consequences for all of us. Our rapport will be tainted by uncertainty, even mistrust. We will no longer be able to distinguish with confidence who is a true friend and who is a resentful former ally. In our search for reliable partners we will find it easy to dismiss as opportunists those who disagree with us and convenient to praise as friends those who tell us what we want to hear.

This depressing scenario is not preordained, nor is it a self-fulfilling prophecy. What we have in common is of greater moment than our controversies. The values we cherish have a power of their own. The principles that unite us endure and compel. They have been given different names, at different times, by different people: truth, liberty, moral decency, respect for human freedom, opposition to tyranny. In fact, these are the principles on which European civilization was built and which Europeans later brought to America. Today, we still share a belief in all of them.

Our differences are not of principle, but of practice. They arise from our histories and our fashions. Nineteenth-century visitors to the Old and New Worlds wrote about continental ways and American manners. Modern travelers continue to discover them. Europe and America have not been built in the same way. Our attitudes have been shaped by our experiences.

Most of us, however, are unfamiliar with the origin of our differences. Often we do not even know what they are. Our neglect contributes to misunderstandings, and our ignorance to disagreements. When this occurs our quarrels become divisive, and we react with impatience. Rather than listening, we sermonize. It is, too often, a dialogue of the deaf.

It is this colloquy that has become the hallmark of recent times—since the end of the Cold War in 1989–1990, and especially since the attack on the World Trade Center in 2001. Our approach has soured the satisfaction we derive from our undertakings, and has injured the pride we take in our accomplishments. We have forced the conclusion that the interests of the Old and the New World have become so fundamentally contradictory that partnership is no longer possible. Some contend that our relationship was never based on common values, and that what divides us is of infinitely greater weight than the substance of our friendship.

Americans and Europeans, dancing together in the dark,[1] is a depiction of what often happens when we seek a harmonious relationship. While we hold one another in a fond embrace, we step on each other's toes and try to lead at the same time. Our conversations are full of conviction and rich with opinion, but we talk at cross-purposes. Seldom do we discuss the striking contrasts between the Old World of Europe and the New World of America.

Yet we both gain by developing knowledge of our historical legacies and cultivating respect for them. It takes time, and exertion, but that is part and parcel of nurturing a relationship that is more than just a marriage of convenience. We did so during the twentieth century, and we learned that the effort was worth the investment. To do so successfully in this new century, however, requires greater resolve than we have been willing to show to date.

We do not have to look far to find the reason why. Most Europeans understand much less about America than they think they do, and today's Americans are blithely unaware how little they know about Europe. In both cases the product is often arrogance: on the one hand, arrogance born of condescension, and on the other, arrogance born of naiveté. The predictable result is that many of us, with real confidence, misjudge each other's motives and behavior, just as we look forward eagerly to our next dance.

This book is a consideration of our differences and affinities and our interests. Consisting of seven essays presented in three parts, each is related to the next; thus, they should be read in order, beginning with the essay on "Differences" in Part One and concluding with that on "The Force of Things" in Part Three. As a whole, the parts form an account of those attitudes, approaches, and affections which give shadow to the past and provide substance to the present. It is with their force, also, that the future of our relationship will be written. The past, indeed, to paraphrase William Faulkner from his novel *Requiem for a Nun*, is never dead nor ever past.

The "Continental Contrasts" presented in Part One are introduced with an essay on *the essential difference* between us. It is found in how Europe and America were built—from the top down and from the bottom up. The difference is profound in its impact, because it marks our history and continues to affect how Europeans and Americans conduct their private and professional lives. This difference is part of the heritage which shapes our views of the world, as seen from our respective backyards. Our horizons, too, are seldom the same, because they are cast and colored by geography, distance and space, by art and music, and by our manners, customs, and traditions.

The stage is thus set for the discussion in Part Two of the influence of the essential difference on our modern interests; interests to which we have committed ourselves since the end of World War II. These are properly called the pursuits of peace and prosperity, the guardians of the values we hold dear in Europe and America. In many ways we describe them with the same words and terms. But our attitudes concerning how the principle of human freedom should be reflected in our qualities of life produce different approaches to how we define and protect them, and on occasion result in dramatically conflicting orders of priority.

The contemporary contrasts are most jarringly apparent, not in our debates over power and weakness, but in how we speak about our concepts of equality, opportunity, and stability and in how we view the purpose of competition and assess the propriety of free and open markets. Hence, the first essay of Part Two treats, (1) the post–World War II origins of "The European Model," built from the top down after 1945 and influenced to a significant degree by the politics of socialism, and (2) "The American Model," which reflects a commitment to a quality of life built from the bottom up, marked by individual liberty and responsibility and molded in the arena of competition for ideas, goods, and services. The second essay considers (1) the forces which transformed the European model into a common market and drove its expansion into a broader European Union, and (2) whether that union will lead to a trans-Atlantic relationship of constructive competition, or to destructive rivalry between an isolated America and an irrelevant Europe.

The subject of Part Three is the future of our undertakings. The first of the three essays focuses on our respective legacies, ancient and modern, and therefore on who we are and on what we may become. The second addresses the effects of the fly in the soup of our relationship; namely, our impatience with each other's approach to life often results in explanations of each other's motives which are simplistic and foolish, and undermines the significance of what we have forged together. The concluding essay clarifies the essence of our most important foreign policy asset. That asset is our joint and several commitments to common values. It may be poetic justice that they come from the very histories whose defining differences still lead us to different paths on our journeys to the same place. But if this is so, it is also the essential difference that obligates us to reject the temptation to trivialize the nature of the principles which unite us. These, born out of our past, must become both the shadow and substance of our future.

Some of the people with whom I discussed the subjects in this book asked whether it is difficult to write in general terms about Europeans and Americans. The answer, of course, is yes. Europeans are not all the same, nor are Americans. Nevertheless, Europeans share a great many judgments in their estimation of Americans and America, just as Americans, who also differ tremendously from one region to another, hold remarkably similar views of Europe and the Europeans.

My colleagues at the Hoover Institution also raised a concern which defines the inquiring scholarly environment. Although few of them know Europe well, most of them are curious about what separates and unites Americans and Europeans. What evidence, they wanted to know, did I have for my conclusions? What criteria have I used to select the differences and affinities, the interests, and the habits of life discussed in these pages? Theirs are legitimate questions, and the straightforward answers are short.

My own experiences are the evidence. I am the son of William Carroll

Bark, cited further on in this book, who was a professor of medieval history at Stanford University. Both he and my mother, Eleanor Carlton, encouraged my interest in Europe, initially at home where my brother and I grew up as the sons of medieval parents in the modern world, and later on as well, when they encouraged without reservation my wish to earn my Ph.D. in history at the Freie Universität Berlin.

Since 1970, when I left Germany after living there for more than four years and became a fellow at Stanford University's Hoover Institution, I have spent my professional and private life discussing trans-Atlantic differences, interests, and affinities with European statesmen, politicians, businessmen and -women, scholars, writers, and journalists. In the course of my research and writing I have often found the thinking of my European interlocutors familiar, but I have also encountered surprising contrasts in outlook between Europeans and Americans. For many years I have recorded our habits of private and professional life, and decided finally that it would be worthwhile to distill my observations into some general principles. The selection that follows is based on what my life, spent almost equally in America and Europe since the age of twenty, continues to teach me are the telling aspects of the bewildering nature of our relationship.

This book is written for those who would examine this puzzle, which is what it truly is, and for those who would seek to understand how the pieces fit together.

The pages which follow are for Europeans who admire what their descendants have accomplished in the New World, for Americans who keep the Old World in affection and regard, and for Europeans and Americans who recognize each other's strengths. It is also the intention that the discussion of the relationship, which has continually shifted and changed since Europeans first arrived in America, will appeal to those who are neither European nor American, who stand outside the Atlantic sphere and view it from farther shores.

This book, finally, has a specific purpose. It is to recall to life the words of English statesman Edmund Burke that "nothing is so strong a tie of amity between nation and nation as correspondence in law, customs, manners and habits of life. They have more than the force of treaties in themselves. They are obligations written in the heart." That is to say, this book is written with the belief that the amity between Europe and America is irreplaceable, and with the conviction that those who argue otherwise are guilty of promoting a fatal conceit.

PART ONE

Continental Contrasts

Preface

It is the essential difference that separates us. It is found in how our societies were created. Europe was constructed from the top down and America was made from the bottom up. How Europe and America were built affects how Europeans and Americans think, how we behave, and how our governments rule. It affects ambition, and defines our spirit of competition. It writes our interpretation of history. It influences how we talk to each other; Americans are direct and Europeans are indirect. It changes the way we see things; Europeans in shades of grey and Americans in black and white. It is reflected in how we describe the meaning of freedom, in our interpretation of it, and in our willingness to defend it. In short, the essential difference profoundly affects the private and public lives of us both, Americans and Europeans.

CHAPTER I

Differences

The Essential Difference

E UROPEANS AND AMERICANS do not refer to the essential difference by name, but we know it is there in the form of continental contrasts. Americans wonder why European governments have so much more patriarchal authority over matters which in America are private responsibilities. Why, they ask, do Europeans trust government to satisfy private desires better than private citizens? It seems to many Americans that many Europeans have traded a portion of their liberty for economic security, and are willing to give up some of their personal freedom in exchange for stability.

This perception draws attention to a striking distinction in how Europeans and Americans generally view the purpose of government. Americans of all political persuasions are committed to individual freedom, and believe it is the government's responsibility to protect the freedom of the individual, not to limit that freedom. Vehement and sometimes strident political debates take place between Americans on all kinds of subjects, from taxes and regulation to the proper obligations of the state versus those of the individual. But in spite of strongly held differences of opinion most Americans consider too much government unhealthy, and many believe that Europe has too much of it.

Whenever Americans and Europeans do discuss the essential differ-

ence, which is not often, they point out that it runs throughout the histories of Europe and America, but that it is easier to explain as it concerns
the New World. What they mean is that America, in its youth, is still very
much aware of the principle on which it was founded. In fact, as Europeans often comment, Americans talk about the principle all the time. They
call it freedom, and independence; and some Europeans call it a history
of winning. From the ground up Americans celebrate it with a birthday
party every year on the fourth of July, and they express their appreciation
for it each year on a national day of thanksgiving.

In the Old World, however, no celebration is held in honor of a European principle; indeed, if there were such a principle what could it be?
Some Europeans caution that the explanation of the essential difference,
from the continental perspective, is not so straightforward, because their
history is one of losing.[1] It takes much longer to tell, because Europe is a
tree with many branches that has been growing for more then twenty
centuries.

From the Top Down

What marks American and European history appears in stark relief.
America was built by European immigrants, and their descendants, who
eschewed social, political, and economic practices they resented. Their
purpose was to form their own government themselves, from the ground
up. Europe, on the contrary, was built by Europeans who enjoyed social,
political and economic privilege, and who had a great deal to gain from
participating in government rule from the top down.

This explanation, however, makes little sense without reference to two
subjects seldom mentioned when Europeans and Americans are together.
The first is *the role of aristocratic rule in Europe*—that is to say, rule provided by Europe's royal houses and the nobility. The second is *the practice
of patronage*—that is to say, the financial and political support given to all
manner of cultural, educational, and social undertakings by the ruling and
noble classes. Today these two subjects do not receive much attention.
But they merit a great deal, especially when Americans and Europeans

begin their periodic hand-wringing as they criticize each other's attitudes and behavior.

It is impossible to understand Europe and the Europeans without knowing how Europeans see themselves and their rights and responsibilities in their respective countries. Over centuries the role played by Europe's aristocracy and the practice of patronage established a hierarchy of governance and also contributed to a regimented class structure. To this day the exercise of rule from the top down remains largely unchanged, and much of Europe's class structure remains intact as well.

Americans, by comparison, have never had an aristocracy. There are, of course, some Americans who boast of having aristocratic European friends with titles like Baron or Count; although on that subject European "social climbers" follow the same practice. In this regard we are very much alike. But the point is that America has never been ruled by a class born to nobility. Americans have been governed by their own elected officials; in other words, by themselves, which is why Americans have never enjoyed patronage of the European variety. On the contrary, Americans have a history of giving, not receiving, a history of charity and volunteering, a history of social mobility and job mobility, a history of idealism, hope and openness, a history of individualism and toughness in order to survive, and a history of solving problems privately rather than turning to government.[2]

The history of European rule has produced dependence by the ruled on those who govern. It is true that by the end of the eighteenth century, marked by the French Revolution, much of the absolute power of the old aristocracies had slipped from their grasp; and a little more than a century later, by the end of World War I, the power held by the Austro-Hungarian, German, and Russian monarchies had disappeared too. But during the nineteenth and twentieth centuries, as the authority of aristocratic royal houses was gradually replaced by that of political parties voted into office by the citizenry, the practice of rule from the top down nonetheless remained.

Today rule from the top down is exercised by what should properly be described as *the new aristocrats*. They are the current government elite, in the form of large cadres of civil servants, functionaries, government officials, and members of parliaments and national assemblies. Their influence is well illustrated by their numbers; for example, in Sweden one in three is employed by government, and in France it is one in four. Common to both the old and the new aristocrats is their impact on economic, political, and social life. Whether it is called big government or the welfare state the guiding principle of politics in contemporary Europe is rule by an elite.

This is not to say that there is no difference between governance by European royal houses in the eighteenth century and democratic government in Europe in the twenty-first. To cite the most glaring contrast, Europe's kings and queens ruled by divine right, while contemporary Europe is governed by elected leaders. There are, indeed, conspicuous differences in practice, but not in the basic relationship of dependency of the ruled on the rulers. One can properly emphasize that European voters elect their leaders, but once elected responsibility for the design and rationale for public policies is the closely held private preserve of the new aristocrats.

This practice, as it were, is exactly the opposite from that in America, where electorates continually challenge whether government policies serve the interests of the citizenry. American voters decide who will govern, monitor the performance and judge the effects of public policies on a continual basis, in every conceivable non-governmental forum. The implicit faith of Europeans in the ability of government to alleviate the miseries of the human condition is absent in America, and very much present is the conviction that strength is found in individual responsibility. This one difference gives an order of substance and meaning to our respective cultures. Nothing remains untouched.

Aristocrats, Old and New

The telling distinction between Europe and America appears in how Americans and Europeans view freedom and individual responsibility, and in how they define the proper role of the state. In America probably no one, in recent times, has cast the distinction more dramatically than an American president whose ancestors came from Ireland. To paraphrase from John Fitzgerald Kennedy's inaugural address in 1961, American social, political and economic culture prompts Americans to ask "What can we do for our country?"—whereas European social, political and economic culture prompts Europeans to ask, "What can our government do for us?" Although President Kennedy did not refer to the essential difference by name, its existence is reflected in the questions. From both can be drawn numerous comparisons between how Europeans and Americans conduct their private, public and professional relationships.

This is not to conclude that Americans love freedom more than Europeans do, or that all Europeans merrily follow government pied pipers. The disagreements Europeans have among themselves, about social, political, and economic issues, as well as the fervor of their disputes with each other, belie such an interpretation. Discovery of a fly in the soup is a daily event, but seldom is fault found with the soup itself, made, flavored and served by the new aristocrats.

Europeans and Americans, however, while they use the same words, do not always mean the same things. This applies to Europeans' attitudes toward freedom. They do not love it any less, but many conceive of it in a different way. This explains why Americans who have never studied aristocratic rule and the practice of patronage are often mystified by European attitudes toward authority. The history of both is closely linked. Although the governing role played by the aristocracy is well treated by historians, much less has been written about the equally influential role of patronage.

Europe's rulers—that is to say, those who controlled wealth via the ownership of land and the collection of taxes, whether it was the aristocracy of princes, dukes, counts and barons, or the church—practiced patronage in every corner of society, and most notably in the humanities, arts, and sciences. In eighteenth-century Europe the Germans called this principle of rule *Mäzenatentum*. It is an old word which can be translated as patronage, and which might be replaced today with the German word *Kultur-staat*, which means literally, "state culture." Either way, the effect in the twenty-first century is remarkably similar to the result in the eighteenth. The state provides the financial base for all kinds of cultural, educational and social activities, rather than private individuals and foundations.

This applies to Europe generally, although in the case of England and Scotland the practice of rule has evolved differently. It is true that the experience of the English and the Scots has no counterpart in the rest of Europe. As my English colleagues point out to me, aristocratic rule, beginning with the Magna Carta in 1215 and followed by the Declaration of Arbroath in 1320,[3] gradually became subject to significant legal limitations. Further, they rightly emphasize that it was English common law, not Roman law, that was brought to America, along with the name of its most famous city—first called New Amsterdam by the Dutch in 1624 and renamed New York when the English captured it in 1664.

For continental Europeans the English case warrants a separate discussion, one which is tangential to the subject addressed in this book. There are, today, many Europeans on all sides of the political spectrum who consider the United Kingdom to be America's Trojan Horse in Europe, some of whom knowingly cite the remark attributed to George Bernard Shaw that America and Britain are two nations "divided by a common language." Indeed, the principle of rule discussed here developed differently in England than it did in continental Europe. But lest there be any mistake about it, the English have just as royal a history and just as rich a patronage as the continental Europeans. Rule from the top down was no more foreign to Britain than it was to the continent.

This conclusion should not be construed as a dismissive response to the legitimate complaint that it is irresponsible to lump differing national histories into an amorphous concept of "Europe." The purpose here is simply to emphasize that patronage in Europe, including England and Scotland, was part of control and influence from the top down.

There are countless examples. One of the most impressive—because the practice has lasted so long and continues to this day—was the birth and development of Europe's great universities. It began with the University of Bologna in Italy in 1088. It is the oldest in Europe and boasts such alumni as St. Thomas Aquinas, Dante and Petrarch. Bologna was followed during the next 300 years by, among others, Paris, Salamanca, Cambridge, Oxford, Prague, Florence, Krakow, and Cologne in 1388. They all had wealthy, and in most cases royal and aristocratic patrons, whose financial and political support underwrote the development of higher learning. One result was the emergence of what we call the humanities and sciences. But individual explorers, artists, architects, writers, and scientists were the beneficiaries also.

There are hundreds of them, such as the explorers Columbus, Vespucci, Magellan, da Gama and Drake. Artists like Titian, Michelangelo, Rembrandt, Dürer, Vermeer, David or Rubens. Philosophers and writers like Kant, Voltaire, Racine, Molière, Cervantes, Chaucer, Dante, Shakespeare, Goethe and Schiller. Composers like Mozart, Chopin, Bach, Puccini, Debussy, and Beethoven. And of course scientists, such as Galileo, Leonardo da Vinci, Newton, Lavoisier, Linnaeus, and von Humboldt.

Most of the extraordinary examples of architecture in Europe are the fruits of patronage. The beauty of European buildings and the grandeur of continental monuments are less a symbol of openness and magnanimity than they are of aristocracy, nobility, and authority. Consider St. Paul's Cathedral or Buckingham Palace in London, or the cathedral (*il Duomo*) in Milan on which both Leonardo and Bramante worked; the Florentine Cathedral Santa Maria del Fiore with its magnificent cupola designed by Filippo Brunelleschi; St. Peter's Basilica in Rome built by Lorenzo Bernini and the Sistine Chapel as well as the Sforza Chapel with paintings of Michelangelo, Botticelli and Perugino. Without the patronage of great noble families—such as the Medici, the Borghese and the Corsini in Italy—none of these magnificent creations would exist. Patrons determined, to a large extent, which artists and artisans survived and which disappeared from view.[4]

Although the examples just cited are Italian, Italy was not an exception. French art and architecture are equally well-known, symbolized by the museum of the Louvre, Les Invalides, and the Château de Versailles. There are an equal number of noteworthy examples in Germany, such as the baroque palace of Würzburg built by the Schönborn family and the parks and palaces of Potsdam outside Berlin, where the most famous one has a French name, Sans Souci, and was built by the Hohenzollern, a family which still exists in Europe. And there is the classical city of Weimar, built by German dukes, where Goethe, Herder and Schiller lived.

It is impossible to know what they all would have achieved without patrons; but patronage accounted for much of the history of Western civilization. Munificent patronage not only enhanced the influence and prestige of those who provided it, but also built an extraordinarily rich European culture which had been in full bloom for centuries before the American idea of freedom was put into words in 1776, just a little more than 230 years ago.

A principal consequence was creation of a well-educated European class that became an intellectual elite, very much aware of the world beyond the borders of their own countries. Alongside this group, of course, existed another level of Europeans, poor in wealth and education, and largely ignorant of the world beyond their own villages, towns and cities. Of the countless millions of this class thousands risked the perils of the trip across the Atlantic; those who made it laid the foundations of modern America.

Patronage also provided, in a sense, a long-term and presumably unintended legacy. Little by little the beneficiaries became dependent on their patrons. As long as patronage continued, and was conducted on a broad scale and in an enlightened manner, there seemed to be no reason to take issue with why it was provided, or to condemn those providing it. Nor did it appear worthwhile to challenge whether, as a matter of principle, it was a wise thing to do, or if in fact, it might be producing an unanticipated consequence—namely, turning the beneficiaries into permanent wards of the patron. But the result was that patronage in the humanities, arts and the sciences eventually became a state responsibility, and part of an overall system of rule and control.

The practice worked well, until the end of the eighteenth century. The French revolution, and later political upheavals throughout Europe in the nineteenth and twentieth centuries, destroyed, for all practical purposes, most of the political and financial power of Europe's nobility. The decline was long and slow, and also, some would argue, inexorable. The aristocracy—and, of course, the Church, in which members of aristocratic families played major roles—lost most of its land, much of its income, and major influence. With that loss the form of patronage as practiced by Europe's noble and privileged classes for more than eight hundred years vanished. But as the exercise of power and influence acquired new names and shapes, the entrenched principle of rule from the top down remained intact.

Following the French Revolution the royal courts of kings and queens were transformed, one by one, into nation-states with presidents and prime ministers, and with parliaments, legislatures, and national assemblies. That is to say, the patrons themselves, once individuals, were replaced by institutions of the state during the nineteenth and early twentieth centuries, created by those who controlled government. Public monies, whose source was taxes, were substituted for private wealth, no longer available on the same scale. Rule from the top down was now exercised by those elected officials who controlled the expenditure of tax monies, and no longer by members of royal families and aristocrats. Creation of the nineteenth-century state was seen as a liberating moment. The state, created to protect the people, would become the antidote to the rule of nobility and to the tyranny of princes. What changed in reality, however, was not the practice, but the names of the rulers and the patrons.

The effects were the same. The largesse of patronage engendered dependency on the patron, whether it was an private individual, a government employee, or the state itself. Comparisons are found everywhere today, and one of the most startling, from an American perspective, is the relationship between universities and their graduates.

Europe, as America, has great universities, but on the continent few of them are private and almost none have alumni associations. In the view of most Europeans and their political leaders there has never been a need for private universities, since those governing have always funded them. As a result graduates of European universities do not assume a debt of gratitude for their education, and in fact few make financial contributions to their respective alma maters. "Why," a European might ask, "should I make a gift to the state for providing me the education to which I am entitled?"

The contrast with the practice on the other side of the Atlantic is sharply drawn. Americans had no choice but to create private colleges and universities. They did it independently of government, because the government was not there to do it for them. They built their system of higher learning themselves, with their own effort and with their own money. In doing so, they cultivated a tradition not only of excellence—Harvard, for example, was founded in 1636 and Stanford University as recently as 1885—but unlike the Europeans they also introduced the practice of supporting their college or university long after they had finished their education. In fact, hundreds of thousands of graduates of American colleges and universities make financial gifts to their alma maters every year, and many do so throughout their lives. And even though Americans later developed great public universities as well, all of them, both public and private, rely for financial strength to a significant degree on alumni who want to "give something back." It is an original American concept that does not have a Europe counterpart.[5]

The foregoing description should not be interpreted as either condemnation or praise. It merely illustrates why many Europeans do not look to themselves, but to the top and hence to government, to rule, to decide, to control, to determine, to underwrite, to patronize. Patronage, of the ancient or of the modern variety, is part of Europe's culture, and European culture is a product of European history. Europe's history makes Europeans who they are. Or, to put it in a deliberately provocative way, Europe's culture of authority is what remains after Europeans have forgotten the historical details of the development of their civilization.

An example of this approach is to contrast the Massachusetts Institute of Technology (MIT), founded privately in 1859 in Cambridge, with the European Union's intention, announced in February 2005, to create a European Institute of Technology to rival MIT in innovation and initiative. A second, French example, illustrates the same approach. In the summer of 2006 the president of France announced the government's intention to finance creation of an Internet search engine, called Quaero, to rival Google.[6]

⊂❦⊃

In the twenty-first century patronage is no longer called *Mäzenatentum*, and the word *Kulturstaat* is not used frequently, either. There really is not a specific name for it today, but patronage is provided by every government in Europe, in the form of subsidies and grants for all manner of endeavor. The beneficiaries are not only the arts, humanities and the sciences. They are also government employees who enjoy pension plans more generous than those available in the private sector, families who receive mandated child support subsidies, and government employees who receive year-end salary bonuses. The result is that the state is both a popular provider, and a generous employer which, unlike a private business, can spend more money than it takes in, without declaring bankruptcy.

The visible hand of the state touches business competition and labor markets, medicine and health care, law and justice, agriculture and the environment, communication and transportation, information and the media, housing and urban development, social security, child care and retirement pensions, and state monopolies for electric power and gas. In short, every aspect of artistic, cultural, economic, intellectual, political, and social life in twenty-first century Europe is affected, in one way or another, by the financial generosity of the state.

The state—in other words, the politicians and civil servants who operate it—determines what serves the public and the private good. Needless to say, not all Europeans applaud this practice because some believe that the extensive powers of government limit individual freedom and stifle personal initiative. In fact, the late Austrian economist Friedrich A. Hayek published a book about it in 1944, entitled *The Road To Serfdom*. He did not refer to the new aristocrats, but that is whom he was writing about. Although the book has been translated into a number of languages, it never captured the continental imagination; and received little attention in 1944–1945 when distraught Europeans were blaming capitalism and free markets for the violence of Nazi Germany and its effort to impose its own brand of serfdom on the continent.

Whichever way one looks at it, however, there is little public discussion about what should be considered acceptable obligations of government versus the right of individual responsibility. On this issue few European politicians encourage national dialogue because the utility of their monopoly of political and economic power might be called into question. If that Pandora's Box were opened, it would be difficult to close. What does take place are demonstrations and strikes about how much vacation time there should be, how early one can retire, how much funding the state should give to pensions, how long the state should provide unemployment payments, and how much money should be paid in subsidies to businesses. The arguments are seldom about *whether* the government should be involved with these matters, nor are they about the right of the individual to work as long as he wishes, or to fund his own private retirement program, or about his right to take less rather than more vacation.

In Europe there are few private entities with sufficient financial means to initiate and sustain national debates on the principle of more government versus less government. Indeed, the "think tank," privately funded and directed, is the exception. In America it is the rule, where different philosophies of public policy are discussed in think tanks large and small, and where ideas compete with each other every day in the intellectual arenas of American colleges and universities.

Irrespective of how one may judge the relative merits of the comparison, there is little dispute about the result. Over time, the Europeans have become, almost without recognizing it, economically dependent on the state, sometimes described, euphemistically, as *the public sector*. Many, though by no means all Europeans, complain about it, but few seek to change it because the alternative of being without it is even less appealing. Thus, today rule and patronage are managed by "the new aristocrats." If you will, *the power of government obligates*. Over two centuries ago both were managed by "the old aristocrats"—and the consequence was the same, rule from the top down. *The power of nobility obligated*, and the French nobility had a phrase for it, *noblesse oblige*.

The juxtaposition of *the state* versus *the individual*, of *the public* versus *the private*, has more than just philosophical meaning, because the distinctions between public and private responsibilities in America and Europe affect how Europeans and Americans see themselves, and define who they are. Lest there be a misunderstanding the contrast is drawn to explain why Europeans and Americans often see things differently. Does the difference mean that Europeans consider the power of *the public sector* to be in conflict with freedom? Most would disagree. It would be an error to conclude that they do not care deeply about their individual freedom. But they do not think it is threatened by rule from the top down. They view the state as the protector and the banker of their entitlements, such as the right to work less but to be paid as though they were working more, or the right to retire earlier rather than later, with the same benefits.

This is why since 1945, with the dramatic exception of Margaret Thatcher in England, no European leader has successfully dismantled the public sector, privatized government services, broken up state monopolies, reduced regulation, and decreased taxes. Europeans are, for the most part, loyal to the unwritten concept of rule from top down. This loyalty affects, in turn, their concept of freedom. They describe it as something in which they believe, not as an inalienable right, but as a government responsibility and not an individual one, to be managed and protected by the state. On the other hand their judgment of freedom in America is less clear. Some Europeans admire it and value it as Americans do. But many argue that Americans have too much of it, practice freedom as a free-for-all, exercise it without responsibility, use it to justify survival of the fittest, exaggerate its advantages, and employ it as though freedom were the cardinal rule governing the game of life. These Europeans have learned it is more comfortable to live within the prescribed limits of their freedom rather than to use freedom to challenge those limits.

The result, for many Europeans, is ambivalence about where their loyalties lie. They find themselves looking at a paradox. If they support political leaders who wish to weaken the power of the new aristocrats, and therefore reduce entitlements, they will bite the hand that feeds them, and most Europeans will not do that; economists call it self-interest. Yet if they remain loyal to the state, they also remain dependent on the state's financial largesse. Some European leaders—most notably in France and Germany—proudly describe the result as *the European socio-economic model.*[7]

Many Europeans thus struggle with a dual loyalty—to the largesse of the state, and to their individual liberty. Because their governments take so much in taxes, it is difficult to accumulate wealth, and economic freedom eludes them. That explains why tax fraud is so widespread in Europe. Europeans have developed black markets for goods, labor and services to avoid paying high value-added taxes which generate enormous revenues for the state. Tax avoidance, if not a matter of pride, is a matter of course—in Germany, ironically, tax evasion is sometimes described as a *Kavaliersdelikt*, which is a historical reference to a misdemeanor to be ignored because aristocrats were not held accountable for minor offenses. This practice puts Europeans in the position of applauding the largesse of the state on the one hand and trying to defraud it on the other.

Americans tend to associate freedom with loyalty to America, while most Europeans do not see a connection between freedom and loyalty to Europe. Some Europeans would say that this may change in the future, as the European Union (EU) grows together in power and expands in influence. Indeed, there may well be a day when Europeans consider Europe to have concrete, definable, patriotic meaning rather than just being a geographical term. But, for the time being, few Europeans define their nationality as European, nor are they heard singing "God Bless Europe."

Europeans are loyal to their respective countries, but they do not generally express it the way Americans do; although that can differ significantly. For example, it is with real conviction that the English sing "God Save the Queen" and with genuine pride that the French say "Vive la France." But the Germans do not say "God Bless Germany." Nor do Austrians have a song called "God Bless Austria," even though the famous American film *The Sound of Music* would suggest that Austrians do. The film has a romantic message for many American viewers who think that the song "Edelweiss" is the Austrian national anthem. In fact, it was written in 1959 specifically for the Broadway musical. For Austrians, however, the story is a chilling reminder of a tragic side of Austrian history.

To make the difference even clearer, Americans often say and sing, "God Bless America." They bless their country because it is theirs, even though the image of the home of the brave and the land of the free is sometimes tarnished. They take great pride in the American flag. This is not to say that Europeans are not proud, too, or that they do not show their flags. Europeans take immense pride in their respective cultures because they represent an old and rich heritage. Cultural nationalism is alive and well in European countries, but political nationalism as Americans express it, with what sometimes seems to Europeans as endless emphasis on the value of freedom, does not exist. In January 2005 President Bush used the words "freedom" and "liberty" in his inauguration speech forty-one times in the space of about seventeen minutes. There is no equivalent European usage.

Nor are there many Europeans who understand how Americans interpret the symbolism of their flag, including those who know America reasonably well. One of them, Parisian writer and philosopher Bernard-Henri Lévy, published an article in the *Atlantic Monthly* in May 2005, entitled "In the Footsteps of Tocqueville." It was the first of several commissioned by the magazine to celebrate the bicentennial of the birth of the Frenchman who wrote *Democracy In America*. Lévy's introduction begins with observations on "A People and Its Flag" from which the following excerpt is taken:

> It's a little strange, this obsession with the flag. It's incomprehensible for someone who comes from a country where the flag has, so to speak, disappeared, where any nostalgia and concern for it is a sign of an attachment to the past that has become almost ridiculous.
> . . . Or is it something else entirely? An older, more conflicted relationship of America with itself and with its national existence? A difficulty in being a nation, more severe than in the flagless countries of old Europe, that produces this compensatory effect?

Few Americans would draw, much less understand Lévy's interpretation of the flag's meaning. For Americans the flag is important precisely because "it is a sign of attachment to the past." It symbolizes freedom won in the American Revolution, but it also stands for freedom nurtured in the present, and to be defended in the future.

It is our histories that present the context and provide the perspective with which Americans and Europeans see the world, whether it concerns the importance of a flag or a description of who really won America's liberty in 1776. "Don't ever forget," a German friend reminded me in Berlin in the spring of 2002 when we were discussing differences between Americans and Europeans, "that the American Revolution was a war fought by freedom-loving Europeans against high taxes imposed by a German king sitting on an English throne." When I later recounted this story to a businessman who had emigrated to America from Italy shortly after the end of World War II, he gave me an annoyed look and said, simply, "It was freedom-loving Americans who fought the American Revolution, not the other way around."

It may seem strange to Americans, generally unfamiliar with the history and practice of continental politics, that European socialists deny that freely elected European governments rule from the top down and argue, on the contrary, that it is precisely the injustices of privilege found in rule from the top down that socialism wants to remove. There is, however, a specific European hook in the argument that is applied by both socialists and nonsocialists alike.

Socialists refer to the injustices of privilege as "the evils of capitalism" as practiced in America. Opponents of socialism, predictably, argue that they want to limit the arbitrary rule of socialists who seek to impose from the top down their view of justice and equity at the expense of individual liberty. Both socialists and many nonsocialists, however, with a novel twist of inventive logic, assert that *the American model*, without giving it precise definition, is inappropriate for Europe. What they recognize, but do not say, is that *the American model* is freedom built from the ground up, and it is that model which represents a threat to those who rule from the top down, whether they are of the left, of the center, or of the right.

The issue is a straightforward one. What this comparison highlights is that America and Americans have, indeed, followed a different path. Although the conclusion may be obvious, it should not be taken for granted, nor should its significance be underestimated. What concerns the new aristocrats is that they alone wield the power of the state, an approach for which some Europeans have a specific name. They refer to it as modern-day enlightened despotism whose motto is "everything for the people but without the people."[8] The new aristocrats, however, dress up this reality linguistically, and rename rule from the top down *the European socio-economic model.* They then place it in a favorable democratic light by contrasting it with *the American model,* which by inference, is callous, manipulative, and unjust. Thus, when Europeans, but also some Americans, wish to draw a negative comparison between America and Europe they focus their criticism on the imperfect *American economic model* as a dream without a future.[9]

They do not argue the merits and consequences of *the essential difference,* they ignore the existence of the new aristocrats, and in the case of socialist and former French prime minister, Lionel Jospin, they invent the theorem to fit the theory. Jospin did exactly this in his book entitled *The World as I See It,* published in French in October 2005, as he proudly described his discovery of "a new aristocracy," and defined it as follows, according to one French reviewer.

> . . . an implicit alliance between major corporate leaders, the world of finance, entrenched interest groups in industry and the public sector, high-ranking federal civil servants, and privileged individuals from the media. . . . this group [the new aristocrats] demands that other social groups make sacrifices in the name of global competition or [in the name] of economic stability, but is unwilling to even consider making an effort or sacrifices itself.[10]

From the Bottom Up

An accurate description of American life is almost always surprising to Europeans, and they often doubt what they are told. From the continental perspective America was born yesterday. This judgment accounts for what many Europeans view as erratic, free-wheeling, and over-zealous behavior, which they criticize, dismiss or forgive as a characteristic of immaturity. But there is another, more significant side to America's birth which many

Europeans do not see, or perhaps ignore. Whichever is the case, there is much about American behavior that Europeans cannot explain accurately and it begins with how America was built.

The American difference is not caused by the oceanic divide, but by her youth, a nation forged not so long ago by men and women of mixed backgrounds with varied skills. Grassroots Americans formed their communities and shaped their society themselves. They established their institutions in the same way. They were, by choice and heritage, democratic and not aristocratic. The right to govern was not vested in a king, but rested with Americans who created a "government of the people, by the people, for the people."

This phrase is not a trivial description. The principle it contains is not only a part of the political air Americans breathe, but it also underscores a telling historical fact with a European connection. Of the authors of the Constitution one was named James Wilson. He was born in Scotland in 1742 and came to America in 1765. His confidence in the idea of popular sovereignty led to the substitution of "We the people of the United States . . ." for "We the people and the states . . ." in the Constitution's Preamble.[11] In its consequence it was a decision which continues to represent a key element of the essential difference between America and Europe.

In 1787 the framers of the Constitution took great pains to define the relationship of the individual to the state, and created a Bill of Rights to codify it. They forbade the government, and the states, from granting titles of nobility, and also wrote into the Constitution that "no person holding any office or profit or trust under them [the government], shall, without the consent of the Congress, accept any present, emolument, office, or title, of any kind whatever, from any king, prince, or foreign state." Indeed, George Washington rejected the idea that he be given the title of "King" with the unforgettable explanation that he hadn't fought George III in order to become George I.

The absence of an American aristocracy has a number of subtle effects which are commonplace in daily American life, but which are noticed much less often in Europe. One of them is that class distinctions generally make Americans nervous, as for example, in the relationship between a master and his servants. This unease has a public side as well. Being waited on often makes Americans feel uncomfortable. It is hardly a coincidence that in American restaurants waiters arrive at the table, introduce themselves by their first names and do not call themselves waiters or waitresses: "Hi, my name's Steve. I'm your server this evening." A waiter in a Viennese restaurant, on the other hand, does not arrive at a table and say, "Hi, my name's Heinrich."

Unlike Europeans, Americans tend to minimize formality and understate its usefulness. The result is that they normally behave as though social differences are unimportant and class differences do not exist. Americans, whether they know each other well or not, usually call each other by their first names. Europeans, on the other hand, consider that an invasion of privacy. They believe their first name belongs to them, and that no one else has the right to use it without their permission.

Europeans do not practice the kind of easy and relaxed camaraderie between social classes that exists in America. No country in Europe comes even close to the mixed-salad relationships Americans have created, which is a reflection of the continuing and largely successful efforts to break down racial barriers. Indeed, there are Europeans who remain highly critical of America's social and racial problems, as though they had none themselves. But in fact they do. Europeans are divided into highly stratified social classes, and national and ethnic groups. There is little intermingling of either classes or races, although there are, for example, almost twenty million Muslims living in Europe. This is one of the striking, but seldom discussed differences between Europe and America; namely, the absence in Europe of any significant debate on such matters as affirmative action. Ask the English how tolerant they are of nonwhites, or ask the Germans if they really are fond of the Turks, or ask the French whether they would like to welcome more Muslims and Jews into France—a country which already has the largest Muslim and Jewish populations in Europe. Americans do not ask these questions, of course, and the Europeans seldom discuss them.

Another comparison, with a different consequence, relates to patrons.

Patrons have always existed in America, but the practice of patronage has been and is of a private and voluntary nature. Government largesse has not been doled out by aristocratic rulers, noblemen, civil servants and politicians to create and preserve a so-called American culture of rule from the top down. America has never had old aristocrats or new ones. It does have a meritocracy of wealth and social position, with great differences between the very rich and the very poor; a divide which is found in every society on the planet. What distinguishes America from Europe is that the social and economic ladder is climbed on the basis of merit. That is truer today in America than it has ever been.[12] There exists the hope and the dream that the poor can become rich, with hard work and a little luck, because they are part of rule from the bottom up. The hope and the dream, however, are elusive in a system of rule where there exists a hierarchy of authority and a culture of class.

Despite occasional assertions to the contrary, there still exists in Europe a powerful class structure of many levels which is experienced by anyone who lives and works in Europe; for example, the political elite, the educated elite, the intellectual elite, the labor union class, the business class, and also the factory workers, the assembly line employees, the seamstresses, and the farmers. These groupings exist in America, too. But there is a difference. Americans believe that respect can be earned, that you are judged on what you achieve, not on what social class you come from. This confidence in merit breaks down social barriers and promotes social mobility in all kinds of ways. It is, in fact, something peculiar to America which Europeans often notice and speak about when they visit the New World.

What is remarkable, from a European's viewpoint, is that America's social system is so pliable. It has within it the capacity to change, to overcome old prejudices, and to address the possible. America is the story of the self-made man. Anybody can operate a business. Anybody can succeed. Anybody can earn respect. Anybody can send their children to college. Anybody can be president, which in fact, is what former president Bill Clinton said he wanted to be when he was growing up.

Indeed, the so-called anybodies can and do become president. Since World War II America's presidents have included a former clothing salesman, Harry Truman, a former peanut farmer, Jimmy Carter, and a former actor, Ronald Reagan. Europe does not know this kind of mobility, and European leaders do not have this kind of background, because continental standards, expectations, and experiences make it practically impossible. Neither do many Europeans have great respect for this mobility. It suffices to recall the ridicule heaped on Ronald Reagan for being a former "actor" when he was first elected in 1980, a common European bias which was repeated when former actor Arnold Schwarzenegger was first elected governor of California in 2003.

This latter illustration is especially ironic because Schwarzenegger is an Austrian who emigrated to America and became a naturalized citizen. Austrians are both envious and proud of him, a former movie actor married to a relative of John F. Kennedy. But Europeans looked on both men with condescension, because neither of them were perfected political products of rule from the top down. They both emerged from the bottom and moved upward, and one of them, Ronald Reagan, led the Europeans out of Cold War bondage. Who in Europe, in 1989–1990, would ever have thought that one day the former prime minister of Great Britain, Margaret Thatcher, and the former general secretary of the Communist Party of the Soviet Union, Mikhail Gorbachev, would be sitting next to each other in Washington Cathedral, to attend the funeral of former actor Ronald Reagan in 2004, or that Gorbachev, when he paid his final hommage to the deceased president in California, would reach out and gently touch his coffin?

The qualities of American leaders are reflective of how Americans have built their country, and of how they are still shaping it. Class structures do not prevent a successful businessperson, for example, from becoming an admired donor to charitable causes in education, medicine, the arts, or the sciences. Americans who create foundations and give to charities are honoring the freedom of opportunity that allowed them to make enough money to help others. An American can earn respect in this way, and thereby change his or her social status in the community as well as help build the community itself. They are contributing to causes that define what America is. It is part of the ongoing construction of America, and cuts across ethnic divisions. It is an American habit of life.

Europeans, in contrast, are very aware of the social class into which they have been born, and find it much more difficult to move from one to another, to break down the barriers with which their history has endowed them. In Europe "getting rich" brings more economic freedom, as it does in America, but honoring the freedom of opportunity that makes wealth possible is not considered an obligation of being wealthy. Helping others less fortunate is the responsibility of the state, which explains why there are so few private foundations in Europe. Moreover, it is counter to the purpose of the professional political class to weaken the state's benevolent monopoly by encouraging philanthropy. And for those Europeans who do appreciate the practice of financial giving in America and who wish to establish a foundation, legal barriers and obstacles await them at every turn, with the exception of Britain.

It is true that American society consists of the very rich, those of a middle income, and the very poor, but Americans have not yet accepted the proposition that it is the government's responsibility to equalize differences in income. The whole idea of rule from the bottom up is freedom of opportunity and freedom of choice, the possibility that anyone can become a successful part of the American dream, which Europeans, who profit from rule from the top down, derisively describe as *the American model*. It is the search for the American dream that brings about 1.5 million immigrants each year to America, coming from, among other places, Europe. For them *the American model* means the opportunity to succeed. One hundred years ago an Englishman described America as "an oyster which the individual can open with many kinds of knives."[13] Immigrants to America today believe the description still applies, to which the presence of thousands of young Europeans in California's Silicon Valley attests. To this day migration to America is a one-way street. It does not take place in the opposite direction.

The Essential Difference, Again

For both Europeans and Americans there is, on the one hand, Europe. It is the Old World; namely, the European continent from which came men and women of different nationalities and religions to settle in America. There is also, on the other hand, America, which takes its name from a European explorer. It is the New World, where European immigrants built a nation of united states. When Europeans and Americans speak of Europe and America in one phrase, it is a reference to a history that spans more than five centuries. But it is the essential difference with which we can decipher the enigma of our exceedingly complex relationship.

Some Americans, of course, are very conscious of this, and recognize that Europeans and Americans have known each other especially well since the eighteenth century, when life in Europe was defined as an age of enlightenment and reason, and life in America was still one of discovery, not yet defined. Since Benjamin Franklin's first visit to Paris in 1767, just nine years before the American Revolution, the European character and the American spirit have been entwined, one with the other. That spirit and character are an inseparable part of the European-American relationship. It is one that is historically, uncommonly close. No other relationship like it exists anywhere in the world.

One of the reasons, of singular importance to the nature of the relationship, is found in the heritage of western civilization. It is faith in what Austrian economist Friedrich Hayek recited as "those values on which European civilization was built;" namely, "the sacredness of truth . . . the ordinary rules of moral decency . . . a common belief in the value of human freedom . . . an affirmative action towards democracy. . . . opposition to all forms of totalitarianism." These values have been called "the principal ingredients of classical liberalism," but in fact, they are also the principles of civility and liberty. The allegiance to these ingredients of Western civilization, and to their defense when threatened, are part of the substance of the European-American experience.

A history of trial and tribulation characterizes this relationship. It is one that has never been dull, that has often been difficult, and that has proved uniquely rewarding. In spite of ourselves and more often because of ourselves, the discord caused by our cultural, political, and economic quarrels is much less significant than the strength provided by the values we have in common. Hayek called them European. But they are also the values that European emigrants brought to the New World, and put at the heart of their resolve to build a new life.

What binds these values together is the thread of Christian heritage. In the Old World "no one," wrote the religion editor for *Newsweek*, "can visit the medieval core of any European city without encountering evidence of the Christian humanism that gives Europe its enduring cultural identity."[14] In the New World this thread became what medievalist William Carroll Bark described with the phrase "the Christian ethic," a thread peculiar to America which ties American lives together.

What is meant is respect for the unique nature and intrinsic worth of every, single individual. It was the belief that individual liberty embraces respect for the dignity of man and for the dignity of his labor. It was the conviction that each individual is important, that each individual matters, that each individual counts. It was an equality which is the exact opposite of what Europeans mean when they speak of social equality guaranteed by the state. It was an ethic which provided Americans with the strength and confidence to build America from the bottom up.

Expression of the idea did not just appear once, in America's Declaration of Independence in 1776. It has been repeated with conviction on countless occasions, including in Abraham Lincoln's Gettysburg Address of 1863, and in the Liberty Oath of 1950, signed by seventeen million Americans. That oath, together with a full-scale replica of the Liberty Bell, was presented by General Lucius Clay as a gift from the American people to the people of West Berlin in 1950, following the end of the Berlin blockade in 1949. Thereafter, as the West Berliners struggled as an island of freedom in the middle of a red communist sea, the first line of that oath was read on the radio every Sunday morning just before noon, and is still read on *DeutschlandRadio* today: "I believe in the sacredness and dignity of the individual. I believe that all men derive the right to freedom equally from God. I pledge to resist aggression and tyranny wherever they may appear on earth."[15]

It can be persuasively argued that the influence of Christianity on European life began to wane significantly in the latter half of the twentieth century. Today, in Western Europe, only in Italy, Ireland, Portugal and Spain do more than a third of the population go to church on a monthly basis—in France an estimated 5 percent of Catholics attend church—and many Europeans on the left of the political spectrum associate religion with "political reaction."[16] It is true that a decline has taken place in America as well, but it has been to a much lesser degree, as the idea of 'the Christian ethic'—no matter how it is defined, explained or phrased—continues to leave its indelible mark on American life.

From the idea came a fabric made not of self-righteousness, but of the principles of freedom and individual liberty. And even though the fabric was woven long ago, it is still very much intact. Part of it is made of the wisdom found in the Ten Commandments, even though today it is illegal to post them in public school classrooms. Although few Americans would refer to strength, justice, prudence, and temperance as "the Cardinal virtues," these too make up part of the fabric. And part of it is a commitment to love, hope, faith and charity, symbolized in America by the phrase "In God We Trust." In the first decade of the third millennium "In God We Trust" is written on all American paper currency, and on every American coin.

The phrase itself did not appear on American paper currency until 1957. But the words are the modern reflection of trust in the old idea of the Christian ethic. Europe's emigrants were looking for a new order of the ages that would include freedom of worship, political independence, and economic opportunity. They did not find the new order waiting for them. They created it, and reaped what they sowed. They were free to give thanks, as they chose, for a bountiful harvest. And when they began doing so in 1621, they called it giving thanks. More than 150 years later, in 1777, the Continental Congress declared the first national Thanksgiving, and 86 years after that, in 1863, Abraham Lincoln proclaimed the last Thursday in November national Thanksgiving Day.[17] Whether described as a giving of thanks, or as a prayer, that national day celebrated confidence in strength, justice, prudence and temperance, and in the conviction *that all men derive the right to freedom equally from God.*

Today Europeans are generally unaware that Thanksgiving is one of America's most important holidays together with Christmas and Easter,

nor are they aware that separation of Church and State was conceived as
an affirmation of freedom of religion rather than condemnation of the
Christian ethic. America's immigrants insisted on a clear distinction because they believed that the State should not dictate an established national church of worship. The reason to separate the Church from the
State was to establish freedom for religion, not freedom from religion. At
the end of the eighteenth century Americans wrote into their Constitution that Congress shall make no law prohibiting the free exercise of religion. But the Founders of the American republic—which included
Episcopalians, Lutherans, Methodists, Quakers, Presbyterians, Deists,
and Roman Catholics—also embraced the idea of "the Christian ethic"
in their New World as part and parcel of civility and liberty. On Christmas Day 1789, to be sure, the new American Congress was in working
session and not on vacation. Eighty-one years later however, in 1870,
Congress declared the day of the birth of Jesus Christ to be a national
holiday in America.

Throughout all their toils Americans sought to make "the principal ingredients of classical liberalism" a part of their daily lives. They did so con-
sciously, not only with confidence in faith and reason, but also with the
hope inherent in their vision of a new order of the ages. They did not
always succeed, to which the extended American history of slavery is ago-
nizing testimony, as is also the struggle for the right to vote. The American struggle for freedom would be marred by racial discrimination. But
as Americans in the New World they moved continually forward, one
slow and often painful step at a time, to create an American age of enlightenment, guided by idealism, and by a belief in hard work that became
part of the American spirit. Their effort was far from perfect and the New
World they created was not, either. But it was far, far better than the Old
World they had left behind, a world in which, long before, the concept
and practice of slavery had been adopted and a world in which racism
would have catastrophic consequences in the twentieth century.

Those who came to America from Europe, with some inevitable and
also notable exceptions, were not the Europeans of wealth and privilege.

Early immigrants—sometimes described today as "the sweepings of Europe"—sought a refuge from territorial wars, ethnic prejudice, and religious bigotry and persecution; nineteenth-century immigrants sought to escape poverty and famine. They were looking for equality of opportunity and equality under the law as signposts on the road to the pursuit of individual happiness. In the eighteenth century Americans already considered it important enough to declare all three inalienable rights in their Declaration of Independence in 1776. They all suffered the emotional pain of leaving Europe and members of their wider families, the dangers of storm and illness while crossing an endless ocean, and the hardships of starting a new life in an unknown world. But once there, they persevered. They gave their spirit, their conviction, their hearts, and their lives.

What European emigrants to America wanted to create was defined, deliberately, when the Great Seal of the United States was designed in 1782 by Benjamin Franklin, John Adams, and Thomas Jefferson. On it are written two inscriptions, both in Latin. The first, *Novus Ordo Seclorum*, is translated as "A New Order of the Ages." In seeking a new order, in a new world, Europe's emigrants looked to Divine Providence during the creation of the republic for which they stood. Hence, the presence of the second Latin inscription, *Annuit Coeptis*. In English it means "He (God) has favored our undertakings." And to one of the authors of the Constitution, James Madison, it meant the following,

> We have staked the whole future of American civilization, not upon the power of government, far from it. We have staked the future of all our political institutions upon the capacity of mankind for self government; upon the capacity of each and all of us to govern ourselves, to control ourselves, to sustain ourselves according to the Ten Commandments of God.

The enterprise became a republic, a state in which government is carried on from the bottom to the top, nominally and in fact by the people through their directly elected representatives. To describe it a Greek word was chosen, *demokratia*, and less than a century later the republic was christened by Alexis de Tocqueville, an aristocratic visitor from Europe, in a famous book he called *Democracy in America*. Of the Americans he wrote, "they brought with them into the New World a form of Christianity which I cannot better describe than by styling it a democratic and republican religion. . . . [F]rom the beginning, politics and religion contracted an alliance which has never been dissolved. . . . [The Americans] combine the notions of Christianity and of liberty so intimately in their minds that it is impossible to make them conceive the one without the other." For millions of Americans this continues to be the case, and for millions of Europeans the fabric of the American character remains a mystery.[18]

If Tocqueville had also written of the Europeans, the description would have been a fundamental contrast in how Europeans and Americans view the purpose of government and the origin of government authority. Europeans considered legitimate authority as coming from God to the Sovereign, who then delegated authority to his officials, to thus rule the citizenry. Americans viewed legitimate authority as coming from God to the citizenry, who then redelegated authority to government officials, who governed as servants of those who elected them.

This was a simple distinction, profound in its consequence. It described American and European behavior better than any other explanation, and affected the structure and hierarchy of all of our respective relationships, private and public. In twenty-first century America and Europe this continues to be the case—and it applies to everything we undertake, whether it is business, education, or government.

⟨✦⟩

Americans, unlike Europeans, think in terms of ongoing change, rather than in terms of historical periods and distinctions. While many signs of European heritage are present throughout America, the cultural and ethnic influences which define American society today are broad, rich, complex, and constantly in flux. Continuous movement, in fact, defines America just as strongly now as it did during Tocqueville's nineteenth-century visit.

Influences on American life from abroad are still predominantly European. But they are also clearly Judaic, Oriental, Middle Eastern and African. Indeed, the history of those Americans who trace their ancestral origins to Africa is a major part of American life, and not only of American life. Their creative artistry in music has been exported around the world as an American cultural ambassador called jazz. Another example is located on the western coast of America where California is defined, every day, by Asian, Hispanic, Latin and Native American influences. Further illustrations are found in food, music, art and language, in the names of California's towns and cities, such as Palo Alto, San Jose, Los Angeles, and Sacramento, and in the cosmopolitan communities of the Chinese and Japanese in San Francisco. All of these aspects of life are an irreplaceable part of America's heritage.[19]

Americans are not generic. But whether they live in the north or south, in the east or the west, or in America's breadbasket, the Midwest, and whether they call themselves New Yorkers, Bostonians, Virginians, or Texans, they are all Americans by choice. Individuals of all cultures, whatever they may be, are Americans in America, where speaking English with an accent is commonplace, just as it was one hundred years ago. Some Europeans argue, with the intention of being critical, that there is no such thing as an American, that they come from everywhere. That, of course, is precisely the point. Part of being an American in America is that, indeed, they are from everywhere, but once they get there they become a different type of human being in how they look, how they act, and in how they think.[20]

As Europeans observe the varied and colorful ethnic landscape of America today, they can recognize that the impact of things European remains more pronounced than any other. The explanation is found not only in the historical ties between America and Europe. It is also seen and experienced in the daily habits of American life which have been, in so many different ways, affected by European culture, customs, and traditions. In fact, European influences are so widespread that they tend to be regarded as American rather than European.

One of them is seasonal. It has become without question the most important commercial holiday in America, as well as the birthday celebration of Jesus Christ on December 25. The greeting of "Happy Holidays" may be heard more often than "Merry Christmas," but December is still that time of year when America, devoted to its tradition of decorated Christmas trees, carols and the gaiety of Christmas Eve, is most intimately affected by European art, literature and music.

American Christmas customs, including postage stamps depicting European paintings of the nativity, recall much of the Old World. One of the most popular carols in America is "Silent Night," written and composed by an Austrian in a little village outside of Salzburg. The story of *A Christmas Carol*, by English author Charles Dickens, is performed in theaters all over America each December, as is sung the *Messiah* by German composer George Frideric Handel. And in both America and Europe one of the most popular songs ever, written by American composer Irving Berlin and made famous by Bing Crosby, is sung in English and in almost every European language. It is called "White Christmas," and has even been translated into Latin.

Many other influences, not seasonal, are present each day in sights, sounds, tastes and names. They are seen in paintings and heard in music, read in literary and dramatic works, reflected in philosophy and science and religion, and are part of the art of a simple family meal around the dining table in millions of American homes every day of the year. European words are found everywhere in American language, beginning with the name of the pre-school to which all American children go. It is called *Kindergarten*, a German word which means a children's garden. And when the children grow up and send an invitation to a party, they very often put on the bottom of it RSVP It is a French phrase, *repondez s'il vous plaît*, which means "please reply." The Old World is symbolized by the names of American towns like Berlin—there is a 'Berlin' in no less than eleven of the fifty states. And there are hundreds of other towns with European names, like London, Rome, Madrid, Paris, Stockholm, and Vienna.

For millions of Americans, too, favorite foods and drinks throughout the United States are of European origin—German beer and bratwurst, Italian pasta, English roast beef and Yorkshire pudding, Swiss cheese and fondue, Danish aquavit and pickled herring, beef steak and French fries,

Polish sausages, Spanish gazpacho and paella, Austrian schnitzel and noo-dles. All of these things are found in shops, in markets, and in restaurants throughout the United States, as are foods of other cultures such as chut-ney and curries, egg rolls and fried shrimp, tacos and burritos, and salsa which has replaced catsup as the most popular condiment on American tables.

Cultural and religious influences of Europe are especially striking in America's Middle West. In the state of Iowa, as one example, a complete list would be overwhelming, but its length is a powerful illustration of Europe in America. In Cedar Rapids there are superb Czech restaurants, a Czech National Cemetery, and a National Czech and Slovak Museum, opened in 1995. "The New World Symphony," by Antonin Dvořák, was written in Spillville, Iowa. The impact of Scandinavia is found in De-corah, where the Norwegian Museum has been visited, more than once, by the King of Norway. Americans as well as European tourists find the influence of the Dutch at Jaarsma's Bakery, the Strawtown Inn and at the Tulip Festival in the town of Pella. The French name of Iowa's state capi-tal is Des Moines (The Monks). The list of Iowa towns with European names, if continued, could go on for several paragraphs and would in-clude Lourdes, Hamburg, Waterloo, Cambridge, and Harcourt, the name of one of the oldest families in France, dating from the eleventh century.

The European tourist can also visit magnificent Catholic churches in eastern Iowa, in Petersburg, Dyersville and New Vienna. One of them is a basilica, and they all contain stained-glass windows made in Westphalia (in Germany), then shipped to Iowa in the nineteenth century. Today many of the parishioners of these churches still have German names. Fi-nally, there is Dubuque, Iowa, one of the so-called Five Flag Cities found on the Mississippi River. Over Dubuque flew the flags of first the French, then the Spanish followed by the English, then the French again during the Empire, and finally the Americans. Indeed, the first Bishop of Du-buque came not from America, but from France, where he was born in 1792, in Lyon, during the French Revolution. He arrived on the Missis-sippi as a newly ordained bishop in 1839, seven years before Iowa became a state, and served until his death in 1858.

The remarkable nature of the European influence is that it is found everywhere in America. There are influences of the Spanish in California, Arizona, and Texas, of the French in Louisiana, of the Polish and Norwegians in Wisconsin, of the Dutch in Pennsylvania, of the Swedes and the Finns in Minnesota, of the Irish in Massachusetts, of the English in Virginia and New York, and of the Germans who traveled by packet boat from Lake Erie or up the Mississippi River from New Orleans to the Middle West of America. By 1860 almost one-third of the immigrants in America were from Germany. Fifty years later, in 1910, 8.3 million Americans, out of a total population of more than 92 million, were German born and more than one million had arrived from Sweden. The modern history of the Middle West is European, and those who live there encounter the European influence daily whenever they speak the names of their cities like Marquette (Michigan), Eau Claire (Wisconsin), Upsala (Minnesota), Paris (Illinois), Glasgow (Kentucky), Lafayette (Indiana), Steubenville (Ohio), or St. Louis (Missouri).

Places and things American and European cannot have the same degree of significance for everyone on either continent. But irrespective of the degree, American and European culture, politics, and economics are inextricably tied together. There is no question that the vision of the American dream and the soul of the American spirit, was laid first by Europeans—by men and women of widely different parentage and nationalities, who came originally from the Old World speaking foreign languages when they arrived. And thereafter, in terms of the essential difference, they followed their own path as Americans.

Many of them formed their own ethnic enclaves—such as the Spanish, the Italians, the French, the Germans, the Poles, the Czechs, the Dutch, and the Swedes. They were proud of their heritage and they preserved it—to this day there are Germantowns, and French quarters, and Little Italys in American cities. Many also continued to speak their native languages at home, and in some cases taught them to their children. But, they deliberately chose English as the language of their new country, and they taught English literature to their children. And they also did something else it had not been possible to do before. They gave their new country their loyalty, and their allegiance. There they were their own rulers in their new nation.

Once in America the idea of freedom was no longer just a dream. It was a reality. They became American citizens, and entered a public realm of both privilege and responsibility. American society was thus given a unique dimension. Citizenship was a private choice, which often found the individual occupying the role of hero, whether it was a fireman saving a life, a policeman protecting a child, or a soldier awarded a Purple Heart. They did not refer to each other as English-Americans, or French-Americans, or Swedish-Americans. While they had strong disagreements and did not always act as one out of many, they shared a single goal. They pursued their new undertakings as Americans, building one nation. They knew who they were, and what they wanted to become.

Whether it was the Pilgrims in seventeenth-century New England or the Irish fleeing from famine in the nineteenth century, life in their New World became the history of courage and achievement. "The Irish experience in America," to quote from the introduction to a documentary for American public television produced in 1998, "is a story of trial and triumph. For all Americans, and for all of us, it's a story about America itself. It was a great victory. This is what they came here for. They didn't come to stay together as Irish-Americans. They came to find something else. And in the end they found what they were looking for."

What they sought was called many things: freedom from want, freedom to worship, freedom to dream, freedom to choose. They also found a way to describe the spirit of the nation they built, and wrote it down, not in the European language of English, but in the European language of Latin, as *e pluribus unum*, out of many, one. Drawing on this principle, individual Americans created a symbol, by themselves, without government oversight: the American flag. When Americans today "fly the flag" they are expressing their loyalty; they are reminding themselves, and the world, that pride in their nation is still part of the American enterprise. It was a surprise to no one in America that the "Stars and Stripes" appeared everywhere, throughout the United States, following the attack on the World Trade Center in New York City on September 11, 2001. Flags were hung from the windows of buildings, flown from the radio antennae of cars and trucks, waved from front doors, and made into lapel pins.

The force and importance of this symbolism, however, was difficult to understand for many Europeans unfamiliar with American history. Journalists in Europe ridiculed this simple pageant of patriotism as a naive and "typically American" public display of private grief. But Americans thought it the most natural thing in the whole world to use a national symbol to show that, as individuals, they stood together as *out of many, one*. It made sense in terms of their loyalty to the American idea of freedom, whether the color of their skin was black, white, brown, or yellow.

It is on that common ground—the commonality of the American experience—that Americans of all backgrounds have since built their lives, and make their lives today. Even though Americans seldom speak, any more, of the enormous impact of Europe on American life, the formation of the American character is inconceivable without it. Yet that character, in all its essentials, is not European but uniquely American.

CHAPTER II

On History, Heritage, and Habits of Life

Geography, Distance, and Space

GENERAL DIFFERENCES, significantly influencing American and European life, begin with geography, distance, and space. Americans are very much aware that Europeans come from individual nations, in the sense that when a European visits America and is asked where he comes from, he will not say Europe. He will give his nationality, such as Belgian or Dutch. When an American goes to Europe his response to the same question is different. He will normally respond, the United States, a few will say America, and some will just say "the States."

When Americans visit Europe they understand that they can only be in one country at a time, and that each country is unique. But they are sensitive to the fact that they are in Europe, to which more than two thirds of America's population can still trace its ancestry. When Americans speak of the Europeans they usually think of them as one group, and when they return home they often say they have been in Europe.

Although most Americans cannot provide detailed explanations, they know that there are geographical differences among Europeans of a kind that do not exist in America. But general knowledge infrequently goes beyond that point—and, of course, the same conclusion applies to European familiarity with America.

Most Americans are unaware, nor should they be expected to know, that Europe's most western point is Dunmore Head, Ireland, although some might argue it is Iceland, and that the Ural Mountains in Russia mark Europe's eastern border. The northernmost point of Europe is North Cape in Norway, inside the Arctic Circle, and the southern border, which can be debated, is the northern coast of the Mediterranean, but the islands of Malta and Cyprus are included in Europe, too. A point of contention is Turkey, at the eastern end of the Mediterranean. There are those, such as former French president Valéry Giscard d'Estaing, who aver that Turkey is not a European country, but its western border is hundreds of miles west of Cyprus, whose Greek part became a member of the European Union.[1]

To take this description a little further, Europe has 48 countries—50 if the Faeroe Islands and Gibraltar are counted—in which more than 140 languages are spoken. There are approximately 100 different ethnic groups represented in the Europe of the twenty-first century, not counting the more obscure minorities such as the Vlachs in the Balkans or the Ingrians in Finland. Individual countries are small and densely populated. Geography varies enormously, and distances between great cities in Europe are short in comparison to America.[2]

Differences in size between individual European countries and American states are dramatic. Germany can fit into the state of Montana, Italy is approximately the size of Arizona, France is twice the size of Nevada but smaller than Texas, and the Low Countries (the Netherlands, Belgium and Luxembourg) can fit into the state of Pennsylvania. The United Kingdom is about as big as New York State, but the U.K.'s population of around 58 million is almost four times as large.

Many of the characteristics Europeans call American have been shaped by geography. It goes without saying that the same point applies to Europeans, but in a more complicated way, because what might be called continental traits are influenced not only by geography but also by language and national borders. In both Europe and America geography is the story of how distance is perceived and space is used, but in precisely opposite ways.

The sheer size of America has a tremendous effect on how Americans behave, and also on how they think. For Europeans this is difficult to understand, because their countries are so small by comparison, and because it is not easy to visualize distance and imagine space. The observation may sound elementary, and even silly to Americans, but when Europeans talk about Florida and California many imagine these states are right next door to each other. This was not an unreasonable assumption at all for the lady sitting next to me at a dinner party in Berlin, when she asked if I would describe Florida. She had heard of the white beaches that went on forever and wanted to know what they were like. When I told her I had never been there, and had no idea how big Florida was, she gave me a look of incomprehension that meant, "Well, why haven't you?" Of course, she had never been to America and had no idea that Miami is more than 3,100 miles or 4,960 kilometers from San Francisco.

Americans who travel are aware, in general terms, of the great distances between major American cities in comparison to short distances between European ones. Many know, for example, that it is about 3,000 miles, or 4,800 kilometers, from San Francisco to New York City and some may be aware that the distance between Vienna and Berlin is about the same as between Los Angeles and San Francisco. But many Americans struggle when they try to explain the size of the continental United States in a way that helps Europeans envision the distance separating the oceans of the Pacific and the Atlantic.

If we use the passage of time as a measurement, however, because both Americans and Europeans understand it, the explanation becomes easier. The following comparison presents a picture that both Americans and Europeans can imagine: a Dutchman can board a plane in Amsterdam in the morning, fly to Paris, get out for lunch, and fly back home in the afternoon, but an American traveling from San Francisco to New York City will still be on the airplane. This illustration is helpful to Americans and Europeans alike. But if Europeans have not actually traveled across America, and most have not, it is difficult to expand beyond this relationship between time and distance.

How, for example, can Europeans comprehend the effect of the country's size on the American character, the American spirit, and on American behavior? The answer is that they cannot, because the European concept of size has no complement in America. What is big to Europeans is often small to Americans, and what is big to Americans is often of huge proportion to Europeans. There are, in addition, many other aspects of American life that have been, or are influenced by continental distances and vast landscapes, such as American film, music and painting, as well as the American concept of what time means and how it is used.

The contrast between wide-open space in America, and the lack of it in Europe, is, like many other differences, simple in explanation and significance. The effect is captured perfectly in a small story of just several lines from the *International Herald Tribune*. It seems that in May 2003 a trip was taken by a group of Germans on a boat down the Missouri River, a waterway of more than 2,300 miles in length (3,700 kilometers). Their American guide, at one point, said to them, "This river must be really boring you," and they answered, "No, you have something we don't have in Europe—wild, undeveloped land."[3]

Americans may take this comment for granted, or dismiss it as stating the obvious. But for Europeans wild, undeveloped land is a symbol of the New World's frontier, and also of its self-containment. It is not surprising that Europeans have been making such observations for a long time, and there are a number to choose from. A recent one, however, is preferable because it addresses the present and not the past. It is striking in its conviction. It comes from a German, in his late forties, who lived in communist East Germany until the Berlin Wall fell in 1989. In 1991 he and his wife visited America for the first time and spent the next two years in California and Maryland. During the mid-1990s they returned several times to drive across America, and since 1996 they call to wish us a happy Thanksgiving, an American holiday they now celebrate in Berlin.

Burkhard's view of America is not unique, but his earnest expression of it is unusual in its strength and clarity. In early 2002 he wrote to me,

Your country is big enough that you don't need to go outside for very much, and our countries are so small we are always stepping into someone else's backyard. Most of the natural resources you need are in America. But I know there is a lot more to it than that. Being self-contained also has a lot to do with being free to choose from many alternatives for work and pleasure. Your mobility comes from that freedom, and both give you self-confidence. We see it when we visit you in America.

For example, and maybe this will surprise you, for me there is just one word to describe you. It is "openness." In German we call you *zugänglich*. That is another way of saying that Americans are friendly and accessible, and willing to help others in ways that we Europeans find both wonderful and overwhelming, because we ourselves are much less outgoing. That is why some Europeans who don't know you think your reputation for friendliness is superficial, or naive. Some even think you make it up.

But, and I hope you know it, Europeans who have visited your country find your warm welcome a breath of fresh air, to borrow an American phrase, which we do not breathe nearly as deeply at home. As a European, new to this difference, I am always startled by it, and before I met you I had never even thought about it. When the Wall was standing I could never leave East Germany to visit America.

There is no question in my mind that most European visitors to your country look on America as a place where anything is possible. Many Europeans also see frontiers in America still waiting to be found. The recent revolutions in communication and computer technology, and in biotechnology, are real examples and they explain why so many young Europeans move to your country. They know there is still the pioneering spirit, there are still new opportunities awaiting those willing to take a chance, and that the American adventure is not yet completed. This attitude, if that is the best word for it, is not found as often in Europe, because we live on a continent where bureaucracy and government make it hard for us to move, to get past the barriers that are put in our way.

Our frontiers were conquered long ago, and our building was transformed into reconstruction by the wars of the twentieth century. If you want to you can point to the fact that we have rebuilt our towns and cities many times over, but that is not the same thing. Look at the urban landscape in Berlin since German unification in 1990, for example. Construction cranes dot the city's skyline. It is enormously exciting and is giving our city a new life, as hundreds of American visitors tell us. But it is, also, a re-building.

When I think of America the words "opportunity" and "openness" are part of my vocabulary, but that is also because I know your country now. Most Europeans, unless they have driven from the Atlantic to the Pacific or from the Canadian border to the Gulf of Mexico, cannot possibly imagine the breathtaking vistas of America's "wide open spaces." That is why Erika and I took the bus across the country to see America. In Iowa and Nebraska the land goes on forever; the first time we saw it we could hardly believe it. Everything is flat. Europeans can look at maps, but that does not help much. There just is not a substitute for driving across the Great Plains. Erika and I wonder if you can really be as aware, as we are, of how much the reality and practice of "openness" defines Americans? You are used to it. But, for us, it is a way of life, an outlook on life we will never have.

There are many reasons for this difference, and because you have spent so much time in Europe, you are familiar with them. You have told me that you are going to begin your book with a description of what you call the essential difference. I agree that the difference exists. But do not overlook that there are many other unusual characteristics, and all of them are important. Among them is the connection between your geography and your openness.[4]

Those Europeans who study the bent and bias of Americans and their behavior will find Burkhard's conclusions useful. They also, however, suggest additional observations. The romance of American geography is about the uncertainty of what may be found in the wide-open spaces, and is about the idea of freedom underneath the western skies. This is not as trite as it sounds. Rivers, plains and mountains have unquestionably left their mark on American behavior. More than one hundred years ago, in 1893, a well-known American historian, Frederick Jackson Turner, made this argument about expansion westward, and its effect on the American character. He presented his thesis in a now famous speech given to a gathering of historians in Chicago, entitled "The Significance of the Frontier in American History." In it he attributed "that restless, nervous energy that dominated individualism" to the influence of the frontier.[5] His writings called attention to "the pioneering experience as one of the causal forces responsible for the distinctiveness of the nation's social order."[6]

The unexplored American West that so many Americans discovered following the California Gold Rush of 1849 gave more than just symbolic meaning to the words open and expansive. More than one hundred and fifty years later European visitors react in much the same way to American geography. Nothing exists in Europe like the overwhelming beauty of the Rocky Mountains, the Wind River Range, or the Grand Tetons. The Alps are beautiful, but not since Hannibal have they presented the daunting challenge that was met by American pioneers trying to cross the Sierra Nevada Mountains in covered wagons in the nineteenth century. The feeling of majesty the mountains gave to those who saw them has been memorably described by a naturalist who came to America as a little boy from Scotland with his father in the 1840s. Of the Sierra Nevada John Muir wrote: "Oh, these vast, calm, measureless mountain days, in whose light everything seems equally divine, opening a thousand windows to show us God."

Wide-open spaces made America an open society in more than just a geographical sense. The country was so big that when Americans began settling it—whether it was in the valleys of the east, on the great plains, or in the wild west—building required the labor of many hands. No one could do it alone. The settlers, the farmers, and the cowmen could not wait for a construction company because none existed. Americans had to help each other. They did not have time to make distinctions between their private and public lives. Nor could they spend a lot of energy indulging the doubts and second thoughts they may have had about their neighbors. Their daily worries were an open book as they built America.

They spoke bluntly. Sometimes they did it loudly and they did not always get along, either, to which notorious range wars between cattle ranchers and farmers were violent testimony. But Americans were, to a great extent, dependent on each other. They had to develop social relationships that were based on the need to work together, not on the basis of who had done what to whom in Europe in the past. They could not afford to live in a European world that was closed and rooted in suspicion.

They did not have time. Their world was full of hardship and demand, but it was also a world full of opportunity. They took risks because that is how they made progress. Sometimes the risks were too great, and they failed, and sometimes the risks were overcome and the rewards were rich.

Americans developed what is variously called rugged individualism, independence, and self-reliance. They had to be strong and resourceful, whether it was building New England in the seventeenth and eighteenth centuries, or moving westward in the nineteenth and twentieth. The challenges of survival had to be met quickly, because there was no other choice. Time was in short supply. Americans were in a hurry to solve their problems, so they could move on to the next one. In doing so Americans depended on each other to build their communities, together—to clear the land, to plant, to gather the harvest, and to construct their houses, schools and churches.

They used weapons for hunting and protection, not only on the frontier but everywhere. Initially, law and order came out of the barrel of a gun, as they struggled to create a standard of justice and enforce a rule of law. The rigor of life in the New World taught Americans that to succeed they had to be independent. They defended their liberty with weapons, which is the story of the American Revolution and why the right to bear arms is inscribed as the second amendment to the American Constitution. They bore arms against the British during America's war of independence because there was no one else to bear them, although there was a good deal of help from the French who were just as determined to defeat the "the perfidious Albion"[7] as the Americans. The year 1776 was the American turning point, the end of the colonial struggle, and the beginning of America's belief in itself.

Some Europeans, as well as some Americans, criticize today what they see as an American preoccupation with guns, but are unaware that belief in the right of the individual to protect liberty and independence, with force if necessary, is as old as the republic. Others, however, understand the point very well, and make the distinction, such as an English businessman in Cambridge who wrote in 2001 that "the American instinct is to trust the person and be wary of the government, in the belief that it's much safer to have a gun in the hands of an individual citizen rather than weapons in the hands of the government. . . . Europeans tend to think in just the opposite terms."[8]

The spirit of the individual, building from the bottom up, was a reflection of America's youth vis-à-vis Europe's age. There was no government to call on for direction, so Americans sought each other out, and developed a commitment to one another that also helps to explain, to a great degree, their generosity. That spirit of helping continues today in the form of private charities and voluntary organizations which provide services all over America, and abroad as well. In 2003, for example, Americans gave $241 billion dollars to approximately 1.3 million charities, equal to the gross domestic product of Austria.[9] This spirit, which Europeans experienced with the gift of millions of American CARE packages after World War II,[10] was demonstrated on an unprecedented level, following the December 2004 Tsunami disaster in southeast Asia. By the end of February 2005 Americans had raised, privately, more than one billion dollars to help the victims.[11]

American history has been described many times over with the same clichés, as a display of challenges to be met, of obstacles to be overcome, and of frontiers to be explored. Today, of course, most of that is over in a geographical sense, and America's critics conclude that Americans have nothing left to exploit, since their insatiable appetite, abetted by impatience, has consumed everything. But the entrepreneurial initiative they developed is still very much a part of how Americans think, whether they live in the country or in villages, towns and cities. Americans still see their society and their lives as wide open, and the possibilities as still endless. Some see this spirit, described by historians writing about the American frontier, as stronger today than it has ever been.[12] American farmers and ranchers overcome obstacles of the present every day, American businesspeople expect challenges they have not yet discovered, and American scientists are still newcomers to the exploration of space in comparison to what it will be like one hundred years from now.

The foregoing is not intended to romanticize the idea of the American spirit, not all of which, historians accurately conclude, is made of freedom, openness and independence, such as the tragic and brutal treatment of Native Americans. The explanation is presented because the influence of geography, distance and space on American history, and on American behavior, represents a sharp contrast with the European experience. The contrast is also drawn, deliberately, in general terms because there are millions of Americans and Europeans who do not think about the effects of geography, distance and space on their lives, much less about why the effects are different in Europe and America. But significant differences are there, nonetheless, as Burkhard concluded in his letter to me, and ignorance or categorical dismissal of them does not make their reality any less dramatic.

In his second letter to me in mid-2002 Burkhard again wrote about openness and geography from a European perspective:

American public and private life—your strengths and your weaknesses, your successes and your failures, your personal worries and your professional problems—is one big, open book. It is one of your great virtues, even though sometimes it makes you look childish, or worse, foolish. Your openness allows you to stare adversity in the eye, and overcome it. It gives you an abundance of possibilities, many of which you turn into riches.

You could well say that we have met adversity successfully, too. For me the peaceful unification of Germany and the rebuilding of Berlin are obvious examples. But I do not need to remind you that here the word adversity refers to a period in our history we would rather forget. Our trials were of our own creation. That is very different from the tribulations Americans dealt with, which were met with a positive spirit of surmounting obstacles to create something new, not rebuilding what we ourselves had destroyed.

Because our countries are small, and are so close together, we are always aware that Europe is a complex collection of peoples and a contradictory map of custom. Sometimes I think that the confidence and assurance you get from your vast and rich land allows you to forget that your abundance of mountain greenery does not exist in the same way in Europe. We do not have any wide open spaces. Our geography does not open our societies and present our lives with the vision of boundless opportunities. It keeps them closed and reinforces our provincialism. We find security in "our corner" much more willingly than most Americans realize. And we know a lot less about our continental neighbors than you assume. You have only two of them, Canada and Mexico. We have many. Austria, for example, shares common borders with eight countries: Germany, Switzerland, Italy, Liechtenstein, Hungary and now Slovenia, the Slovak Republic and the Czech Republic.

Americans travel about constantly, not because they are innately restless or unhappy, but because they have the freedom and the space in which to do it; thus, many have lengthy daily commutes to get to their jobs and about forty million Americans each year change their address. On average they drive 12,000 miles each year, or about 19,200 kilometers, partly because it is convenient and partly because distances make it impractical to walk or use a bicycle. In comparison to the practice in America most Europeans do not move about in the same way. Some, of course, travel a great deal, and the spirit of exploration has European origins, not American ones. But Europeans do live with some constraints Americans do not. Gasoline costs much more than it does in America, and automobiles are expensive. Europeans pay more attention, as a consequence, to how much gasoline they consume, and to how much wear and tear they put on their cars. Few drive eighty kilometers for dinner in a restaurant, but Californians living in Palo Alto think nothing of driving that distance for dinner in San Francisco. The number of cars per capita is also distinctly different. In the EU it is about 470 cars for every thousand inhabitants, while in America it is about 760 per 1,000 people.[13]

Europeans love their fast cars, as every American knows who has driven on German autobahns, but rarely do Europeans drive them for three or four hundred miles at once. But if they do, and travel the same distance that separates San Francisco from Los Angeles, they may cross two, or even three different national borders. That makes them conscious, quickly, of changes in language, dress, and food, as well as in history, heritage and habit. A road trip of three or four hundred miles in America does not put the traveler in another country. And if Americans drive through the mountains of Utah and across the expanse of Wyoming until they come to the continental divide, where water flows in opposite directions, they can experience a feeling of measureless calm that does not exist anywhere in Europe. If Americans are in the Rocky Mountains and look east, or west, they still see America while Europeans in the Alps can see not just different vistas from one spot, but different countries.

Space in Europe means something confining, not something expansive, and, during much of European history, it has meant something threatening as well. More than one hundred years ago this concern was the subject of an unusual conversation between the French ambassador to America and President Theodore Roosevelt's wife. During a discussion of pacifism Mrs. Roosevelt is said to have suggested that France might learn from the relationship between America and Canada:

> "We have a three-thousand-mile unfortified peaceful frontier. You people arm yourselves to the teeth."
> "Ah, Madame," the ambassador replied, "perhaps we could exchange neighbors."[14]

The meaning of the response is self-explanatory. European geography, for Europeans, is more than just picturesque. The plains of Poland, for example, have been called a stepping stone separating Germany from Russia, while those living in Luxembourg describe their country as the marble between the elephants of France and Germany. The border dividing France and Germany is another example. How many times have the French and the Germans fought each other? A visitor to the Alsace-Lorraine, where the European Parliament meets in Strasbourg, will encounter German and French names everywhere as a reminder that this magnificent region also has a tragic past, dating from the battle of Tolbiac in A.D. 496. What the visiting tourist, however, is unlikely to experience today is the tone of conversations among French families in Alsatia whose homes were occupied by Germans twice during the twentieth century.

European populations live much closer together. The consequence is that privacy is more prone to invasion and difficult to protect. In America population density is about 32 people per square mile, but in Europe it is

134, more than four times as great. One can argue that problems of privacy in large cities are the same, whether in Europe or America. But European attitudes about privacy, whether one lives in the city or in the country, have been significantly shaped by battles over space, and hence, by the lesson of European history that it is wise to be wary, if not suspicious, of both neighbors and government. This explains in large measure why there is a side to Europeans which is protective, private and closed. It is behavior that has nothing in common with American practice.

This line, drawn between what is private and what is public, is not exaggerated. It is also a difference with which most Americans who have European friends are well familiar. It was put in a vivid way by a British visitor to America at the end of the nineteenth century. Since then, of course, an entire century has passed, but James Muirhead's conclusion is even more valid now than a century ago, thanks in large part to how we communicate with each other publicly, especially via radio and television. He wrote that Americans ". . . have as a whole not only less reverence than Europeans for the privacy of others, but also less resentment for the violation of their own privacy. The new democracy has resigned itself to the custom of living in glass houses and regards the desire to shroud one's personal life in mystery as one of the survivals of the dark ages."[15]

Another area of contrast, very much related to space, is the subject of land. Europeans regard the utility and define the meaning of land differently from Americans. Because there are few large private holdings, anywhere in Europe, land is precious, both psychologically and in real terms. Through centuries of inheritance, as well as war, land ownership has been reduced to smaller, and smaller morsels. The history of Germany is a good example, but all European countries have similar histories.

Vast tracts of land and open space are part of the American countryside. In a manner of speaking land is all around Americans and they buy and sell it frequently. Europeans, however, do not sell land often, because most of them own very little of it, if any. It is looked upon as something of unique value, and Europeans, if they are fortunate enough to have a small piece, not only keep it but consider its size a private matter. One of the effects is that Europeans seldom ask, "How big is your farm?" or "How many acres do you have?" But Americans ask this question all the time, because property is considered a sign of wealth and success. So they ask the question in Europe as well, blithely unaware that Europeans consider the question rude.

When, however, Europeans do tell their American visitors how many acres they own, most Americans are unable to put the answer into any meaningful context. For Europeans 100 acres, which is about 41 hectares, is enormous. But that number is small by American standards. In 2002, for example, the average size of an American farm was 436 acres, which is about 178 hectares, while the average size of a farm in the European Union was 29 hectares, or about 71 acres. That makes the average American farm about six times as large as a European one, a comparison which fits nicely with another statistic of equal importance. Almost three times as many farms existed in Europe as in America in 2002, but on about one-third as much cultivated land.[16]

Those Europeans who have never traveled across America are not in a position to understand the reasons for American curiosity about the size of a land holding. But those who have sometimes describe it as reflecting a mentality of bigness. In a sense it is part of American culture, and Europeans recognize it everywhere—in big cars, big refrigerators, big water heaters, big houses, big supermarkets, big skyscrapers, and even in big hearts. But in Europe it is quite the opposite. European hearts are warm but reserved, European spaces are neither open nor large, and land ownership is a private matter.

Art and Music, Language, Manners, and Habits of Life

Geography is only one of the many differences that define the open and closed societies of America and Europe. Another is artistic form, such as painting, film and music, but also drama and literature. Considered in general terms, because there are notable exceptions, European art and music, as it has been created and written since the late Middle Ages and which many Americans know well, is a reflection of the taste and values of patrons. The quality of art of the Old Masters is timeless, which is why several million Americans go to Europe each year to visit museums and art galleries. The same point applies to composers. The music of Bach, Beethoven, Couperin, Mozart and Vivaldi is played throughout America.

Americans, as well, have contributed more than their share to music, art, and literature, and they have also added forms which are characteristically their own. The arts in Europe stand in sharp variance to what has been created in America during the past 150 years, such as jazz, film, and the American musical theater and, to some extent, American landscape painting. The observation also applies to music popular on both continents, such as rock, rap, and hip-hop. The quality of European art and music has survived the taste of centuries, and Europeans are justifiably proud of it. But it recalls primarily the past more than the present.

American arts send a message dealing with the present, and also, in a sense, with the future. Many of the themes are about things that dreams are made of: imagination and hope, spirit and adventure, courage and success, the triumph of good over evil, of the positive over the cynical. This is especially striking in western films and in the musical theater of the twentieth century. But the message has its artistic origin in American landscape painting of the nineteenth and early twentieth centuries. There is found what has been variously described as a feeling of "awe and wonderment," a power of "untamed nature," an excitement at what the artists were seeing.

Those familiar with American art have little trouble identifying American from European landscapes, signed or unsigned, even if they do not have figures or buildings in them. Landscape painting reflected the vision of limitless opportunity in America. Artists like Thomas Moran, Albert Bierstadt, Frederic Church, John Kensett, Jasper Cropsey, George Caleb Bingham, and Alfred Jacob Miller all painted scenes of what inspired American imagination.

These paintings were often of panoramas with endless rivers and mountain ranges. American painters celebrated America's geography, whether they were in the east or in the west, or in the Middle West, because they could not ignore it. An extraordinary exhibit of these paintings, entitled "American Sublime—landscape painting in the United States

1820–1880," was held in London, at the Tate museum in 2002. Of the ninety works just three were from museums outside America. A reviewer for the *Financial Times* in London wrote of the exhibition that "what sets the Americans apart is the sheer scale of where they were, and what they saw. Where the Europeans would have had to search out their wilderness sublime, for the Americans it was simply enough to be where they were, for it was all about them."[17]

Europeans generally are not familiar with American landscape artists or with the American musical theater, and know little about the message of the American "western" film. But those who do find in them a distinctly American approach to the adventure called living. What struck French writer Françoise Giroud about the difference between both continents was "the degree of optimism, the exhilaration. . . . There is a strength in the United States that we in Europe constantly tend to underestimate."[18]

American landscapes are about pursuit of the American dream, in a pictorial and romanticized way, and fill the imagination with stories of hope. Similar stories, however, are also told in American film and in American music. Both art forms tell tales about the triumph of good over evil. The frontier spirit is given life in films called "westerns," with titles like *High Noon* and *The Man Who Shot Liberty Valance*. They starred actors like Gary Cooper and John Wayne, whose names are household words. "Westerns" are stories of American lives, where the "good guys" win and the "bad guys" lose on the frontier. American generations of the 1940s, the 1950s, and the early 1960s grew up with "westerns." And some of them were directed by European immigrants to America; the director of *High Noon* was an Austrian originally from Vienna, Fred Zinneman.[19]

Today American children no longer watch movies about Cowboys and Indians very often. But, although much of what they do watch is considered by many Americans, and by even more Europeans, to be cultural trash, the lessons of the "western" are still found in American films which draw enormous audiences. Excellent examples are the Star Wars series and the Lord of the Rings trilogy. The themes are the same as they were when the "bad guys" were punished by the "good guys" in the American west. They are about the virtues of independence, the spirit of adventure, the strength to persevere, the courage to overcome all odds, and the ultimate triumph of good over evil.

Stories of America, similar to those suggested in painting and told in film, are found in infinite variety in American music and song—such as in bluegrass music of Kentucky, Negro spirituals, Dixieland jazz and New Orleans jazz, country and western music born in Nashville, Tennessee, and songs from the American musical theater.[20] All of it, in one way or another, celebrates different aspects of the American character, such as the Kansas state song, "Home on the Range," which was President Franklin Roosevelt's favorite song. Much of this music is also a romanticized reflection of America's history of social change, movement, and mobility. While many Europeans are familiar with rap and rock, comparatively few have ever heard the songs of Stephen Foster or Hoagy Carmichael, like "My Old Kentucky Home" and "Camptown Races," or "Stardust" and "Ole Buttermilk Sky." Other examples are the music of George and Ira Gershwin, of Irving Berlin, of Jerome Kern, and of Cole Porter, made famous on the American stage by such singers as Ella Fitzgerald and Frank Sinatra.

The names of the latter two singers are well known in Europe, but the words of the music they sang, familiar to older generations of Americans, are not. One of the very best examples is Cole Porter's song about the wide open spaces, called "Don't Fence Me In." The song, which may originally have been written as a parody, reflects nonetheless an American attitude toward life. It was recorded by Bing Crosby in 1944, toward the end of World War II. Since then it has sold millions of copies in America, and is still popular. Its lyrics speak to the spirit found in wide open spaces:

> Oh, give me land, lots of land under starry skies above,
> Don't fence me in.
> Let me ride through the wide open country that I love,
> Don't fence me in
> Let me be by myself in the evenin' breeze,
> And listen to the murmur of the cottonwood trees,

Send me off forever but I ask you please,
Don't fence me in.

Just turn me loose, let me straddle my old saddle
Underneath the western skies.
On my Cayuse, let me wander over yonder
Till I see the mountains rise. . . .

American musicals are dramas of American life in all its freedom and in all its contradiction. They are stories of romance and hope, of the land, and of how Americans invented themselves, with names like *Carousel*, *State Fair*,[21] or *Annie Get Your Gun*. One American musical critic, Ethan Mordden, captured the spirit when he described the meaning of Rodgers and Hammerstein's 1943 musical *Oklahoma* as being about "Americans: their morality and government and spirit, how they learn the arts of compromise and tolerance in order to deserve the liberty that democracy fosters."[22] The lyrics of the songs are about the fields, the sky, the beauty of corn as high as "an elephant's eye" and the message they send is about the freedom of the open prairies.

Not all musicals, needless to say, are about "the wide-open spaces." Many, like *1776*, *Show Boat*, *Porgy and Bess*, or *West Side Story*, tell very different stories of American history, and in some cases are social criticism set to music. All of them, however, are about confronting challenges, and succeeding; they are about making life from the bottom up, not about directing life from the top down. Some of them illustrate as well an American inclination to cultural inferiority vis-à-vis Europe. This is conveyed perfectly in a song from *South Pacific* in which an American nurse from Little Rock, Arkansas, sings about a French plantation owner with whom she has fallen in love. The song is a fascinating American-European contrast: "We are not alike," the heroine sings. "Probably I bore him. He's a cultured Frenchman, I'm a little hick." While the message may be outdated today—*South Pacific* opened on Broadway more than half a century ago in 1949—it remains powerful because many Americans, both young and old, are sensitive to the cultural differences, which of course is one reason why they like to visit Europe.

Europeans rightly think of America as young in comparison to Europe, but how difficult it must be for them to imagine how wild America really was, and how young it still is, if they have never seen it. There is, of course, no substitute for traveling across America, but if that is not possible there are other introductions available. Among them are exhibits of landscape painting, "western" films, or the excitement of a visit to the American musical theater on Broadway. And it is especially in the American musical theater that words set to music tell powerful American stories. Few Europeans are familiar with any of them, but there is a little-known and remarkable exception. An Italian who composed such famous operas as *La Bohème* and *Madame Butterfly*, Giacomo Puccini, understood the power of the musical theater well. Almost one hundred years ago, in 1910, he entitled his new opera *The Girl of the Golden West*.

꧁꧂

There are, needless to say, all kinds of cultural influences found in American society today. Some of them are contained in art, music, and film and some are not. Many of them, of course, have nothing to do with the western frontier and trace their origins to the frustrations of life in crowded cities. The influences of urbanization are bringing about dramatic and not always welcome changes in American society, and in European cities as well. Crime, violence, drugs, and poverty are just the beginning of a long litany of problems which Americans see in films, hear about on television newscasts, and read about in their newspapers every day.

European critics of America are well familiar with the litany. They often recite it, as though Europe had no list of its own, and sometimes give the impression that they understand American problems better than Americans do. Many lives in America, they argue, are stories without a future. Many Europeans, for example, can cite Martin Luther King's famous phrase, "I have a dream," as a dramatic symbol of American's history of discrimination, of the inequalities of American life. But while the phrase was uttered in the context of racial struggle, it was spoken as an affirmation of hope. And that is exactly the point.

Europeans are well familiar with the troubles that vex Americans, but few Europeans are acquainted with the American conviction that the dream is possible and that Americans believe in it, whether it is a rugged frontier or a racial one. Day in and day out the belief is honored and given life, in a myriad of ways, and not only in movies, music and theater. Another one of those ways makes its appearance each year in January when Americans travel to large cities in "Freedom Trains" to celebrate a national holiday in honor of Martin Luther King.

Europeans live in societies which are far more narrow and much more provincial than Americans imagine. American tourists looking in shop windows, visiting museums and dining in restaurants always register new sights, sounds, and smells, but they cannot recognize what lies underneath the surface unless they live in Europe for a long period of time, and are able to speak at least one European language.

The elementary difference between the American and European experience with language has varied ramifications. Only one out of five Americans can speak, read and write a foreign language—any language—but for 16 percent of Europe's population English is the mother tongue and a further 31 percent claim they can speak English well enough to carry on a conversation.[23] That difference tilts the scale of perception and judgment. Europeans, partly because of their ability to understand English, think they know America well, and Americans, because so few of them can speak any European language, are much less sensitive to European custom and fashion. The following statistics, provided by the U.S. Census Bureau following the 2000 census, speak for themselves. In American households the language spoken most commonly at home, after English (215.4 million) and Spanish (28.1), was Chinese (2 million), thus eclipsing French, German and Italian over the decade of the 1990s.

The matter of language accentuates the differences between us. Americans call their language English, but Europeans call it American. They see two languages where Americans see one. To the amusement of some Americans and to the chagrin of others, this difference is referred to pointedly in Lerner and Loewe's musical *My Fair Lady*, based on a play by English dramatist George Bernard Shaw. The character of Henry Higgins, played in the film version by the English actor Rex Harrison, tells us about language in a now famous lyric: "There even are places where English completely disappears! In America, they haven't used it for years!" But whatever Europeans think it is, language in America has one characteristic that is unique. It unites. That is, indeed, amusing when one recalls that it is a European language. It becomes ironic when one considers that language in Europe achieves the opposite effect. Europe's many languages divide.

In the European Union, for example, there is not one common language that unites, but more than twenty different official languages which divide, including Gaelic. There is also a significant grammatical usage in many European languages which separates the personal from the professional. In French and German or in Spanish and Italian, for example, there is a formal and an informal address. It amounts to a public and a private way to say "you," a usage still very much observed. Most Europeans would never dream of addressing someone they do not know well, with the personal and private "Tu" in French or "Du" in German. It is a distinction that is not made in modern English usage.[24]

There is also a more obvious reason why Europe's languages cannot play the unifying role that English achieves in America. On the continent different languages create different worlds in countries that are right next to each other. One consequence, of course, is that some Europeans learn to speak several languages—half of Europe's population is bilingual—and for many Europeans one of the languages is English because their professional lives demand it; in continental high schools 89 percent of the students study English. This ability is often interpreted by Americans as a sign of the sophisticated European. Many Americans are envious, and sincerely regret that they cannot speak French, for example. Europeans, for their part, are not without humor when they consider this difference, and are fond of telling a story about it in the form of the following question and answer:

Question: "If a person who speaks three languages is called 'trilingual,' and a person who speaks two languages is called 'bilingual,' what do you call a person who only speaks one language?"
Answer: "American!"

Of course, Americans could learn a second language, but most Americans do not see a persuasive reason to do so. Few Americans make an effort to learn, because whether they live in Alaska or Florida, they do not need a second one at home or abroad. The result is that less than eight percent of American university students today study a language other than English. American travelers can get along quite well in Europe, and elsewhere, just speaking English. Thus, not many Americans really know from experience, and are not prompted by geography to consider that "to possess another language is to possess another soul," to borrow a phrase from Alexander Solzhenitsyn.

Nonetheless, sometimes Europeans give the scornful impression that because most Americans can only speak English, they are either arrogant or culturally deprived. In fact, often when Europeans point out that Americans speak "American," they also condescendingly observe that if Americans spoke English "English" it would be easier to understand. For Americans, however, the only basic difference between English spoken in England and English spoken in America is one of accent, even though it is possible today to find separate dictionaries for English and for American.

Americans and Europeans can argue, if they wish, over the definition of cultural deprivation, but there is no valid dispute on the matter of arrogance. It is just a fact that English today is the language of the western world, just as Latin was the principal language of European law, religion and science during the later Roman Empire and throughout the Middle Ages. In France, for example, Latin was not officially replaced by French as the national language of law until King François I did so by ordinance in 1539, followed by the first French dictionary, which was not published until sixty-seven years later, in 1606.[25]

As it affects science and technology, international law and trade, we are again seeing the domination of one language, English. Many of the technologies invented since the end of World War II, used today in America and Europe, generally require the use of just English. The language has become, in fact, the linguistic standard of the Information Age and is also becoming a corporate language around the world.

English, indeed, has always been America's language, even though European immigrants brought with them many other ones. A perfect example, because it illustrates a common practice, is the case of a Swedish immigrant to America in the 1870s who settled in Seattle. He married the daughter of an Irishman, and they communicated in the language of America. Their children—the second generation of Americans in this family—learned little Swedish at home, but more about Swedish and Irish customs and traditions. In turn some of those were passed down to the third generation, whose members spoke of them proudly. But they learned no Swedish at all. For America's European immigrants, to be American meant you spoke English, which explains why many early immigrants refused to speak their native languages with their children, at least in public.

Today times have changed. In parts of the state of California for example, election ballots are printed in Spanish, Chinese, Japanese, Vietnamese, Tagalog and Korean, as well as in English. There are, of course, disagreements, large and small, about whether deliberate emphasis on linguistic diversity unites or divides.[26] But irrespective of the merits of being multilingual, the language of culture, commerce, and politics in America is English.

It is here that an asymmetry differentiates Americans from Europeans. Americans who move to France, for example, and master the language do not become French, because being bilingual is not a sufficient condition for being bicultural.[27] But emigrants to America who all learn to speak English, including Europeans, become part of the American pageant. They become Americans.

The role of language, as one of the threads tying together the patchwork quilt of Americans in the New World, is not an idle matter. It is true that many European immigrants to America held on to their native languages, and wrote and conversed in them in a wide variety of ways, and still do. But they also deliberately chose to learn English because there was no other practical alternative. Because they spoke many different languages and came from different backgrounds, English gave them something in common. No matter where they lived, throughout the entire history of

America, they have been able to communicate with letters and newspapers, first carried by the Pony Express and later by trains, cars and airplanes, as well as by telephone and telegraph, by radio and television, telex and fax, and finally today, via e-mail and the Internet.

Americans, however, have always been and still are a nation of many languages and accents, which is why Americans, unlike Europeans, do not take exception to how English is spoken and seldom comment on how it is pronounced. A European visitor to America can, indeed, go to New Orleans and speak French, to the Amana colonies in Iowa and speak German, or to Los Angeles and speak Spanish. But the point of significance is that Americans do not have to change the language they speak when going from one part of their continent to another.

"Languages," as German writer Peter Schneider puts it, "also serve to smuggle values, cultures and philosophical systems."[28] This proposition, in America, is not high on the list of national concerns. But in Europe, language is a matter of both politics and pride. The most striking example is spoken French, about which myths abound. One is that this language of diplomats is dying. But after English it is the most frequently taught language in the world.[29] Another, also found in the musical *My Fair Lady*, is Professor Higgins's observation that "the French don't care what they do actually, as long they pronounce it properly." Added to that is the old and often repeated myth of legendary French rudeness to language-impoverished American tourists who cannot speak French. The myth makes great cocktail party stories, few of which are true.

These myths obscure concerns considered legitimate in Europe, but in which most Americans have little interest. One is the consequence of pride taken in one's national language by members of the European Parliament, in which twenty-seven countries have elected representatives, thus creating enormously complex and expensive translation requirements. Another is what seems, to many Europeans, to be the relentless spread of English in all matters cultural, economic and political. In Europe the French, but by no means only the French, look upon English as a cultural invasion coming from America, dominating diplomacy and the global marketplaces of trade and commerce.

The growing adoption of English as the corporate language in European boardrooms is hardly an example of an American conspiracy, but for many Europeans the use of English is nevertheless seen as a threat to preservation of a cultural heritage. Those Europeans who feel strongly about this matter face a Hobson's choice from which there is no escape, because professional life in Europe requires, increasingly, a command of English. Thus, in early 2005 the municipal government of Madrid, which was competing to host the 2012 Olympic Games, announced that the city's taxi drivers must be able to speak English by the end of the year or forfeit their licenses.[30]

A more subtle difference, setting Europeans and Americans apart, and indirectly related to language, is how we hold a conversation. Americans get right to the point. Normally a guest in an American home has not been through the front door five minutes before he is asked what he would like to drink. Then hosts and guests go on from there, happy to see each other and to learn how things are going. It is a custom whose purpose is to put guests at ease, right away, and to assure them that they are welcome.

Europeans get to the point, too, but in an indirect way. They are just as delighted to see their guests, but usually they inquire first about their families, about how everyone is, and about what they are doing. And after a while they ask what they can offer their guests, but they do not do so right away, and seldom say, "What would you like to drink?"

Americans, as well as some Europeans, may consider this point to be so insignificant that it deserves no attention at all. And many Europeans and Americans would surely say, "If you live in a large city, it's always about the drink, whether you're in London or New York, Paris or San Francisco." But the difference is not of minor importance, because how Europeans and Americans talk, with friends and with each other, informally and formally, illustrates how they see relationships, both private ones and professional ones. They both know where they are going, but the path they take to get there is not the same. The paths they do follow really reflect two different concepts of an order of politeness and approach, two different habits of life. Each defines distinctly how Europeans and Americans treat everything they do.

The explanation for these differences in habits of life is simple, but also subtle; and that is the way it was expressed to me when I asked a French acquaintance, Elisabeth Burgess, to describe how we converse:

> Talking is about knowing how to live. In French we call it *le savoir vivre*. We think life is about receiving friends and acquaintances, about listening to what they have come to say, about being with them. It is about how we speak to each other, to old friends and new ones, about trust, and about how we communicate. It is about living life. It's not about having a drink.

My response to Elisabeth could be called a classic case of rising to the bait. I pointed out, with more vehemence than necessary, that the drink is not the issue for Americans, either. On the contrary, the point is to make your friends feel at home, which is why they were invited in the first place. But it is true that Europeans take more time to get where they are going. They start, as Elisabeth put it, with *le savoir vivre,* and often follow what seem to be, to Americans, indirect and circuitous paths. They get from point A to point B but, in a manner of speaking, they often stop at a café along the way. Americans, on the other hand, operate on the principle that the shortest distance between points A and B is a straight line; that is to say, they use time to get where they are going as fast as possible.

This difference is often apparent in how Americans begin telephone conversations. They call each other up and get right to the point, "Hello David, this is Bob. I've got a problem. Do you have a few minutes?" This approach is taken every day in America. But Europeans would invariably begin the conversation with a question, "Hello Horst, this is Henning. How have you been? Tell me how your family's doing." Then, they listen for the reply.

By itself, whether a conversation is begun with American practice or European habit, is not of great moment. But knowledge of the difference, and the willingness to respect it, improves the quality of the exchange, which is an academic way of saying that it builds trust and confidence.

The difference in approach—the direct versus the indirect—may seem irrelevant to Americans, some of whom have told me they do not have time for this kind of game and are unwilling to play it. That attitude is one I understand very well. But whether it is a game or not, there is a valid point. When Americans speak directly, in private or professional dealings, Europeans often find it offensive, although they seldom say so. They do not think this way.

It is true beyond any doubt that most Europeans do not appreciate why Americans are so straightforward. Unless they are well familiar with American history and habit, they often draw the wrong conclusion; namely, that Americans are rude and insensitive. Either way, however, the comparison illustrates a point of importance to us both. It is that even though we often leave a lot of broken glass along the edges of the different paths we take, each of us, in our own fashion, eventually arrives at the same place. In getting there, it may be helpful to us both to recall that how we communicate with each other affects the outcome of what we are trying to achieve. How carefully are we prepared to listen to each other?

Manners include not only what we say in a conversation and how we say it, but also how we behave. For historical reasons, already touched upon, Europeans live in societies which are far more structured than their American counterpart. Their behavior in public is more circumspect, more cautious, friendly to be sure, but also standoffish. They draw a clear line between what is obviously public and properly personal. For most Europeans it would be inconceivable to discuss personal problems with the utter abandon with which they see it done on American radio and television talk shows. Even though some Americans consider the display vulgar, most Americans draw little distinction between private and public life, and talk about both all the time irrespective of where they are. In Europe, American informality is legendary. Some Europeans do understand the reasons for it. But for many it is so public and so ostentatious that they are genuinely baffled by it.

Europeans, however, are far from alone in this reaction. Many Americans traveling abroad, who are conscious of the public-private distinction, often cringe at the insensitivities of their fellow countrymen. Their embarrassment sometimes leads Americans to apologize, as in the case of an American friend waiting in line at an Air France ticket counter in de Gaulle airport outside of Paris.

In front of him was standing a tall and well-built man, in a broad-brimmed Stetson hat, talking at the top of his lungs, in a rude and peremptory tone of voice, to a petite and attractive French airline clerk behind the counter. When he left, my friend moved to the head of the line, and said,

> "Excuse me, but I want to apologize for the behavior of my fellow countryman. The Americans I know are not rude and we do not pardon that kind of performance. It was insulting and unnecessary."
>
> The young French clerk answered, "Please, sir, do not worry about it. It does not happen often, and we understand that flying can be stressing."
>
> My friend responded, "That is very nice of you to say that, and I thank you for your patience. By the way, where is he going?"
>
> "Well, sir," she explained, "he is going to Dallas." After what seemed to be a very long pause, she continued, "but his luggage, it is going to Seattle!"

Manners, or the lack of them, sometimes have unexpected consequences, as the foregoing story illustrates. In fact, many Europeans convey in their tone of voice and in their body language that American money is welcome, but American behavior is not. Why is this? Are American manners that coarse? Is American disregard for the social graces of the countries they visit really so blatant? Is the fact that young Europeans like American films, dance to American music, and eat American hamburgers, a capitalist conspiracy, for which American tourists should be blamed? It is especially this latter question that strikes at the nerves of the American traveler, and for good reason.

American guests at European dinner parties do not appreciate being asked, in an accusatory manner, why America has exported its "culture" to Europe, and they often respond awkwardly. Few, indeed, are aware that Hungarian-born Arthur Koestler answered the question, long before

McDonald's existed, in the early 1950s: "Who coerced us into buying all this? The United States do not rule Europe as the British ruled India; they waged no Opium War to force their revolting *Coke* down our throats. Europe bought the whole package because Europe wanted it."[31]

Koestler's logic is just as applicable today as it was fifty years ago. To take McDonald's as an example; the company had sales in Russia during 2004 of about $310 million, and was serving more than 200,000 customers daily in over one hundred different locations. These figures become more significant when it is noted that Russia is only McDonald's fifth-most profitable market in Europe, after Britain, France, Germany, and Spain, in that order.[32] The point is that Americans and Europeans do not always share the same tastes or the same standards of behavior, but they are quick, often too quick, to criticize. The consequences emerge often as feelings of contempt and resentment.

As is the case with many things, the significance of differences in behavior can be overdone, but it is nonetheless enlightening to hear a European talk about the way Americans dress, and describe how Americans approach the matter of a meal. The following view comes from a couple in Vienna, a professor of finance and his wife, an art dealer in nineteenth- and twentieth-century paintings, in a letter written in early 2004:

> Millions of Americans visit Europe each year. They go to our restaurants, buy things in our stores, visit our museums and galleries, attend concerts and the theater, and admire our churches and cathedrals. And, of course, as you do in America, if we see an American who looks a little lost understanding a menu or reading a map, we ask if we can help. But it seems to us, and we think to many Europeans overall, that American tourists sometimes forget they are guests in Europe. They don't demonstrate complete disregard for our sensibilities, but they make little effort to respect our ways of life. For example, how do they dress? Well, you know the answer to that. We understand that most Americans in Europe are on vacation. They want to relax, and we recognize that. But how they are dressed, in T-shirts, Bermuda shorts, and tennis shoes, is often more suitable for the beach than for cities whose beauty they have come to see.
>
> We don't like it, and you can hardly blame us if we judge Americans by what they wear. We recognize that neither Europeans nor Americans walk

around all day in suits. But when we see Americans eating in a fine restaurant, dressed as though they were going to a rock concert, it makes us wonder whether you have any respect for standards at all. But it may be that on this point European tourists are just as guilty as Americans. We know that standards of dress are changing everywhere, in Europe just as in America.[33]

As I read this it reminded me of a colleague in Ann Arbor, Michigan. Several years ago he and his wife were visiting the wine country in Burgundy. On a late morning in October they found themselves in a little town outside of Beaune, and decided to stop for a quick lunch. So they went into a restaurant, which, unbeknownst to them, turned out to be a top restaurant with one star in the *Guide Michelin*. He was not wearing a coat and tie and his wife was wearing pants and tennis shoes for the car trip. Although his French was not very good, he was able to explain successfully that they just wanted to have salad and a sandwich. They were seated at a table, located near the drafty entrance. While the food was good and the waiter was polite, David and Ann both felt a chill in the service they could not explain.

When David had finished telling me this story I said to him, "Look, I know you didn't intend to insult anyone, but quite frankly what did you expect? You were in a restaurant where dining is considered a pleasure, not a question of how quickly you can eat salad and a sandwich. Moreover, I suspect I know how most of the other people were dressed. Probably a good deal better than you two." He nodded his head, and I told him, "If you ever have occasion to go back, make a reservation, wear at least a sport coat, tell your wife to skip the tennis shoes, and see what happens. I'll bet you will see a difference." And in fact, that is exactly what happened, when they deliberately returned two years later. They were there for more than two hours, in the middle of the wine country of Burgundy, and took the time to enjoy a wonderful meal. They were also treated with greater respect, a result which a coat and tie produces throughout Europe.

Taste, of course, as well as appreciation of good food, is not a European monopoly. Americans often encounter Europeans traveling through

America looking very casual in their Levis and sandals, happily stopping at every fast-food place along the way. But there is, nevertheless, a major difference in how we both approach a meal. For most Europeans, whether they live in a big city or in the country, lunch or dinner is something special. The dining table exists to serve that purpose. It is not a time to hurry. It is a time to slow down, to appreciate the company of those at the table, to savor the effort given to preparing a meal, whether it is at home, or in a restaurant.

Europeans are proud of their table, and the table is where 75 percent of the French eat dinner together as a family, whereas in America it is about 33 percent.[34] In a few words, eating is a celebration of life, not a tiresome inconvenience. One way to interpret the meaning of this difference was put in the form of an analogy by a former counselor to the secretary of commerce in the Reagan administration, who wrote in 2003 that "food is to European culture what free speech is to American culture."[35]

These predilections do not apply to all Europeans any more than they describe all Americans. The American habit of "eating on the run" has spread to Europe, too. Twenty years ago it would have been inconceivable to see Europeans eating sandwiches while walking down the street, because that is not enjoying something. It is saving time; moreover, it would have been considered uncouth. But even though Europeans are adopting the same practice, they still resent what they see as American culture infecting their continental *savoir vivre*.

Whether this conclusion is fair is beside the point, because Europeans use it to condemn an American way of life they do not respect. Manners give Europeans, so they often conclude, something of value in common. What Americans have in common in this area is that they often ignore the art of living and replace it with the art of movement. Perhaps few Americans or Europeans think of it in this way, but the distinction affects how they interpret the messages being sent by each other's behavior.

A similar comparison applies to the concept of time and how it is used in America and Europe. In Europe it is a state of being. In America time is a commodity. My Viennese friends made this point in the same letter in which they wrote about manners:

> To us, Americans are in a hurry. You are always going from one place to another place, and are constantly preoccupied with what can be bought and consumed. But how often do you stop to enjoy what you are doing? The historical elegance of Old Europe is not an empty phrase. Time moves more slowly on our continent. We delight in it and recognize the beauty and mysteries the passage of time brings with it. Some Americans, of course, can easily describe us as living in an "Art Musem" if they wish, but most of us believe that the hour does not strike for those who are happy.
>
> The iconoclastic culture of the New World is not elegant, and much of the artistic genius you admire in your museums and hear in your symphony halls was created by Europeans. We know that American pop-culture is exciting, but it also has a short life because it quickly runs out of images to break. It is superficial, too fast, and too loud. It allows no time to consider what has already been achieved. Your emphasis on speed, on always moving quickly, reminds us of a poem written long ago by a European, William Wordsworth. It begins with the lines,

> > The world is too much with us: late and soon,
> > Getting and spending, we lay waste our powers:
> > Little we see in Nature that is ours;
> > We have given our hearts away, a sordid boon!

> That poem, entitled "The World Is Too Much With Us," was written about us, almost two hundred years ago, in 1806. But today the world is very much with you, in how you talk to each other, and in how you eat and dress. It is especially with you in your waste, and in your pride in getting things done, now. What we mean is told in a story about time. It is a conversation between a Texan and a French taxi cab driver in Paris. It speaks for itself, we think.

> A Texan was picked up by a French taxi and driven through the streets of Paris.
> "What's that?" the Texan asks.

"It is zee Louvre, Monsieur!" the driver replies.

"How long did it take to build?" asks the Texan.

"It took over one hundred years, Monsieur," said the driver.

"Well, we have one just like it in Texas and it took only ten years to build."

There was a silence for a bit . . . until the Texan asked, "And what's that, over there?"

"It is zee Arc de Triomphe, Monsieur!" said the taxi driver, proudly.

"And how long did it take to build?"

"Ah, monsieur, zat one took seven years," the driver replied.

"Well, we have one just like it in Texas and we built it in only seven months."

Another silence, which lasted until the Texan pointed again, this time to the Eiffel Tower.

"And what is that structure over there?"

The taxi driver, after a long pause, replied, "I do not know, Monsieur. . . . It was not zere last week!"

Klaus and Elizabeth know America and Europe well. They both speak English fluently and raised their four children in Palo Alto, California, between 1982 and 2002, and their comments, for me, were of more than just passing interest. This was the second time they had written to me at my request, and my response to them, long overdue, was an attempt to explain the contrast.

. . . I think Americans genuinely appreciate that you deliberately make the effort to enjoy your privacy, your families, your meals, the calm beauty of your villages and countryside. We do recognize it, and it is something American visitors to Europe find enormously appealing. Why we find it so, of course, is simple to answer. It is because in America we always seem to be going somewhere, and more often than not, we complain that we are running out of time, as though it were merely a commodity. You may be familiar with the many phrases we have to deal with time, such as "a stitch in time saves nine," or "make hay while the sun shines," or "there is no time like the present." And you have often heard, I suspect, the famous phrase "remember that time is money." It was coined by Benjamin Franklin, a man who later became a great American friend of France, in an essay written in 1748 and entitled, "Advice to a Young Tradesman."[36]

I can understand why it may seem to Europeans that the pace of our lives is much faster than yours, but I also want to remind you, for the record, that a healthy respect for the value of time is not our invention. A Greek scholar and friend of Aristotle who lived during the fourth century B.C., Theophrastus, taught his students that "time was the most valuable thing that a man could spend."

. . . It is true that our concept of time is a reflection of many of the things we have often discussed together—America, a country that is not very old, and Americans, who are in a hurry to go forward, who want to solve problems quickly so they can tackle the next ones, who look at what can be accomplished in the short term because they fear there may not be enough time.

Your concept of time, in Europe, is based on a different history. Your concept of scale is measured in centuries, not in years and decades. Like Americans, you have a long memory, but unlike Americans, you also have a historical memory full of the lessons your history has taught you for over two thousand years. In Europe time is a balance of age and antiquity, of history and maturity, of prudence and wisdom, and of great success and disastrous mistakes. In America, wrote Oscar Wilde in 1893, "youth . . . is their oldest tradition. It has been going on now for three hundred years."[37] Perhaps that is what a French friend of my wife's meant when she told me that "the difference between America and Europe is that Americans do things, and Europeans see things."

I have always liked her comment because there are some fascinating elements of truth to it. Generally speaking you do draw on your history and heritage to see things we do not, and you tell us so. Americans use the experience gained from their history to justify doing things you do not want to do, or cannot do. Americans speak of freedom, and they will tell you why it is necessary to defend it. Europeans do not talk about freedom often, but when they do it is normally a discussion about what people are entitled to, and seldom about the opportunities freedom offers.

Finally, let me conclude by agreeing with you both. Yes, we are still doing things and we are still in a hurry. But we have a sense of the importance of history and heritage, too. Excuse the American tourists who are without manners, remember that we visit Europe because we feel drawn to it, to where many of our ancestors came from, and because we consider you our friends. Even though many of us cannot speak even one of your languages, and are not well familiar with your traditions, we have great respect for how you live. You celebrate life and European culture.

We know that our art, music, literature and architecture are young, and we are very much aware of just how young they are in comparison to the long history of Europe. But I hope you recognize that it is our understanding of our short history that explains why we still celebrate personal freedom. For us everything flows from that. That is why we are anxious to talk about it all the time—from the man on the street to the president of our country. Freedom is our life, and is the foundation of our culture. Some Europeans are fond of saying Americans have no culture. They are wrong. America's culture is freedom. And, Oscar Wilde notwithstanding, it is also our oldest tradition.

Views from the Backyard

The phrase "the American spirit" is used frequently in American discourse, and most Americans would agree that there is such a thing, formed by our history, youth and customs. It is a marvelously romantic image, and it is also a strong one that does not have a European counterpart. As a phrase "the European spirit" does not exist. But a European "spirit of history" does roam the continent nonetheless, even though it does not have a proper name. It is a way of looking at things, affected by the essential difference.

How are these two spirits interpreted? Or, to put it another way, what are they made of? "The American spirit," and the European one without a name, are sometimes explained in the context of the backyard. Readers of the European press know that some Europeans—active in business, politics, education, entertainment and journalism—subscribe to the following interpretation: Americans are provincial, their country is so big they do not have to pay attention to what is going on outside of their own backyard. Europeans are worldly, their countries are so small they do not have a backyard, they must look outward and therefore have developed a sophisticated view of the world around them. It is the nature of our so-called backyards, they imply, that explains why Americans and Europeans see the world differently.

Is this an accurate description? Opinion is divided on this subject in Europe. Burkhard Koch, when he responded to my request to tell me if he could recognize a spirit unique to America, drew an unusually sharp and very different conclusion.

> Americans live in a world full of anticipation. You are forward looking, courageous, adventurous, spontaneous, open, and young. We Europeans live in a world full of cynicism, and are reflective, pensive, skeptical, suspicious, closed, and old. Americans accept differences between people, but Europeans do so much less willingly. So Americans look for an approximation of perfection, while Europeans are always seeking perfection itself, but they don't try often because they are unwilling to take the risk of failure. So they settle for the status quo.

I suggested to a French acquaintance that Burkhard's claim was overstated and she said, "No. The French are like St. Thomas. They doubt, until they see the wounds." A second explanation was given me by a French artist who told me that the French nature is that of "the cashier." She is a young woman who has a job. But it's not great, although it provides a steady income. She doesn't really like her job, and she seldom smiles when she is working; yet she is afraid to change jobs because she may end up with something worse. So nothing happens. Her life goes on, without much satisfaction, day after day, and when she leaves for work each morning her family says to her, "take courage."

A third response came from an Italian businessman, who is a large producer of food products in California. He reacted to the comparison by making a note in the margin of this manuscript. He wrote, "on this attitudinal difference here is an old Italian peasant/bourgeois saying that captures how people felt and feel: *Miseria stabile, Ricchezza mobile* (poverty is constant, riches are fleeting)." The note continued, "This saying is a reflection of the inherent skepticism that even when things are going well, it probably won't last! Related to it, for the purposes of your book, is another expression Italians use among themselves to describe someone who has had good fortune. The words *Ha trovato l'America* (he found America) speak directly to what Italians imagine is a land of plenty."

Which is it? Provincial versus worldly, open versus closed, courage versus suspicion, or something else? Accurate descriptions of our backyards are not easily found, anywhere, because they are difficult to describe and because ignorance of them is widespread. Those Americans who have been able to live in America and in Europe—not just travel there—share the observation that what most Europeans think America seems to be, and what it really is, are two very different things. Most Europeans have never lived in America; thus, their knowledge of American life comes from television, film, magazines, and newspapers. This is especially true for impressions gathered from films; American movies capture more than seventy percent of the European film market, and half of dramatic shows on European television come from America.[38] A similar conclusion applies to Americans. They have little idea of European manners and customs, because few American travelers to Europe speak European languages, because European private life is closed to most American tourists, because American media pay little attention to European affairs, and because many Americans have never been to Europe.

What is the proper definition of the backyard? The explanation is not self-evident, because so many different experiences define our perspectives. But one thing is certain. What we see in each other's backyards determines, in large measure, the respect or disdain we have for each other, and shapes our desire to excuse or to accuse. What we believe our respective backyards are made of, therefore, is extremely important. Americans and Europeans have a responsibility to represent them, accurately, but seldom can they do so.

Some Europeans, who consider Americans to be rich and without culture, see a self-contained continent and therefore, a country whose domestic affairs and foreign policies are formed in a vacuum, without regard for the interests and affinities of Europe and the Europeans. Those who choose this interpretation believe that America is all about greed and consumption, about having a whole lot of everything, about money and wealth acquired at the expense of others, in Europe and elsewhere. They do not know, and some do not wish to learn, that riches are not what define America or Americans. Riches are the result of what America is about. And what is that? If you asked Europeans this question, some would say America is about power, dominance, and violence, and others would say it is about freedom, hard work, and prosperity.

There is some truth in both answers, but each is incomplete. America is not about riches that can be measured on a scale, because America is about making an idea reality. It is about making choices, about finding opportunities and seizing them, about taking responsibility for success and also for failure. It is about the liberty of individuals to develop their own abilities. Some call this the American spirit, and others call it American selfishness. But whether the description is positive or negative, freedom is the ingredient that makes possible all parts of the American character.

Recently I asked a German friend of mine to tell me what she thought about freedom in America, and she said to me, "You single out freedom, time and again, and it is boring. America is about many things." And she is right, of course. Life in America is about many, many things—contradictions and inequalities, waste and abundance, disparities between rich and poor, the sorrows of failure and the joys of success. But so is life in Europe and on this point Americans and Europeans are very much alike.

Where they part company is the way they display the essential difference between them, which explains, in part, why so many Europeans disparage what they see as simplistic American patriotic behavior. Europeans find signs of it everywhere in America, not only in the use of the American flag, but in the names like "Liberty" or "Freedom" Americans give their boats and airplanes, in the parades which mark American holidays, and in the creation of patriotic societies such as the Daughters of the American Revolution or the Colonial Dames of America. Some time ago the Greeks did the same, but the practice has long since disappeared.[39]

Europeans use names in similar ways. But European names draw first on centuries of history, not on centuries of freedom. Consider the names of public squares, or even of subway and train stations. Some names do celebrate the accomplishments of famous people or reflect cultural achievements, but many of them also recall historical events, such as the train station in London called Waterloo which commemorates the defeat of Napoleon in 1815, or the name given a metro station in Paris called Tolbiac. It is a place near Cologne where Clovis, the first king of the Franks, defeated Germanic tribes in A.D. 496 and took possession of Alsatia.

European use of names is a reflection of age and time that is absent in youthful America. But Americans do draw on the significance of an idea, which is why the words "liberty" and "freedom" are used as proper names. Americans consider this to be perfectly natural, but seldom does it seem self-evident to Europeans.

Americans do not find the idea of freedom boring, at all, because they believe American history tells the opposite story. But, nonetheless, the conclusion is drawn by many Europeans, again and again, that American preoccupation with the idea of freedom blinds them. Sometimes it is presented as a statement, as is the case with German writer Peter Schneider, who argues that "the impressive integrative power of American society seems to generate a kind of obliviousness to the world, a multi-cultural unilateralism. The result is a paradox: a fantastically tolerant and flexible society that has absorbed the whole world, yet has difficulty comprehending the world beyond its borders."[40] At other times the tone of the conclusion suggests an accusation, as though Americans are unconcerned with anything outside "fortress America."

The suggestion is not entirely without merit. There are, after all, more than 295 million Americans and not all of them are fascinated by world affairs. News coverage of events abroad takes up less than 2 percent in the average daily newspaper in America. Less than 1 percent of all American students enrolled in college, for example, study abroad and less than 10 percent of students are required to take college-level language courses. Moreover, in 2004 only about 17 percent of Americans, not all of whom go to Europe, had passports; that means millions of Americans have never been introduced to life beyond America's borders.[41]

Young Americans today, those between the ages of 18 and 24, know relatively little about world geography, not to mention Europe. On this point the results of a survey on geographic literacy published in late 2002 are enlightening: 87 percent could not locate Iraq on a map, 76 percent could not find Saudi Arabia, 49 percent could not identify New York City even though they knew it was the site of the 9/11 "ground zero," and 21 percent were unable to locate the Pacific Ocean. Slightly more than a third knew where the island featured most recently in the American television reality show *Survivor* could be found.[42] The only possible conclusion to be reached is that younger generations of Americans are appallingly ignorant of the geographical world around them.

American life has always been acted out in its continental backyard, but for much of that time Americans have also taken an active role in world affairs. That role has not always been played perfectly, and Americans recognize that they have made mistakes aplenty. But they can also look with pride on the contributions they have made toward making the world a freer and safer place in which to live. It was not out of naiveté that America came to the aid of Europe in the twentieth century, nor was it because Americans were hopelessly idealistic, a condescending observation Americans hear from European intellectuals on a regular basis, and not only from them. America went to the aid of Europe, on the contrary, because most Americans believed in the cause of European freedom, and had the courage of their convictions. American men and women did so because they wanted to, not because they were ordered to do so by their government.

Some Europeans find this difficult to believe, because their long history reminds them that warfare is conducted by government conscripts not by volunteers. In European societies built and ruled from the top down idealistic volunteerism is not a distinguishing characteristic, so it may be understandable that many Europeans ignore the comparison with America.

On occasion, indeed, it is even dismissed out of hand, which occurred during a conversation I had in late 1999 with a member of the French Senate in his mid-seventies. We were talking about American soldiers in Europe during World Wars I and II. He had a lot of questions, quite cynical in nature, about American policy and about why America had entered both wars so late. I said to him, "But you've forgotten the most important question." "And what's that?" he asked. I said, "Why did Americans go?" He looked me right in the eye and said, "Because your government told them to." I responded, "No, they went to defend freedom, some as volunteers and some as conscripts." He just shook his head and said, "It was in America's self-interest. You saw the danger of a spillover."

My French host made it clear he was displeased and did not pursue the matter further. I remain certain that he thought I did not recognize how the real world works, and I do not know if he heard or understood the point I was trying to make. But there is a consideration here that my French host should not malign; nor should it be blown out of proportion by a sympathetic American reader. It is, once again, the impact of the essential difference on how we think.

If I had continued our conversation, I would have argued that the majority of Americans take pride in the idea, vision, and reality of "the American spirit." They are adamant in their conviction that it is more than just an ideal. It is not something they wish for, it is something they practice. They believe personal freedom is both a privilege and a right, and that defending it is a responsibility. It is a commitment they have made throughout their entire history. It would be foolish to say that America has always been right, and most Americans know that no country is in perpetual possession of the truth. America's critics, of course, are fond of drawing attention to the mistakes, and loath to observe that Americans have also tried to learn from them.

Americans, however, have also learned from European mistakes. Of the many lessons Europe's history has taught Americans it is that there is always someone trying to take away freedom from somebody else. When this occurs, and it has been a recurring aspect of European life for centuries, Americans want to help, if they can. They could during World Wars I and II, and thereafter. That is why they went to Europe. They did not go because "their" government "told" them to.

American students of literature are well familiar with a famous poem written by English poet and theologian John Donne, entitled "No Man Is an
Island."

> No man is an island, entire of itself;
> every man is a piece of the continent,
> a part of the main; if a clod be washed
> away by the sea, Europe is the less, as
> if a manor of thy friends or of thine own
> were; any man's death diminishes me,
> because I am involved in mankind; and
> therefore never send to know for whom
> the bell tolls; it tolls for thee.

Although it was written almost four hundred years ago, in 1624, its message has not lost either its vitality or its validity. Would Americans be able
to name the author and the title of the poem today? Probably just a few.
But most Americans are well aware that when the subject is freedom, and
its defense, there is no safe backyard and no man is an island. Those Europeans who profess to believe that Americans are spoiled by comfort and
consumption should refresh their memory of American history. If they do
they will discover that what they believe is not true. America did not take
the advice Thomas Jefferson gave to President James Monroe in 1823,
"never to take part in the quarrels of Europe." By the same token, Americans who claim that Europeans are plump with paradise and lean with
power, may recall that the Cold War was won by Europeans and Americans together; neither could have won it alone.

It is not surprising that Europeans describe the backyards of America and
Europe differently. What do they see in their view of the American backyard? When I put this question to my Viennese friends in 2004 they
began their explanation with a question:

> Why don't you admit it? America is self-contained and self-confident! You
> really do not need the Europeans. And you should not be offended if many

Europeans see it that way. That does not mean we admire you less. But we do not like it when you talk about your ideal of freedom as being beyond criticism, as being the only one of any real substance, and that no one can possibly understand the value of freedom as well as you do. We would not call your attitude an arrogance of power, as some of America's critics do. But we would call it an arrogance of belief. We tell you that because we have learned something about Americans from raising our children in California. To put it politely, it is difficult, if not impossible, for Americans to imagine that the idea of "the American spirit" is not as popular everywhere in the world as you believe it should be. And it never occurs to you to stop long enough to think about it.

Your history and heritage tell you that freedom is everything, and that it will prevail. But, that is not always true. You should remember, for example, that it was the English historian, A. J. P. Taylor, who once wrote, " 'Freedom does not always win. This is one of the bitterest lessons of history." We would point out to you, also, that America is not really dependent on anyone else, at least not nearly to the extent that Europeans are. You can afford to indulge your conviction that freedom is an end in itself. Your faith in yourselves and your isolation from foreign shores permits you, and sometimes even encourages you, to draw conclusions and act on them, irrespective of repercussions elsewhere, outside your own backyard.

It is a luxury that we in Europe do not enjoy. None of our countries are independent in the way America is. We believe in freedom and we believe in its defense. But in Europe the defense of freedom means depending on and getting along with a lot of other countries economically, politically, and militarily. We call that obligatory diplomacy and for us it is a two-way street. What country in Europe is self-contained enough, in the American sense, to act unilaterally? There is none, and if there were, we wonder if Americans would like it. In the past there has been such behavior in Europe, and it has always ended in disaster.

Europeans understand the value of freedom, which is why they fought the Cold War with you. But Europe was not built with freedom. Freedom has prevailed in Europe in spite of European history, or perhaps because of it. America, on the contrary, was made with freedom, which is why you talk about it all the time. But we would caution you that many Europeans think you sometimes speak about freedom as though Americans have a copyright on it. You talk about it as though you invented the idea, as though European history were the same as your own.

What you fail to see is that Europeans and Americans do not share "a love of liberty," they share the words. Europeans interpret their meaning very differently, because the circumstances are different. We do not share the same resources. We do not share the same history of rule. We do not share the same experience of relationships with other countries. We do not share the same independence to act. Because that is true we do not always agree with your conclusions that America's idea of freedom is the most important thing in the world, nor that everything else, to quote your national security expert, Condoleezza Rice, is of "a second-order effect."[43] We believe this conclusion is simplistic and unnecessarily condescending.

These observations may try your patience, but that does not make them invalid. We think there is a European message here, and it goes like this: Our painful history has taught us that the world is a complex place; do not tempt fate by seeing only what you want to see. This message is a veiled warning, made out of admiration, not jealously. We are saying that even though you may believe you can afford to pay less attention to balance, to the nuance, to the different shades of grey in the world, you cannot.

Our historical experience has taught us this, and yours has not. Our history is not the story of winning the war of independence as it is in America. We applaud your courageous spirit, and we believe you when you say that no man is an island. But we also caution you to remember that no two islands are the same. Americans associate their backyard with freedom and patriotism; in fact you often use the words as thought they were interchangeable. Europeans cannot. They associate their backyard with war.

Klaus and Elizabeth made their point. The backyards are not alike. Europeans and Americans define them differently because they are different, and they focus on different things when they gaze beyond them. Our separate historical experiences distinguish our horizons, and what we see shapes our perspectives. They concluded their letter as follows:

For some of us in Europe the different backyards mean we marvel at your courage to move ahead, we are envious of your sense of invention and initiative, and we admire your willingness to try something new. We have these qualities, too. But, in a way very different from you, we also are captives of centuries of our own history, burdened by our authoritarian structures, and limited by our geographical boundaries. Change in Europe occurs slowly for these reasons. This does not mean our convictions are weak, or that we do not value political and economic freedom as strongly as you do. But it does remind us that Europeans and Americans do not always take the same road to get to the same place.

So we close with some advice gathered from our European experience. Be a little less self-righteous, a little more modest, and much more attentive to the reasons why we don't always see the world in the same way. We have not always followed this advice ourselves, and we have paid a high price for not doing so. But the advice is sound, and it is well meant. If Americans, as well as Europeans, can follow it, it will benefit us both.

They had touched the main issues, all that is except one, which is a sensitive matter for Americans. Europeans, when they want to attack what they view as a naive American view of the world, assert that wars have never engulfed the American continent and that Americans, therefore, cannot understand the real meaning of conflict. Thus, so goes the explanation, the Civil War, in all its tragedy and destruction, was something Americans started and ended themselves, at home. Pearl Harbor was an attack on an island, not on the continental United States. World Wars I and II, as well as the wars in Korea, Vietnam, and Iraq, were wars that Americans elected to fight on the other side of oceans. They were not fought in the alleys of Cleveland, Ohio, as European wars have been fought on European streets. The inference is that American history has not blessed Americans with the ability to recognize that the world's backyard is more complicated than the backyard of flag-waving, bright-eyed, bushy-tailed Americans.

Many Americans who have heard this interpretation of the legacy of American history do not accept it with equanimity. They know that America's historical time frame is short in comparison to the European, but America's long-term memory about threats to freedom, and about the value of loyalty and patriotism, is very much intact. Both are based on an idea which Americans have never left in the backyard. The idea is a multicultural reflection of a set of beliefs. "Patriotism," American historian Walter Berns has written, "is not place but principle. The word 'fatherland' . . . does not occur in our patriotic vocabulary because our allegiance is not first of all to our native land (the word 'nation' comes from the Latin *nasci,* 'to be born') but to the ideas of freedom that animate it."[44]

Without these ideas the American spirit would not exist, and without that spirit America would never have gone to the aid of the Europeans in the twentieth century. Would Americans go to the aid of Europeans in the twenty-first century, if they again needed help? The answer must be hypothetical, but it can be framed effectively in the form of a question: Would Americans stay home? Would the Europeans go to the aid of Americans, if the roles were reversed? They all did so during the war on terrorism in Afghanistan. And some did during the war in Iraq. What does this tell us? The question calls to mind what American writer James Baldwin wrote in 1961: "Europe has what we do not have yet, a sense of the mysterious and inexorable limits of life, a sense, in a word, of tragedy. And we have what they sorely need: a sense of life's possibilities."

PART TWO

Qualities of Life

Preface

How significant is the contemporary influence of the essential difference? In a word, immense. Nowhere are its effects more evident than in how we ordered our post-1945 worlds in Europe and America, and in why we chose the paths we took. In both cases the explanation is the same.

In drawing on our respective practice and experience we rebuilt our lives from the top down and from the bottom up, because it was the only way we knew how. The consequences remain far-reaching. Today we live with these dual approaches to the organization and management of our lives. In Europe it is the institutions of the state that rule. In America government is by the people via their institutions. The twentieth century origins of how this came to pass are found in the desperation and rubble left in the wake of World War II.

In Europe, attachment to rule from the top down allows those who govern to define the relative importance of different qualities of life and how they should be ordered. In turn, a European by-product of this order is criticism of American faith in economic freedom and equal opportunity as misplaced and oversold. In contrast, the singular American approach to life—that freedom is always the first priority, and that everything else is of "a second-order effect"—also has a by-product. Americans have little patience with the European view that, because economic trials and social tribulations are made of many colors and affect everyone, they are too important be left to the unchecked chaos of free markets. Yet in France, for example, few politicians know how markets work. So, the task of managing free markets is assumed by political elites, most of whom have never held full-time jobs in the real world of hard work. Specifically, in France in late 2006, only 30 of 331 members of the French Senate had ever been active in private industry. So, in October French senators left "their Paris sanctuary in the seventeenth-century Luxembourg Palace to (visit) factories and offices in search of what Finance Minister Thierry Breton . . . calls an 'economic education.'"[1]

These contrasting attitudes, however, seldom evoke provocative newspaper headlines. These are usually reserved for trade disputes, arguments over defense capabilities, and disagreements over threats to national security. While these matters are important, how we order our qualities of life is far more significant in the long term.

This arrangement is subtle, but because it affects the allocation of our budget priorities, it is profound in its consequence. It is here that debate begins between those who defend the rights of the individual and those who champion the wisdom of the state, and also here that disagreement exists on the priority of equality vis-à-vis freedom, and on the value of equal opportunity versus equality of result.

At the center of our differing viewpoints on these subjects is a struggle. It is between competition and growth versus regulation and stability, between the invisible hand of the marketplace at work and the visible, but often hidden hand of the state at the controls. The result is that each of us extols the virtue and justice of our respective economic and social practices—*the European socioeconomic model* versus *the American model.*

Seen from this perspective the following two essays are neither a truncated history of post-1945 Europe and America, nor are they a recitation of differing views on economics and social science. They are much more than that. They are a narrative of the continuing hold that the essential difference exerts on our pursuit of peace and prosperity.

Chapter III

Equality, Opportunity, Stability

The European Socioeconomic Model, the American Model

EUROPE AND AMERICA, while acting together to achieve many goals following the end of World War II, also pursued different domestic policy priorities. Surrounded by the aftermath of war, Europeans readily accepted the strong role of rule from the top down. After almost a decade of threat and turbulence they welcomed, and valued, the promise of stability. As individuals they voluntarily set themselves free from many responsibilities which they might otherwise have assumed themselves. It is in this manner that they became wards of the state. Those Europeans who found security in this approach had a wide array of political champions to choose from.

The contrast with the American state was dramatic. Americans continued to look to themselves, and not to their government, as the guarantor of their freedom. They kept protection of their personal liberties in their own hands and deliberately limited the federal role. They valued the opportunity to choose how best to provide for themselves, to earn the financial rewards of their own labor, to assure that their government worked for them, and not vice versa. Americans had a relationship with their government which was independent of the state, not dependent on it. This freedom gave the individual primary responsibility for his or her economic health and social welfare.

Not all Europeans today, by any means, endorse rule from the top down, and critics of statism in Europe are growing in number. But, with the invariable exceptions, the basic differences in approach have changed little during the past sixty years, since 1945. Americans and Europeans continue to value opportunity, and assess risk, differently.

One result, and a significant one, was described recently by a columnist in the *Financial Times* in London. He was referring to Germany, but his conclusion applies as a whole to the practice of rule from the top down. He wrote that "in a country where the welfare state has taken almost all risk out of life, people have difficulty not only coming to terms with bad luck, but with good luck as well."[2]

What has just been outlined is what European political leaders mean when they proudly speak of *the European socioeconomic model*—a prescription for regulated result and economic equality. "Europeans claim," so wrote French commentator Dominique Moïsi in 2002, "to stand for a multipolar world that shares European values of pluralism, reconciliation, humanism and tolerance. The reality, however, is that most Europeans dream of turning their continent into what would amount to a large Switzerland—a rich, selfish, boring and largely irrelevant place. They speak of the greatness of their *European socioeconomic model*, of its irresistible attraction. But at the first challenge, they are quick to shut the doors of their fragile paradise even to the closest of outsiders."[3]

Moïsi's conclusion does not garner admiration among many European politicians. They are naturally hostile to such criticisms. But they do not attack the authors. They do not need to, because they have invented a straw man to deflect attention from themselves. They call it the *American model.* This phrase, already briefly noted, is used by Europeans in a negative way to describe a society riven with inequity, with fancy houses for the rich and ghettos for the poor, with health care for some but not for others, with widespread homelessness in the richest country in the world, populated by fat Americans who consume fast food and drive gas-guzzling cars.

An enlightening illustration of this point was sent to me in 2002 by a

Czech mathematician who lives in Prague, and who earned his Ph.D. degree at Rutgers University in the state of New Jersey in the mid-1990s. I asked him if he could give me several examples of things he thought distinguished Americans and Europeans:

> We Europeans cling more to the average, while you Americans tend more to go for the extremes. Here are a few examples. Some Americans are so overweight they would be considered monsters in Europe, and yet you also have some of the finest athletes in the world. Most of the richest people in the world live in America, but you have scores of people spending their winter nights on subway vents. Most of the very top universities and research centers in all fields are in the U.S. At the same time some elementary schools are so substandard that it would not be tolerated in any of the European countries. I guess that this overall tendency to go for the average causes us Europeans to be more indecisive to take any action, more careful in considering all the options, while Americans are more adventurous, whether it comes to moving from place to place, quitting a job and finding another one, or perhaps, even in going to war.

The observations are valid. What the writer omitted, however, is that freedom in America brings with it opportunity, hope, and choice, as well as inequalities. Americans do not claim that theirs is a perfect society, which is why millions of Americans, young and old, serve as volunteers every day of the year to help those less fortunate than themselves. But when all is said and done, Americans place a greater value on protecting their freedom of opportunity than on restricting freedom to assure equality of result.

This is a conscious choice of significant consequence. The guarantee of economic security offered by the European practice of rule from the top down does bring with it greater equality, but greater equality has a specific cost that freedom does not. That price is the creation of individual dependency on the state, and a loss of individual liberty. That kind of economic security regulates opportunity, limits hope, penalizes accomplishment, and restricts freedom of choice. Many Europeans consider this a conundrum. They would like to have it both ways. Of course, they know they cannot, but neither do they want to admit it. And, most do not. Europeans accept the imperfections and restrictions, and European leaders consistently compare their asserted social strengths of *the European socioeconomic model* with their asserted social weaknesses of *the American model.*

❦

Rule from the top down has numerous effects, one of which is the existence of a permanent political class. Instructive in this regard is the rationale for establishment of the School for National Administration (ENA: *Ecole Nationale d'Administration*) in France, founded in May 1945. Located in Strasbourg, it was, by any measure, an attractive prospect, born of the recognition during the war that well-educated civil service administrators would play a pivotal role in reconstructing postwar France.

The idea, however, came not from the bottom up, but from the top down. That is to say, the concept presupposed that an educated, permanent civil-service elite would rule more wisely and effectively than private citizens unschooled in the skills of government. So an institution was founded to educate France's political elite in the art of administration on a nonpartisan basis. The institution's graduates, however, known as the *énarques*, soon learned that they all shared a compelling reason to protect the power of the new class they represented. They held a monopoly, and they have guarded it successfully. For example, between 1974 and 2002 two of the three presidents of France, and nine out of 11 prime ministers had attended the ENA, while in French ministries and government institutions several thousand graduates hold permanent civil service positions.[4]

The ENA is a superb example of state power consolidated in the hands of a few. My colleagues look at me incredulously when I explain it, because nothing like it exists in America. But Europeans generally, and in this specific case the French, do not consider their relationship with the state as one of subservience to an elite. Rather they see it as as a mutually satisfactory arrangement by which to assure the general and common welfare of the individual. This relationship amounts to an economic entitlement, greatly influenced by the socialist vision of society. Although the contract is proudly described as *the European socioeconomic model,* superior to *the American model,* it could well be called *the new socioeconomic freedom* that stepped onto the continent out of the ruins of World War II.[5]

Few Europeans or Americans spend much time analyzing the contrasts between their political and economic cultures, and perhaps it is a good thing, because they are so different. Both are concerned, however, with their private privileges and public obligations as citizens. They are also conscious of the freedom they have to determine their own future. What decisively influences their lives is how they think about their own responsibilities as individuals versus the state, about what they can become, and about what they are prepared to do about it.

Americans think of who they are in terms of what they have accomplished, of what they have contributed to their community, of how well they have provided for the education, health, and welfare of their families. This allows them to look at life in terms of what they can still do, of the opportunities that still await them, of how they can help others. Most Europeans think of who they are in terms of being average, and frequently in terms of what cannot be accomplished, in terms of what is not allowed, in terms of what is not possible.

The logical consequence is self-evident, and it accounts for a major difference between how many Americans and Europeans imagine their respective roles in the societies in which they live. This contrast between American optimism and European pessimism was drawn for me by an investment banker in Paris who cited the example of a glass of water. "Americans," he said, "see the glass half full, figure out how to fill it to the top, and have faith in their ability to do it. We see the glass as half empty, with little hope to fill it, regardless of how hard we try. If the attitude toward what you do, or what you want to do, is positive, the glass is always waiting to be filled. But if the attitude is negative, the glass only contains what is left."

These distinctly separate outlooks toward life influence everything Americans and Europeans do, including how their leaders approach the discussion of problems. Europeans are prone to say what they cannot do, and then offer reasons why it is so. Americans often begin a conversation by saying, "You need to understand that this is a problem, and this is how we are going to solve it." Is this a further example of the different paths Americans and Europeans take in their effort to arrive at the same place?

Socialism in Europe and America

The tale of socialism in Europe has a lot in common with the story of the glass of water. As an approach to managing government, the promises made and the promises kept are a history of mixed results. Nonetheless, socialism continues to exert a tremendous influence on economic and political life, despite the collapse of corrupt and dictatorial "socialist" governments in central and Eastern Europe during 1989–1990.

The development of the post-1945 economic and political order in Europe and America was significantly influenced by socialism; that is to say, it enjoyed tremendous appeal in postwar Europe, and was absent as a major political force in American politics.[6] This is a development of enormous consequence that also has its origins in the essential difference. Few Americans, however, are familiar with the history of socialism. But without knowledge of socialism's influence on the continent, it is not possible for Americans to grasp the rationale or understand the practice of politics in Europe.

It is a common American tendency to equate "socialism" with the phrase "welfare state," and most reject the idea as inconsistent with economic independence and political freedom. There is something in their psyche that causes Americans to consider economic dependency on the state as a sign of weakness. This is why Americans think accepting welfare is something to be ashamed of, including many of those who take it. In fact, some Americans call it a socialist invention designed to create a dependent relationship. While that contention always stirs up squabbles on college campuses, it is also true that socialism appeals to few Americans because there is no spawning ground.

There are socialists in America, of course, but they play no meaningful role in American political life because, to take root and survive, socialism needs exploitation, abuse, class divisions, and inequality, with no hope for change. It cannot thrive in a society where equal opportunity is considered more important than equality of result, where economic rewards come from hard work and not from government, where standards of living rise, and where social mobility is always active. In America one consequence is that socialists have never won a national election.

The history of socialism in Europe is almost exactly the opposite. The story begins in earnest at the end of the eighteenth century, when the power of the old aristocracy was disappearing to be replaced eventually with a new aristocracy in the form of elected politicians. The political and economic changes ushered in during the era of 1789–1815 in revolutionary Europe marked, in general terms, the beginning of changes that took place over decades, until the annexation of Austria by Germany in 1938, when preoccupation with the coming deluge of violence interrupted them.

Measured in terms of years, radical change did not arrive quickly, nor was it "social" or "equal." French revolutionaries, to take one example, succeeded in cutting off many heads belonging to priests, aristocrats and tax collectors—among them the founder of modern chemistry, Antoine Lavoisier—but they did not destroy, at all, the lines separating social classes in that country, nor did class distinctions disappear anywhere else on the continent.

Society remained highly structured as Europe plodded through the nineteenth century. The Industrial Revolution did not merge class differences, but in some cases made them worse, and did succeed in creating a new business and social elite in Europe. It also enriched the ideology of socialism.

In the latter half of the nineteenth century Europeans faced two fundamental choices. One was escape from poverty and drudgery, and in some cases famine; a massive emigration to America took place, to a land of hope and opportunity, not to a land of class divides. The other was to remain in Europe. Many in better-educated and wealthier social and business classes prospered, while some of those who were not of that status were attracted to a political movement whose leaders preached the injustice of markets and competition. In their speeches they spoke of an artificial world of equality of result, but not of the free world of equality of opportunity. They demanded rectification of disparities in wealth, improvement of working conditions, an end to management abuses, and abolition of privilege. This was an attractive prospect, and was ardently pleaded, most notably in the writings of German social and political philosophers Friedrich Hegel, Friedrich Engels, and Karl Marx, but also by self-styled intellectuals whom Friedrich Hayek described in a famous monograph as "the professional second-hand dealers in ideas."[7]

The movement's rationale was the appealing vision of a social contract. Drawn in part from Rousseau's political tract of the same name, the contract between the state and the individual promised to strengthen the authority of the former and promote the welfare of the latter, so both would be served. Socialists argued that those who labored—the proletariat— should have the right to make the rules; in other words, to govern by replacing private ownership and management with public ownership and control.

It was a doctrine of hope, in a non-American sense, that called for "a complete transformation of the economic and moral basis of society by the substitution of social for individual control and of social for individualistic forces in the organization of life and work." The "organization" amounted to a new economic order and political system, deliberately described with the alluring word "social."

Advocates called it "Socialism." Eventually they even wrote a song about it, originally in French, entitled "The International." Few Americans have ever read the words to it, and do not know that they are far more militant that they are social.[8] "The International," in fact, was a siren song about a class struggle that would change the world "from its foundations." The song, however, is out of tune with the history of the socialist promise, still powerful in contemporary Europe.

The promise had tremendous appeal to those who labored in nineteenth-century factories produced by the Industrial Revolution, and who felt excluded from sharing in the fruits of their labor. They saw a much better life in the equality socialism offered. That equality would be assured by a "socialist" government that would possess the political power to control the means of production and the selfless altruism to distribute goods equally to all. And for those who suspected how it would work in practice, socialism also contained a hidden reward, but of a very different kind. It was the lure of enormous political and economic power in the hands of those who controlled the operation of the marketplace, via government; an earlier vision of the power European governments amassed while rebuilding the continent after 1945.

The ruling class—the socialists—would dictate equality of result by establishing state monopolies, by nationalizing major industries via confiscation of private property, by controlling how goods would be produced and sold and distributed, and by deciding how the profits would be shared. To make the vision praiseworthy, rather than politically threatening, the promise was often touted as a democratically controlled economy run by the people. Those whose economic and political freedom of choice would be adversely affected, opposed socialism. But those who wanted to gain political and economic control described the system in a different way. They called it a guarantee of the rights of every man to participate in the creation and distribution of wealth. They did not address the artifice that socialism was a new form of old rule.

Those who embraced socialism for its public promises of equality, or for its hidden assurances of dictatorial power, argued that it would produce a just society, without poverty. Few discussed what was obvious to many; namely, the ideology of socialism was based on the assumption that those controlling government had a better idea of what was in the individual's interest than the individual himself.

Socialism was predicated on the assertion that private businessmen profit and grow rich while exploiting others who remain impoverished, and therefore on the permanent existence of an adversarial relationship between the private interest and the public good. This logic, rather than breaking down arbitrary and exploitative class structures and distinctions, reinforced them. The individual, according to the socialist view of the world, could not change his lot by hard work, could not reinvent himself, could not succeed, and was condemned forever to his social class.

Thus, the glass was never full, but always half empty, and the individual was powerless to fill it to the top. Caught in this web from which there seemed no exit, the individual nonetheless had a right to freedom from capitalist bondage. Indeed, he was entitled to it, if a means could be found to escape. The logic of the argument was that socialism would bring that emancipation. That logic was also the deceptive genius of the socialist promise.

Freedom without definition was an abstraction, so the claim went, but with definition freedom would become real. "Whose freedom?" Karl Marx asked in a speech on free trade in 1848, and answered his own question: "It is not the freedom of one individual in relation to another, but the freedom of capital to crush the worker." From this conclusion followed the elixir. Socialists—the new ruling class—believed in the right of the individual to be free from the stifling burden of capital, and therefore would honor this right to freedom by providing the citizen with a social contract. Socialist government would serve the people's needs; namely, all those needs the people made manifest by expression of their desire to be free, and equal. In other words, socialism would transform the "manifestation" into reality, because mere and mortal individuals were powerless to do so by themselves. The means to do so would take the form of manifestations, demonstrations, protests, strikes and riots, and also of revolution.

The socialist idiom amounted to nothing less, and to nothing more, than a nineteenth-century continuation of eighteenth-century rule from the top down. Given the political conditions of upheaval, which continued into the 1870s in Europe, and the economic turmoil of the Industrial Revolution, it is hardly surprising that, in the course of the nineteenth century, socialist political parties grew stronger until, in the twentieth, socialism gave birth to its heirs in the form of dictators. If there was any doubt that the concept of *social* in socialism had no room for the individual, and that individual lives could be sacrificed for the so-called good of the whole—if necessary, millions of times over—socialism's red and black aristocratic children, born in the twentieth century, removed that uncertainty. In Russia they were part of Lenin's and then Stalin's red Communist Party of the Soviet Union, which ruled for 73 years from 1917 to 1990. In Germany they were members of Hitler's black National Socialist Workers Party, which existed for 12 years, from 1933 to 1945, followed by the red Socialist Unity Party that governed the German Democratic Republic until 1990.[9] And in central Europe, after 1945, they formed communist governments, imposed from above and preserved until 1990 by Soviet military power.

By 1918 Europe's wealthy landowning classes had been, for the most part, politically emasculated. In their stead had arisen political parties. Political power moved from castles and country manors—the "power houses" of the landed aristocracy—to new, government "power houses" in the cities. In turn, the majority of the parties to which the socialist movement gave birth participated in the electoral process, because they recognized in it a vehicle to take them into the halls of government. Whether the parties called themselves socialist, labor, or communist was a distinction without great practical difference. What was important was that their participation accorded them respect. To reinforce that point, most notably in Germany, they called themselves Social Democrats. Today, to elaborate on the German example, the formal name is still the Social Democratic Party, and the former communist party of East Germany, which ruled until 1990, now styles itself the Party of Democratic Socialism.

European parties of the left, however, were far from alone in the desire of their leaders to rule from the top down. They had a great deal of company from political parties of the center and of the right. Their sights were all set on the same goal. They understood that electoral government, as opposed to governing by divine right, was the twentieth century's epaulet of political legitimacy. They were *the new aristocrats* without noble names. And they understood—whether of the left, the center or the right—how rule from the top down worked. Of the many tools they employed in mastering their craft, one of the most valuable was that of taxation—on the sale of goods and services, and eventually on income, capital gains, inheritance, and wealth. Thus, they secured the revenues with which to finance their operation of *the public sector.*

They all recognized the enormous attraction of a social contract between the citizen and government, and they knew as well that those ruling enjoyed certain material privileges. After all, they had been well taught by the social, economic and political practices of their namesakes, the old aristocrats. That world, of course, had never been open to them; indeed, one of its strengths had been that it was closed to all but a few. So the new aristocrats borrowed from the past and operated their political parties as private clubs, to which admission was not guaranteed merely because one wanted to be a member. Approval was required. In turn, out of politicians they made a new class, and membership in it a badge of privilege: in France in 2006 the Socialist Party numbered just 200,000 members, just a little more than 3 percent of the country's population.

By the beginning of World War II Europe's political upper crust had developed politics into a professional occupation. They had laid the seeds for and cultivated new rule from the top down over a period that began in 1789. It grew, for all practical purposes, for 200 years, until the late 1980s, when the revolution in computer and communication technology—known as "the fax revolution" in Europe—began to break apart their monopoly of information, and to undermine rule as practiced by the new aristocrats.

Socialist parties in contemporary Europe, also known as labor parties, play a major role in determining the political, economic, and social agendas of governments throughout the continent. That is not to say that their socialist programs are without opposition. Socialist governments are voted out of office, just as they are voted into office. But they have formed an unwritten alliance with parties of the center and of the right, to preserve the principle of rule from the top down.

Not all European political parties are a part of this unwritten system. The exceptions are Europe's nonsocialist, "liberal" parties, defined in the classic sense that a "liberal" society is one of free markets without the social engineering of government taxation, redistribution and regulation. Of the eight caucuses in the European Parliament, one, the ALDE Group (Alliance of Liberals and Democrats for Europe), is composed of elected parliamentary members from thirty-five different liberal parties of twenty-two member states of the European Union. These national delegations espouse their own respective political and cultural values, but also cooperate together in the ALDE and share a common vision for Europe. But aside from these exceptions, Europe's parties are part of the system which, to varying degrees, they all practice. When in government, whether they are so-called conservatives or socialists, the common approach taken to assure their respective survival is to maintain the social contract.

Real reform—that is to say, reducing the massive role that postwar 1945 European governments play in the lives of the people they govern—seldom comes as an initiative from the major political parties. When elections take place in Europe there are, certainly, always opposing views presented by liberals and conservatives, by socialists and nonsocialists. European voters, in whatever country they may be, do have real choices to make. But the choices are about people and parties, not about policies and principles. Political parties, whether conservative or socialist, operate on the generally accepted premise that the right of the state to define the limits of freedom is part of the political order.

In France the practice is called *dirigist* or *statist*, a state which directs and provides. Its operation may explain why French National Assembly member Pierre Lellouche observed in the spring of 2000 that if there were to be a French renaissance it would have to come "from outside the political debate and independently of the political class. . . . What the political class is doing is foreign to the real world and basically irrelevant."[10]

An example of what Lellouche meant had already been discussed twenty years earlier in the 1980 American presidential election. Ronald Reagan campaigned with a slogan which in 2005, twenty-five years after he first used it, is still largely absent in European political campaigns. He criticized the *more-government-is-better* policies of the Democratic Party for producing a country that was overgoverned, overregulated, overtaxed, and overspent. His simple message was that there was too much government in the lives of everyday Americans. Reagan's slogan expressed one side of the debate about a philosophical issue that seldom takes place in European politics—namely, what is the proper role and size of government.

Change occurs, of course, just as philosophical discussions also take place. But debate on the relationship between the state and the individual is not daily political fare. Even though many Europeans are painfully conscious of the regulated world in which they live, and often reject it in private conversations, few political leaders have the desire and courage to challenge the prevailing order. One who did subscribe to the principle that *less-government-is-better* was Margaret Thatcher, the "Iron Lady" of Great Britain. As prime minister between 1979 and 1990 she was able to transform rule from the top down, and bring about a British renaissance of the kind to which Lellouche would refer ten years later.

That Thatcher was able to dismantle much of Britain's *dirigist* political and economic structure was no accident. She was able to challenge the "Socialist consensus" successfully because she possessed two qualities indispensable to political leadership: courage and conviction. She believed that socialist anti–free market policies, led by labor unions and given life via confiscatory taxes and government monopoly of nationalized industries and services, were limiting opportunity and stifling economic growth. Indeed, in the late 1970s Britain was called "the sick man of Europe," borrowing money from the International Monetary Fund to pay its bills.

She called the struggle "the second battle of Britain," and the result best spoke for itself. The tax system was overhauled and the top personal income tax rate dropped from 98 percent in 1978/79 to 40 percent ten years later. Massive industrial restructuring took place in the seven old, basic industries of steel, textiles, coal mining, ship building, ports, agriculture and automobiles. The cumulative effect was that Britain's standard of living, in 1984 the lowest in Europe's common market, became the highest by 2005.[11]

Since the end of World War II, however, the only major European country to achieve success has been Britain. The principal reason why is that no other political leader has possessed the skill to deal with the resistance that accompanied Thatcher's attempt to weaken rule from the top down, and few have been willing to gamble their political futures on the outcome of such a venture.

Margaret Thatcher was prepared to take the risk and she succeeded. But Europe's politicians understand the significance of the elementary conclusion that if they cannot win elections they cannot govern. So the majority embrace the concept of *the European socioeconomic model*. What they mean by it is old rule with a new name, and when they use the phrase they are delivering a homage to the benevolent state, sensitive to injustice, acting as a force of equilibrium, keeping the different elements of society in balance and the forces of inequality at bay.

In America a balanced partnership between government and the individual, which serves the welfare of the citizen while preserving the power of the state, is a contradiction in terms. *The European socioeconomic model* is the antithesis of the idea and practice of American freedom. Americans talk about all men being created equal in the eyes of God, about equality in terms of having a right to equal opportunity, and about an equal right to liberty and justice. It is a concept as old as the founding documents of the American republic. How the Declaration of Independence begins reflects how Americans think, even if the last time most Americans read it was when they were in school:

> *We hold these truths to be self-evident, that all men are created equal; that they are endowed by their Creator with certain inalienable rights; that among these are life, liberty, and the pursuit of happiness; that to secure these rights, governments are instituted among men, deriving their just powers from the consent of the governed; that whenever any form of government becomes destructive of these ends, it is the right of the people to alter or abolish it, and to institute new government, laying its foundation on such principles, and organizing its powers in such form, as to them shall seem most likely to effect their safety and happiness.*

Government power frightens Americans because they do not trust it. Nor do most Americans believe that it is possible for individuals, in matters of the social-economic commonweal, to be equal partners with the state. This is why the vision of a social contract between the state and the individual, which serves the interests of both, is difficult for Americans to imagine. Or, perhaps it is the opposite. Americans can see it very clearly, and it scares them to death. Either way it prompts Americans to ask such questions as, "How can Europeans let the state take care of them from the cradle to the grave?" "How can bureaucrats and politicians possibly know what is better for the individual than the individual himself?" "Where is their pride of independence?" "Where is their righteous indignation?"

These questions, of course, do disturb some Europeans. That is why there are still Europeans who come to live and work in America; in fact, as a whole more educated men and women continue to emigrate to America than to all other countries in the world combined. They are making use of the right to pursue happiness as they define it and as they make it, free from the constraints of the collective happiness imposed by government control in, for example, Europe.

When immigrants arrive in America they are coming to build happier lives, and they still bring with them, as they always have, their energy and initiative. They bring a will to succeed, and their loyalty to the idea of American freedom. They do not all enjoy success in the same way. Some make good decisions and some make bad ones, and some have more luck than others. But they all are free to choose, to take responsibility for their choices, and to pursue happiness as they define it.

In Europe the principle and practice of the social contract is part of political and economic life. Today, that means all political parties have to finance the contract. The only way they can do that and deliver the contract's entitlements is to use the marketplace as the principal source of income. And that is exactly what they do via regulation and taxes, to a degree unprecedented in America. It is true that nonsocialists advocate far less tax and regulatory control than socialists. But it is also true that most nonsocialists are firmly committed to the idea of *the European socioeconomic model.* To do otherwise and still get elected, is not yet possible.

Winds of political and economic change, however, are blowing across Europe and are turning in surprising directions. In early July 2003 a meeting of European center-right leaders and politicians took place in Strasbourg, the seat of the European Parliament. Then French prime minister Jean-Pierre Raffarin, who replaced socialist Lionel Jospin in the French elections of June 2002, stirred up a hornet's nest when his comments about socialism were widely quoted. He concluded that "France is not yet on the road to heaven, only in purgatory, since we still have Socialists." The response by François Hollande, the secretary-general of the French Socialist Party, may have been less truthful than he intended. "The demonization of the competition," he responded, "reveals a concept of politics that we do not share."[12] It was an ironic conclusion in view of socialist opposition to free and open competition in the marketplaces of ideas, trade, and commerce—a struggle they renewed immediately, following the end of World War II.

The post-1945 Political and Economic Order

In late 1945 Europe and America each faced fundamentally different problems of political and economic recovery and reconstruction. No bombs had fallen on American cities, and Americans were not surrounded with the horrors of physical destruction and the obstacles presented by economic dislocation. But Americans were not free of challenges either, nor were they immune from sorrow; more than 400,000 American men and women died during World War II.

Americans faced formidable problems of their own, as families began to rebuild their private and professional lives. In practice, this meant returning to the operation of a free market economy, and reducing the awesome powers acquired by government to guide the war effort from Washington, D.C. The effort to do so moved forward, little by little; although some historians argue that many of the powers of government amassed during Franklin Roosevelt's administration were never returned to the American people. But the regulatory controls of wartime were largely abolished; Americans resumed competition in the marketplace, and renewed their search for the American dream.

Tremendous social changes would transform many aspects of American society during the second half of the twentieth century, but one element remained the same.[13] It was the primacy of the individual, of equality of opportunity, of the freedom to choose—and one of the things Americans chose was participation in a massive and voluntary effort to assist European recovery. They sent blankets, clothing, and food.[14] America forgave French debts, and the Marshall Plan gave the Europeans the financial means to rebuild their economies.[15]

The challenges of reconstruction on the continent were immediate, and complicated. Whether to rebuild Europe's cities was not merely a question of deciding to do it. The real question was what role the state should play in establishing a peacetime economy capable of producing goods and providing services.

This issue—how should recovery be managed?—joined the protagonists; namely, the advocates of socialism and central planning and the champions of capitalism and free markets. At the end of 1945 the dominant view among Europeans was that some form of state control of the economy was so obviously necessary that it was beyond dispute. Socialism, so claimed its supporters, would lead to greater social justice and to greater efficiency; only under state control could the industrial economies possibly handle the overwhelming tasks they faced.

In a dramatic portent of the struggle to come, British voters, in elections held in July 1945, replaced conservative party leadership headed by Winston Churchill with that of the British Labor Party under the leadership of Clement Attlee. What followed was a grandiose government program of expanded social services combined with nationalization of heavy industry and transportation. The British historian A. J. P. Taylor wrote of the prevailing mood that "nobody in Europe believes in the American way of life—that is, in private enterprise; or rather those who believe in it

are a defeated party and a party which seems to have no more future than
the Jacobites in England after 1688."[16]

Taylor's view was strongly held, and he was far from alone in his belief
that capitalism was morally bankrupt. In Great Britain, the Labour Party
had a receptive audience for its solution to Europe's misery. The party
called it creation of a *welfare state* as opposed to a *warfare state*. This
emotion-laden comparison found wide appeal among Europeans as a
whole, who looked to government, and not to private enterprise, to create
equitable social and economic conditions. Indeed, many Europeans, on
all sides of the political spectrum, blamed capitalism for the Great Depression and held the marketplace responsible for the second European war
of the twentieth century.

There was also another and very different element in play that further
sharpened the struggle. It was the claim of legitimacy. That is to say, socialist political leaders in post-1945 Europe asserted a moral right to govern because they, so they argued, had opposed the dictatorship of Nazi
Germany as a matter of principle, while others had profited from it. Germany's Social Democratic Party echoed much of the tenor of the time in
the language of their party program, formulated in Hannover in May
1946. A key passage contained the following conclusion:

> . . . today's Germany is no longer in the position to carry a private, capital-
> istic profit-economy, and to pay profits from exploitation, capital divi-
> dends and bond income. . . . Just as socialism without democracy is not
> possible, so is, on the contrary, democracy in a capitalistic state in continu-
> ous danger. . . . German democracy must be socialist, or the counter-
> revolutionary forces will destroy it once again.[17]

There were those in Germany, however, who strongly disagreed with this
socialist interpretation of history, just as there were economists throughout Europe who fervently believed in the efficacy of competition and free
markets. Less than a year later, in March 1947, the leading conservative
party in the three western-occupied zones of Germany, the Christian

Democratic Party (CDU), approved a very different program. It struck a balance between the alleged evils of capitalism and the dangers of socialism, wrapped in an embrace of individual initiative:

> . . . the new structure of the German economy must proceed from the assumption that the time of unlimited power of private capitalism is over. But we must also avoid replacing private capitalism with state capitalism, which would be even more dangerous for the political and economic freedom of the individual. A new economic structure must be sought which avoids the mistakes of the past and which allows the possibility of technical progress and creative initiative of the individual.[18]

The clash between two different concepts of political and economic order in Germany mirrored the larger one taking place in Western Europe as a whole. Those political leaders and members of the intellectual and opinion-shaping elites who condemned the inequalities of capitalism and championed rule from the top down recognized an unparalleled opportunity to justify the exercise of great governmental powers. Europe had to be rebuilt. No one, so the logic went, had a greater moral claim to the control of recovery and reconstruction than those who recognized the evils of competition and profit. No one, indeed, was qualified to do so except the state, led by the party of socialism.

In short, these figures saw an opportunity in the requirements of recovery, not for freedom, but for establishment of a postwar ruling class. In central and eastern Europe, behind the Iron Curtain, communist parties had already prevailed with control dictated by the Soviet government. But in Western Europe the die was not yet cast, which meant that the political war between the forces supporting a planned economy versus a market economy, initiated immediately in Britain, was just beginning.

Those in Western Europe who opposed central planning feared that if a new ruling class ever got its political grip on the economy it would never let go. They suspected also that its leaders would develop state power in a way that would make Europe's citizens increasingly dependent on government to provide for their welfare. If this occurred, they argued, such control would become, over a long period of time, exceedingly difficult if not impossible to reverse.

One of the leading critics was German economist Wilhelm Röpke. Given what was at stake, his message was a powerful one. He argued that

> . . . if we seek a pure free market economy based on competition, it cannot float freely in a social, political, and moral vacuum, but must be maintained and protected by a strong social, political, and moral framework. Justice, the state, traditions and morals, firm standards and values . . . are part of this framework as are the economic, social, and fiscal policies which, outside the market sphere, balance interests, protect the weak, restrain the immoderate, cut down excesses, limit power, set the rules of the game and guard their observance. . . .[19]

Although Röpke's concerns were not shared by many, neither was his voice an isolated one, and he enjoyed distinguished company; in fact, at the war's end he and his wife had translated Friedrich von Hayek's critique of socialism, *The Road to Serfdom*, into German. There were also others in Europe known to both men. The importance they all attached to the values of the free market was the reason for the initiative taken by Hayek in early 1947. In April, in the tiny village of Mont Pèlerin in Switzerland, more than one thousand meters above Lake Geneva, he brought together an extraordinary group of almost forty economists and thinkers, primarily from Europe, but several also from America. They included not only Röpke, but Maurice Allais, Bertrand de Jouvenel, and F. Trevoux from France, Karl Popper and Lionel Robbins from the London School of Economics, Alexander Rüstow and Walter Eucken from Germany, Fritz Machlup and Ludwig von Mises from Austria, T. J. B. Hoff from Norway, as well as two young economists from the University of Chicago, Milton Friedman and George Stigler.

They debated whether to name their group after Lord John Acton (1834–1902) or Alexis de Tocqueville (1805–1859) and finally compromised, settling on the name of the village in which they met. Over the next half century—the Mont Pèlerin Society held its most recent General

Meeting in November 2006 in Guatemala—it became the most influential circle of the twentieth century dedicated to the pursuit of individual
freedom and to the operation of market economies. Of those attending
that first meeting, four were subsequently awarded, at different times, the
Nobel Prize in Economic Sciences: Hayek, Friedman, Stigler, and Allais;
and several others who joined the MPS later on have been awarded the
prize as well.

That the meeting in 1947 took place at all is remarkable, given that the
war had ended less than two years before and that traveling anywhere in
Europe posed major logistical problems, especially for the Germans, who
needed special permission from the occupation authorities to leave Germany. Those who came, however, all had a great deal in common. Hayek
had invited them because they had "held on to the idea of liberal thought
during the difficult times of the world wars, of the world economic crisis,
and during the expansion of fascism and communism, and . . . have not
lost their confidence in the power of the free market."

Their agenda was dramatically different from the program of the Social
Democratic Party of Germany. They discussed the problem and the
chances of a European union, free enterprise and competitive order, liberalism and Christianity, employment and monetary reform, wages and
labor unions, agricultural policy, and poverty, income distribution, and
taxation. On the final, and tenth day, they agreed on the Society's principles, which went to the heart of the struggle for the postwar European
economic and political order:

> the position of the individual and the voluntary group is progressively un-
> dermined by extensions of arbitrary power. . . . The group holds that these
> developments have been fostered by the growth of a view of history which
> denies all absolute moral standards and by the growth of theories which
> question the desirability of the rule of law . . . that they have been fostered
> by a decline of belief in private property and the competitive market.[20]

In 1947 it was still far too early to tell how the struggle would turn out
in Europe as a whole. Initially, those committed to individual liberty and

to competition in free marketplaces were able to communicate the power of their ideas. So, for example, in western Germany, thanks in large part to the economic policies of Ludwig Erhard, who later became a member of the Mont Pèlerin Society, the western Germans began to develop in 1948, following their currency reform, the freest market in Europe, after Switzerland.

The operating principle was based on the program presented by the CDU in February 1947. It was labeled the *social market economy* and its achievements were eventually baptized *The Economic Miracle* (*Das Wirtschaftswunder*). The name for this economic system implied a hybrid of the planning and control of the public state with free market policies, serving common social goals. But in fact, it was nothing of the kind. On the contrary, the purpose of the *social market economy* was to enable the individual to participate in all kinds of entrepreneurial activities, in the social, society-related economic life of Germany, and to do so in a country whose government would rule from the bottom up.

Post-war Germany, as post-war Europe, labored under the political pressure applied by those who had a stake in rule from the top down. Slowly, and gradually, economic freedom in western Germany and throughout Western Europe came to be regulated in the form of an unwritten contractual relationship between government and the individual citizen, one imperceptible step at a time.

Battles were fought issue by issue, decade by decade, throughout the 1950s and continuously thereafter, into the 2000s. Throughout, the central question remained the same: government control or private responsibility? Even though it was seldom phrased this way, that is what the struggle was all about, and it touched every conceivable part of society. In the aftermath of the war, all the areas requiring immediate attention were affected, such as housing; transportation by road, rail, and air; road and highway maintenance; communication via mail, telephone, and telegram; and water, gas, and electricity supplies. As time went by the focus was directed to regulation of labor markets, to minimum wages and salaries, to state financing of pensions and retirement plans, to free education, to national health care, to the regulation of the banking and insurance industries, and so on.

Although the outcomes varied from country to country, the predictable consequences were all there, somewhere: weak currencies, arbitrary constraints on labor mobility exercised by labor unions, destructive and expensive public sector strikes, uncompetitive labor markets, opposition to privately financed university education, nationalizations, a multitude of different government monopolies including utilities, transportation and telecommunication, and complex taxation of wealth, personal income and corporate enterprise designed to generate the monies necessary to feed the steadily growing appetite of the social contract.

As governments acquired more powers, a universal social welfare system emerged, in different shapes in different European countries. The consequence, in West Germany, was that Erhard's concept of the *social market economy* gradually lost its meaning. The "social element" in the market economy, as interpreted by those who endorsed the idea of the social contract between the state and the individual, today dominates marketplaces throughout Europe, including Germany. This explains why the phrase *social market economy* appeared early, and often, in the 2004 draft constitution of the European Union.

When compared with the struggle that took place in West Germany, developments in France were in some ways significantly different, but in others very much the same. There, with the exception of the period of 1945–1946 following liberation, France remained continually at war until 1962. French postwar history was one of decolonialization abroad, and unrest within. The war in Indochina ended with the devastating defeat at Dien Bien Phu in 1954, and the conflict in Algeria continued until independence was granted in 1962. The effects on domestic politics, combined with both violent and nonviolent attempts to control the French national agenda, were turbulent and destabilizing. Between 1946 and 1958 twenty different governments ruled the Fourth Republic. Today the history of this period, outside of France, remains largely unread and unknown.

It was not until Charles de Gaulle won election as prime minister in 1958, and succeeded in writing a new "presidential" constitution, that France had strong leadership under what became the Fifth Republic. His ten years as prime minister and then president, until 1969, were marked by his vision of restoring the glory and grandeur of France. But it was an uneasy period. The war in Algeria split the country in two. It divided political parties, the French army, and religious groups as well. It was also accompanied by several failed assassination attempts against de Gaulle himself. His focus on restoring pride and place to France, built on ending the war in Algeria and reasserting French leadership within Europe, is the history of decisions which led to the collapse of the gold standard, to the initial exclusion of Great Britain from the European Economic Community (EEC), and to creation of a French nuclear capability.

This story of postwar France began with opposition to the German invasion, and subsequent occupation. The death of more than 76,000 French soldiers killed during the first six weeks of combat in 1940 had, as one consequence, the development of a French resistance during 1941, while France was ruled by a puppet government with its headquarters in Vichy, where the United States maintained its embassy until November 1942. When American general Dwight D. Eisenhower wrote his final assessment of the war, he recalled those French men and women without uniforms who made a contribution equal to fifteen divisions. The history of the French resistance was one of bravery and sacrifice, but also one of turbulence among the French themselves, between the Left and the Right. In postwar France it became a political combat waged unabatedly, and one which continues to this day. It is a story of pride, prejudice, and tragedy that is well known in France, less so in Europe, and in America knowledge of it is almost nonexistent.[21]

The French left, which included the French Communist Party (PCF), had a socialist agenda which it forcefully pursued. The postwar Fourth Republic was constantly shaken by interminable political clashes over social and economic issues. One consequence was that the intrusion of rule from the top down into French society was systematically expanded year by year. By 1974 François Mitterrand had succeeded in unifying the centrist and leftist parties—except the PCF—into the Socialist Party. When he was elected president of the republic, just seven years later in 1981, the socialists dominated French political life. There was irony in the political comparison with America where, one year earlier, the strongest pro–free market president in postwar American history, Ronald Reagan, had been elected in a landslide victory

In contrast to American Republicans, French socialists embarked immediately on a program of further nationalization of French business and industry, which included 38 banks and financial institutions and twelve conglomerates, including electric power, chemicals and pharmaceuticals, electronics and computers, iron and steel, and aeronautics. Even without the nationalizations, the French government already controlled a major share of French industry, including public utilities, post and telecommunications, gas, coal, airlines, and railways. The extent was staggering. Altogether state-owned businesses accounted for about one-fourth of the industrial output and about 30 percent of industrial exports. Moreover, one-half of French businesses with more than 2,000 employees were owned by the state.

In 2005 France was one of two members of the European Union countries using a common currency—the other was Austria—where public spending accounted for more than 50 percent of gross national product. It is precisely here that Americans familiar with French politics see the dramatic effect of the social contract on the relationship between the state and the individual. A survey taken in France in 2004 indicated

> that more than 70 percent of French youths would be happy to work as "fonctionnaires," or state employees. The appeal of security appears greater than that of risk. More energy goes into preserving acquired rights, including steadily lengthening vacations, than creating new enterprises.[22]

This "contract" and its heavy financial cost affect not only French economic and political life, but every aspect of the relationship between Europe and America—including military capability. The governments of Western European countries have become skilled cultivators of compromise and practitioners of the special exception, although the verdict is still out for those countries which won their freedom with the collapse of communism in 1990. While there are Europeans who would like to see the economic powers of government significantly reduced, such a transformation, if it ever comes to pass, would represent a social and political revolution.

The reason is because the majority of Europe's political leaders benefit from maintaining the status quo. Another way to phrase the same conclusion was given in early 2003 by a professor of social and political theory at Britain's University of Buckingham, Norman Barry: ". . . representative assemblies subject to little restraint will not stand up to pressure groups [such as labor unions]. . . . it is the parties that are now cartelised and it is in their interests to preserve the present order."[23]

There are many examples which illustrate what is meant by "the present order." Among those which set forth major differences between the American and European outlooks are productivity comparisons and the related issues of birthrate and immigration, as well as attitudes toward work and retirement.

The idea of a broad government retirement plan is one illustration. In principle there is little disagreement on either continent that government pensions can serve a useful purpose, and when debate does occur it focuses on how to fund them properly. But on another issue, of equal importance to the success of government pension programs, Americans and Europeans differ dramatically.

Driven largely by socialist rhetoric, but also by government practitioners of rule from the top down, Europeans and Americans have, over the last fifty to fifty-five years, drawn different conclusions about the value and purpose of labor. An instructive illustration is that of a highly competent forester in France, in vigorous health, who retired at the age of sixty. When asked why he no longer wished to work he explained to me that when he was fifty-nine he had been visited at home one evening by a functionary of the French social security office who encouraged him "to make way for the young."

In Europe retirement is a reward and the "right" to retire has become an entitlement, while in America the "right" to work as long as one likes is a matter of choice. In short, in Europe the goal of retirement—whether, from the top down, to create employment or whether, from the bottom up, to cease doing something distasteful—has become more important than the pride taken in work. This manner of thinking is so foreign to the American work ethic that a rational explanation borders on being incomprehensible.

In February 2005 a visitor to the Hoover Institution, an economic reporter for the Italian newspaper *Corriere Della Sera*, asked me if I could account for the difference in productivity between America and Europe. There is a simple answer. Although Europeans produce almost the same amount per hour as Americans, Americans work more. The 35-hour work week does not exist in America—as the American author of *The End of Work* rhythmically puts it, Americans live to work and Europeans work to live.[24]

There are, however, also other ways to respond to this question. One is provided by some astonishing statistics published by the International Labor Office (ILO) in Geneva in September 2003. Americans were working between nine and twelve weeks more each year than Europeans, and about 80 percent of American men and 62 percent of American women worked more than 40 hours per week. One consequence was that average labor productivity in America grew at about 2.2 percent between 1996 and 2003, double that of the growth rate in the European Union.[25] Another way to draw the picture is to note that between 1973 and 1998 American GDP grew at an average rate of 2.9 percent annually, which is 39 percent more than in the EU. During the same period the number of Americans employed increased from 41 to 49 percent, while in Germany and France, for example, the percentages fell to 44 and 39 percent.[26]

A second consequence is waiting in the wings. Europeans are not only working less, but they retire earlier, their birthrate is declining, their immigration rate is low, and they are living longer.[27] Between 1950 and 2000 the average retirement age in the EU decreased to 59.8 from 66. Today, the common practice in Europe is to stop working, at the latest, at age 59 or 60, and often before, at age 55 or even 52, while in America the average retirement age is almost 63 years of age. By 2005 pensions comprised about 21 percent of public spending in the EU while the cost of Social Security in America made up about 4.8 percent.

The problem is easy to see. If Europeans do not change their negative attitude toward the dignity of labor and develop a positive work ethic, which includes reforming their generous pension plans, two things will happen. First, European GDP (gross domestic product = the total value of goods and services produced) will continue to move forward at a snail's pace. It is currently about 1.25 percent per year; on a per capita basis it is around 30 percent lower than American GDP, the same level as in 1975. Second, if this trend is not reversed EU governments will have no choice but to spend more and more of their budgets on pensions. Where will the money come from?[28]

Looming in the future is the prediction of a decline in the annual growth rate from 2.1 percent to 1.5 percent by 2015 and to 1.25 percent by 2040.[29] If the forecast becomes reality, who will finance *the European socioeconomic model*? It will not be Europe's working taxpayers. Today there are four people working for every retiree, but by 2050, unless the culture of retirement undergoes dramatic change, there will be two workers for every retiree and the median age in the EU will move upward, from 38 to 49.[30]

Over the last fifty years European politicians have created what today is the present economic and political order of post-war Europe. That order sets the first budget priority for every single country of the now 27-member European Union. The name of that priority is *the European socioeconomic model*. The model, the result of a deliberate choice, presents European governments with a dilemma: to finance budget deficits with tax increases or to reduce government expenditures and thereby weaken the popularity of those ruling from the top down.

There is a parallel, achieved with the same element of deliberateness, in America's postwar history, but with a difference. The relationship between Americans and their government has also developed systematically since the end of World War II. It could be called the American way, whose characteristics are marked by a continuity of spirit, focus and enterprise. That is to say, Americans also have a model. European critics label it *the American model*. But Americans know it by the words and phrases they use to describe the opportunities the model presents, that is, the challenges of hard work, competition, loyalty, risk and reward, going back to the drawing board when they fail, and finding the strength and courage to succeed.

Europeans might well argue that Americans, with time, will become as jaded in their view of the world as Europeans. But Americans would very likely respond, "That may well turn out to be the case, but we're not there yet." In fact, some take the logic of the response one step further, such as T. J. Rodgers, who heads a Silicon Valley company, Cypress Semiconductor: "Europeans always marvel about how optimistic we are. The difference is that in the U.S. we haven't had a few thousand years of hierarchy to grind out our faith. Here we understand that if we don't like the future, we'll just invent a better one."[31]

For entrepreneurs in Silicon Valley these words all add up to the belief that human capital and individual potential, creativity and invention become real in the arenas of ideas, trade, and commerce. Americans know that risk and reward reign in those marketplaces; they call it the pursuit of happiness. That pursuit is what gives Americans the incentive to get up each morning, to try to make their country, and their lives, a little bit better than the day before. That pursuit is also why they celebrate their day of independence, and why on the Fourth of July many Americans say "Thank You" to all those who have come before and who, each in their own way, have given their hearts, their spirit, their faith, their toil, and their lives for protection, prosperity, and liberty.

This exposition on the political struggle over the postwar European and American social and economic order explains, in part, the historical evolution that draws on different approaches to rule and responsibility as defined by the essential difference. Its effects, in a contemporary context, are not limited to contrasts in our histories, heritage and habits of life. Marks are also left on our economic policies, and found in the operation of our marketplaces and how we use them, but not only there. In Europe, there is an additional aspect of "the present order." This is the concept and the reality of the European Union. It is not a subject of daily conversation at American breakfast tables, but the European Union is changing the face of the continent. Its success or failure will also change the long-term relationship between America and Europe.

CHAPTER IV

Uncommon Marketplaces

The Concept of the Union

WHEN AMERICANS TRY to picture the European Union they may imagine a vague outline of a European market-place, but for most it is easier to recall a favorite city. Some are aware of how and why the EU was created, but there is little public discussion of its political and economic potential. In one form or another, however, the EU is here to stay. This is why American businesses, as well as American government officials, have established working relationships with different EU institutions. Essential to making these relationships work well is knowledge of the forces that motivated creation of the EU. This story neither begins nor ends with the defeat of Nazi Germany. Its roots are buried in the noble loam of the essential difference.

In Europe World War II did not end in 1945. Hostilities, in an unconventional sense, continued until 1989. It was Europe's Fifty Years' War, and one day historians may call it that. As long as the continent remained divided Europe was not whole, but existed as a *provisorium*. The first part of the war was conflict between 1939 and 1945. The second part took place between 1945 and 1989. It was a battle for the hearts and minds of Europeans fought primarily with political and economic weapons. It was baptized the Cold War, but it also had two distinct military elements. One was the nuclear arms race. The other was the protection provided by American military power for the arena in which the battle was being fought. That power preserved both the peace and freedom of Western

Europe, until the war finally ended with the opening of the Berlin Wall in 1989 and with the collapse of communism in 1990.

One of the characteristics of the second part of the war was *how* the Europeans expressed themselves vis-à-vis America on economic, military, and political matters. Their views were often enough straightforward, from time to time argumentative, and in the case of France, sometimes openly confrontational, following creation of the Fifth Republic in 1958. French president Charles de Gaulle withdrew France from NATO in 1966 and alliance headquarters were moved to Brussels. Today NATO's former buildings are part of the University of Paris.

This example of independence was not an isolated one. In the early 1960s, European countries, with France playing a leading role, began to demand redemption of *Eurodollars*—accumulated as a consequence of American postwar European recovery aid under the Marshall Plan—in exchange for American gold. By 1971 the gold supply had dwindled to such a point that the U.S. Treasury was bankrupt, in terms of the amount of bullion left in its vaults as backing for the total amount of paper dollars in circulation. The result was the end of the Bretton Woods agreement of 1944—the postwar international monetary system—which had established convertible currencies, fixed exchange rates, and free trade.[1]

France notwithstanding, there was also always a tone of deference to the primacy and requirements of American military power, if not to American culture. Europeans and Americans understood that as long as the Cold War lasted Western Europe would seek its security under the American nuclear umbrella, and would rely on American armed forces stationed on the continent. There was no other choice. Europe needed America's military protection, and both America and Europe wished to keep the western side of the Iron Curtain free. This conclusion was evident to many, but much less so was an unanswered question of equal importance. Would the eventual outcome of the Cold War change the nature of the European-American relationship, and if so, how?

When the war ended in 1989–1990 it was the indelible mark of a great American-European victory, made possible by the pursuit of common goals built on a foundation of common values. Communism had lost and, for the moment, socialism in the east was discredited, even though rule from the top down continued in the west. But as the iron fists of dictatorship departed the European stage one by one in the course of 1990, something new, which had not existed during the Cold War, made its entrance. It was the figure of an independent Europe.

For the first time since 1938, when the annexation of Austria marked the beginning of German aggression, all European governments were sovereign. No longer encumbered by the rules and preferences of the two superpowers, the Europeans were free to assert their own economic and political aims, and define the world's problems as they saw them. And this is exactly what they did. European leaders moved forward to create the political centerpiece of a new postwar nation, to be built on the existing economic foundations of the European Economic Community (EEC). They named it the European Union (EU).[?]

Its formation, as we know it today, had been impossible as long as the Fifty Years' War lasted; that is to say as long as the Soviet Union maintained the division of Berlin, the division of Germany, and the division of Europe. But once Germany chose to unite in 1990, so too could Europe. The lead was taken by Western European leaders whose predecessors had begun cultivating the idea of political union in the late 1940s, and who had laid the economic groundwork in the late 1950s. When the Cold War receded into the shadows of history in 1990, they lost no time in moving forward. The next year, in 1991, the European Union was formally born when fifteen Western European leaders met in the town of Maastricht, in the Netherlands, to negotiate a treaty to unify Europe that would come into force in 1993.

Formation of the community was the consequence of a lesson Europeans drew from war; namely, how to preserve peace on their continent. They believed the answer lay in the political and economic union of Europe's countries. Whatever label is attached to integration today—some call it an idea, some a concept, some call it building a nation— original momentum was provided by Winston Churchill, who urged creation of a united states of Europe in a speech in Zurich in 1946. The rationale was clear enough. European countries, politically and economically interconnected, would become so dependent on one another that a peaceful union would be far more profitable than a warring Europe. It was a shining prospect that seemed to emerge from the darkness of destruction. The transformation of the idea into reality would carry with it all the risks and rewards, some proudly said, of a noble and tremendous experiment.

European supporters of the idea recognized that the effort, if it were to succeed, would have to be the result of a series of steps. It could not be the consequence of a proclamation. In turn, members of the union would have to set aside elements of sovereignty in order to produce consensus that political and economic, and eventually military union, was in the interest of Europe. They would also have to bridge political enmities, swallow portions of national pride, and create supra-national political and economic institutions to govern a union in which its citizens had confidence, and with which they could identify. It was equally clear that overcoming the obstacles and meeting the challenges would take, at the very least, an unpredictable length of time.

In post-1945 Europe, on a continent where political and social contradictions existed everywhere, the logical spot at which to find common ground was the marketplace. An early milestone was creation of the European Coal and Steel Community in 1951, five years after Churchill's speech. The major step was taken just six years later—a remarkably short period of time in a historical context. In 1957 the Treaty of Rome created the first European Economic Community (EEC). Its members were Belgium, France, West Germany, Italy, Luxembourg, and the Netherlands. They called it the Common Market.

A period of thirty-four years, begun with the Treaty of Rome in 1957, witnessed not only gradual expansion of the Common Market's membership to include fifteen Western European countries by 1991, but also creation of the community's principal governing institutions: the European Parliament, the European Commission, and the Council of Ministers. In the mid 1990s two other events took place which represented additional milestones on the road to a common marketplace. One was the abolition of customs duties on goods purchased in one EU country and shipped to another. The other, known as the Schengen agreement, ended visa controls on fifteen Western European borders in 1995.[3]

By the end of the 1990s the EU had become daily news for European media, and for European leaders the common goal was clear. It was creation of a single market whose purpose, they declared with pride and fanfare in Lisbon, Portugal, in the spring of 2000, was to make Europe the most "dynamic, knowledge-based economy" in the world by 2010. Their commitment was soon known, variously, as the Lisbon Agenda or Lisbon Strategy. Based on agreements made by the EU's members during the 1990s, the EU marketplace would be governed by the same fiscal and monetary principles, and a common currency would be overseen by a European Central Bank. Within the European Monetary Union (EMU) the new "euro" would be used to pay for the manufacture, production and sale of goods and services. In turn, it was envisioned that the members of the EU would eventually become subject to the same tax and regulatory policies. Thereafter "Europe" would take its place in the global marketplace.

In America, at the end of the 1990s, the European enterprise was viewed with benign neglect. The economic significance of *Maastricht*, as the EU is often called in Europe, was not well understood by most Americans. Their attention was focused on the unfolding revolution in computer and communication technology. The Lisbon Agenda ruffled few feathers, because most Americans paid no attention to it. Those who were watching, however, wondered how realistic the intention really was, given the obstacles which stood in the way. Efforts to overcome them would be filled with political risk.

European leaders were aware of the difficulties as well. Tax and regulatory policies, for example, were not the same in all EU countries. Unless, for example, tax policies all became one—EU leaders referred to this goal as "harmonization"—the dream of a single market would remain just that, a dream. Achieving the goal gave rise to questions whose answers were far from evident. How could harmonization possibly occur, given that European governments relied on their tax and regulatory policies to generate the revenues needed to meet their obligations as authors and arbiters of the social contract? In fact, why would those European politicians who coveted rule from the top down have any incentive to do so? If revenues declined, and government leaders raised the specter of increasing budget deficits or reducing social benefits—known in French as *les acquis sociaux*—ferment and unrest would follow. These questions represented puzzles of many pieces, and they touched on two critical points.

The first point was the old and essential difference between America and Europe. In the context of the EU it was expressed as the conflict between the advocates of fiscal discipline versus the defenders of fiscal largesse. The significance of the debate is easier to understand when put in historical context. It was set forth in a letter to me from a well-known American businessman, born in Italy, who is a large importer of agricultural products from Europe.

> In 1957, when the Common Market was created not far from where I was born, West Germany was a manufacturing and exporting powerhouse that needed "market access" for its exports, while protecting its home market from import price competition. France was the "low-cost producer" of foodstuffs *in Europe*, and needed to keep out lower-cost competing foodstuffs from America and the rest of the world. France was not a manufacturing threat to Germany; and the Italians were not a threat to either France or Germany in manufacturing or agriculture. So the *real* goal and *real* problem for *economic* union was how to build a customs wall around Europe—a modern incarnation of an old European practice. This was done via the EEC and it was effectively completed by the early 1970s.
>
> The economic rationale behind *political* union was simple and logical. In the absence of supra-national, "European" hegemony over the EEC countries, each member would be incapable of managing their respective budget deficits and maintaining the value of their currencies without rupturing the "social contract"—with the exception of West Germany, which was the exporting powerhouse. In other words individual European gov-

ernments, in order to pay the financial costs of the "public sector" and therefore stay in power, would continue to increase government deficits and weaken their currencies.

In fact, periodic currency weakness in various EEC countries, e.g. France, provided these countries a competitive edge over other, more fiscally responsible EEC members, e.g. West Germany, and threatened the goal of a single market inside tariff walls. So, how were they to make the common market work? They needed a greater "European" authority to impose *fiscal discipline* over their respective, individual economic policies in order to hold the EEC together. They agreed on this discipline in the form of a growth and stability pact for their European Union when they negotiated the terms of the Maastricht Treaty between 1991 and 1993. The open question was whether they would follow their own agreement.

The second point, affecting operation of a single market, was about old European balance-of-power rivalries, and also concerned matters of political and economic sovereignty and government control. The complexity of the issues was greater than met the eye, because the European Union meant different things to different people. For Germany, it was a balance-of-power vehicle to overcome national sovereignty, to reassure their neighbors that a unified Germany would not pose a threat to their national security. Thus, during the unification year of 1989–1990 the West German government emphasized, time and again, that a unified country wanted to be regarded as a European Germany, not seen as dominating a German Europe. The French wanted a unified Germany that would be forced to keep itself in political and economic balance vis-à-vis its neighbors, and especially in relation to French economic and political leadership within the European Union.

The British objected neither to balance nor to a European Germany, but in the U.K. "Eurosceptics," as journalists called them, had serious misgivings about abandoning the pound sterling, and their fiscal sovereignty, to adopt a single European currency. And some in Europe, including former prime minister Margaret Thatcher, saw in "Maastricht" an effort by European socialists, led by former French finance minister Jacques Delors, to socialize Europe from the top down.[4] Socialists, so the objection went, would seek to control the centralized governing structure of the EU in Brussels, where twenty unelected European Commissioners and upward of 20,000 nameless civil servants make and enforce the rules, served by more than 3,500 interpreters translating the EU's twenty-one official languages.[5]

These strongly held and contradictory views meant that the single market was given different interpretations by different participants. The various political parties within the EU—on the left, in the center, and on the right—paid lip service to the Lisbon Agenda, but they did not agree on how to make a "dynamic, knowledge-based economy" a reality. This disagreement assured the emergence of political battles in the future over, as yet, still undefined issues.

Tied to the obstacles was also a challenge which a majority of the EU's members did meet successfully; namely, formation of the European Monetary Union (EMU). The vision of a common currency was far from new. It was widely recognized as indispensable to operation of a single market, and its creation was addressed specifically in the Maastricht Treaty. One of the first references to it had been made shortly after the end of World War II by French monetary expert Jacques Rueff, whom Charles de Gaulle described as the "poet of finance." In commenting on the idea of European unity, Rueff made the now famous statement that, "Europe will come into existence by its money or not at all."[6]

Creation of a single currency, carefully planned, was given life in the mid-1990s with the founding of the European Central Bank (ECB) located in Germany, in Frankfurt on the river Main, a city quickly nicknamed "Mainhattan." In January 1999 the "euro" was declared legal tender for financial transactions within the EMU. Finally, in January 2002, the long-planned and decisive step was taken when coins and paper money were put into official circulation. On January 2, 2002, the price of a euro on international currency exchange markets was $1.12.

Introduction of the new money was a staggering change which can only be appreciated if one imagines the complexity of replacing the dollar in America, from one day to the next. It was the biggest financial transaction in the history of the world, amounting to the equivalent of $580 billion dollars. The European Central Bank put in circulation 50 billion coins in denominations of 1¢, 2¢, 5¢, 10¢, 20¢, 50¢, 1€, and 2€, and 14.5 billion banknotes in the amounts of 5€, 10€, 20€, 50€, 100€, 200€, and 500€.

Enough coins were minted to build twenty-four Eiffel Towers. Banknotes, stretched end to end, would have formed a line reaching to the moon and back, four times. The notes themselves no longer bore national symbols of great European artists, composers, writers, or scientists, but were decorated with architectural drawings of fragments of fictitious bridges and buildings to serve as symbols of unity. The coins had one face bearing the numerical denomination and a map of Europe, and the other side had a national symbol; so, for example, in Germany the verso bears the German Eagle.

On January 1, 2002, the currencies of twelve European countries, for all practical purposes, disappeared. The French franc, in circulation for more than 600 years, was a victim, as were the Belgian and Luxembourg francs, the German mark, the Italian lira, and the Irish punt. And so were Dutch guilders, Spanish pesetas, Portuguese escudos, Greek drachmas, Austrian schillings, and Finnish markka. More than 200,000 automated teller machines had been recoined, and so had many other machines that took coins—including parking meters, cigarette machines, public telephones, and luggage carts at train stations.

European bankers had already been dealing with the euro for three years when January 1, 2002, arrived, and in a manner of speaking they had become accustomed to it. The introduction of the actual coins and currency, however, was an overwhelming event for Europe's citizens. This was especially true for older generations, in all of the twelve countries. For them the value of the euro was far from self-evident, because they had always measured value with their respective national currencies. Deprived of these they no longer had a meaningful reference point. Although frustration would diminish with the passage of time, it would not happen overnight. For many the loss of their national currency was the cause of anxiety and doubt. For many also the rest of their lives would be spent converting the new euro into the value of their old currency before they could understand if the purchase or selling price of anything was really fair, whether it was a bottle of milk, a newspaper, or a restaurant bill.[7]

In America calculating the value of what the dollar buys is a simple matter. Whether in Florida, North Dakota, Georgia, or California, the customer knows whether the price is fair because the benchmark of measurement is the same. But the disappearance of this respective element of simplicity in 2002 left uncertainty in its wake. In Germany, for example, the euro was far from popular; in the spring more than 50 percent of the population wanted to return to the German mark. They believed that businesses had used the euro's introduction to increase prices. European economists spent a good deal of time emphasizing that, with the inevitable exceptions, it was not true. Thus in May 2002 Otmar Issing, the chief economist of the European Central Bank, reassured an audience in Essen, Germany, that prices had not gone up, and concluded, "I can see from the look on your faces that you don't believe me. My wife doesn't believe me, either."[8]

But there was also another side of the coin, of greater significance. Using a single currency meant that Mr. Issing could put euros in his pocket in Berlin before boarding a plane for Italy and pay for dinner in Rome with the same money. Exchange shops and hotel front desks were no longer in the money-changing business for twelve different currencies. Travelers, and the industry that helps them with hotel reservations, car rentals, and plane tickets, began to find financial arrangements a lot easier too, and the travel itself less expensive. The European Central Bank called this the advantage of transparency, and said so in advertisements leading up to New Year's Day 2002, as in an ad from *Le Figaro Magazine* in Paris in December 2001: "Welcome to a world without borders."

The structure for maintaining peace in Europe was thus given financial shape, from the top down. Confidence in the euro as a currency of stability presumably would grow with development of the single market, to match the symbolic value of a Europe with just one backyard. No currency had circulated so widely on the continent since the Holy Roman Empire. Without the euro a real union of Europe had no future. But with it the dream of union now became dependent on the will of European leaders to make the single European marketplace a reality.

Just as some American observers had doubted the ability of the EU's members to harmonize tax and regulatory polices, here too there were misgivings. The chairman of the Federal Reserve Bank in Washington, D.C., Alan Greenspan, initially predicted the euro would never come to pass. He was far from alone in his skepticism about the wisdom of introducing a single currency. In 2003, Martin Feldstein, professor of economics at Harvard University, argued that British adoption of the euro would be a long-term mistake, because whenever cyclical unemployment increased, the country's price stability would be put at the mercy of an uncontrollable, supra-national European Central Bank.[9]

For European leaders, however, introduction of the euro was much more than just a unique event. It had been driven by political will and marked by a remarkable continuity of resolve. Each of the EMU's leaders had an enormous investment in assuring the success of the undertaking. If it failed, so, surely, would creation of the dynamic union to which they had pledged themselves with the Lisbon Agenda.

Adoption of the euro committed the EU's members to creation of a single capital marketplace in which they would maintain fiscal stability while promoting growth. In practical terms, however, only twelve members gave up their monetary sovereignty to join the EMU—Austria, Belgium, Finland, France, Germany, Greece, Ireland, Italy, Luxembourg, the Netherlands, Portugal, and Spain. Three members, for the time being, declined to participate, led by the UK, and followed by Denmark and Sweden.

In a Growth and Stability Pact, which was first and foremost a tool to enforce budgetary discipline, the twelve agreed that, (1) annual government deficits would not exceed 3 percent of GDP, (2) gross debt would not exceed 60 percent of GDP, and (3) the annual rate of inflation would not exceed 1.5 percent of the average of the three best performing states during the previous year. They, therefore, also established a means to levy heavy fines on those governments which might violate any of the rules in the future, and gave the ECB the power to enforce the agreement.

The pact thus represented endorsement of common fiscal and budgetary principles to protect the value of the euro. The purpose of the tool, created at Germany's urging with strong backing from the Dutch, was to prevent the euro from being weakened by individual countries; the example was Italy, which had exceeded the ceiling for deficit spending for three decades prior to meeting the limit of 3 percent in time to qualify for EMU membership in 1999. In principle, therefore, the governments of the twelve had given up, voluntarily, their power to control the money supply and to set interest rates, and agreed to keep their deficit spending within set parameters.

From the perspective of 2005, the short history of the common European market had progressed quickly; in fact, some Europeans felt, too quickly, when the size of the EU was expanded dramatically from 15 to 27 members in May 2004. The addition of Cyprus (the Greek half), the Czech Republic, Estonia, Hungary, Latvia, Lithuania, Malta, Poland, the Slovak Republic, and Slovenia meant that the union to which six western countries had given birth was now truly a European one. Its 450 million citizens, in comparison to a population of about 295 million in America, generated a gross domestic product of about 10.763 trillion dollars, which exceeded America's GDP of more than 10.170 trillion dollars.[10] The size of the enlarged EU stretched from the Atlantic to the Baltic Sea, and from the Arctic in Sweden to the cusp of the Middle East in Cyprus.[11]

On the EU's agenda remained development of a common foreign policy, a common European security and defense policy (ESDP), and eventually creation of combined European defense forces. Achievement of these goals, as had been the case for every objective since 1957, would occur step-by-step. These would be taken slowly and precisely, and the inevitable setbacks would surely receive greater publicity than the accomplishments. But if the history of the EU was a portent of things to come, the movement would continue forward, not backward. So, for example, under the ESDP initiative the EU's first civilian mission began to work in Bosnia in January 2003, in tandem with an EU police mission to restore the rule of law, and the first EU military mission began operation in Macedonia in April 2003, with the deployment of the European Rapid Reaction Force (EURRF). The steps were modest—some Europeans said exceedingly modest—but they signified a commitment and a beginning.

Americans who are receptive to the simplicity of the *American power versus European weakness* logic scoffed at Europe's talk of developing common and effective foreign and defense policies, and some Europeans did as well. But steps and events contained an unmistakable message. The EU was growing in size and in potential competitive power. Many of its members—although for the moment, not all—fully intended to form a real union, operating within one market, secured by a common defense. It was quite clear, of course, that as the EU pursued its agenda, unforeseen obstacles would appear. But to assert, as some Americans did, that those operating the EU did not know where they were going, and to dismiss the obstacles they faced as insurmountable, ignored the history of the EU.

Yet it was because of this history that both optimism and pessimism held sway. A European foreign policy was absent, and neither a single capital market nor a dynamic marketplace existed. Europe's center of international finance remained London, not Frankfurt. Indeed, making compromises to form a Growth and Stability Pact was one thing, but replacing economic rule from the top down was quite another. If the Europeans succeeded, however, the result would be greater European cohesion. A stronger European voice would become more credible if backed by economic and military power. With such a voice the EU could contribute a forceful and balancing hand to the management of international affairs in concert with America. The vision of "Europe" represented a historic opportunity the Europeans would be foolish to squander. But if they failed the result would be European irrelevance. There would be little of value to be found in the middle.[12]

Either way it was certain that the future would be full of surprises. Reminders were everywhere: such as the continuing debate on the harmonization of tax and regulatory policies, the sharp division of opinion in Europe on the issue of Iraq, and, in the late spring of 2005, the French and Dutch rejection of the proposed European Constitution (a subject addressed in chapter five). Indeed, unpredictable behavior on both sides of the Atlantic recalled Disraeli's observation that, "we moralise when it is too late; nor is there anything more silly than to regret. One event makes another; what we anticipate seldom occurs; what we least expected generally happens." But surprises and moralizing notwithstanding, Europe was embarked on the road to union. And it was entirely possible that vocal political and economic debates would continue to drive integration forward in ways neither expected nor imagined.[13]

The end of Europe's Fifty Years' War created the conditions for establishment of Europe's centerpiece, the European Union. But it was also here that an unresolved set of issues beckoned which were best described by two questions: Could the EU work, and if so, what would be the consequences for Europe and America? How these questions would be answered would highlight the differences between European and American economic and political cultures, just as it would affect our relationship.

When Realities Are Trump

A knowledge of American and European history places in relief the problems the Europeans face. How Europe was built weighs on the efforts to make the European Union succeed.

Europeans are heavily divided between those who, over decades, have become dependent on the social contract as a source of economic security and political freedom, and those who prefer a single, free and competitive market as an arena in which individual liberty and entrepreneurial ability are rewarded. If the EU becomes the world's most dynamic marketplace there will be winners—those who believe in rule from the bottom up. Success will also produce clear losers. The logical consequence of the Lisbon Agenda would be the death knell for European socialism. It would surely weaken, if not break completely, the power monopoly of Europe's professional political classes who rule from the top down. The stakes in the outcome are historic in magnitude. Which realities will trump?

The Growth and Stability Pact limits government spending to a certain percentage of the annual gross domestic product. By doing so the members of the EU agree to make government expenditures dependent on growth in the marketplace; that is to say, to exercise restraint in their spending policies. The reality of the pact is that if EU leaders observe the limits they have set on the size of their respective budget deficits they will have to reform the terms of the "social contract" and reduce social benefits; otherwise they will be unable to finance them. This reality thus also becomes the acid test. Will Europe's leaders be able to follow the Lisbon Agenda and keep their political lives?

Although top-down politicians do not say so publicly, privately they recognize that growth will be significant *only* if they deregulate their marketplaces for products and services, break the lock held by labor unions on artificially high wages, increase labor mobility, and reform their tax codes. Dealing with these four issues is a daunting prospect all by itself, and it is complicated by a fifth. Even though the EU's members have agreed to establish a common market, they are still without common rules of competition for the production and sale of goods and services.

All of these unresolved issues, individually and together, slow growth, impede productivity, generate unemployment, and prevent creation of a free market. The issue of job protection and regulation of labor markets is a good example. A February 2003 analysis of Germany, where wages are the highest in the world, made the case in point: "Before eliminating jobs, companies usually have to justify their plans in talks with employee representatives, and then give workers months of notice and substantial severance packages. Job cuts are often so time-consuming and costly that companies find other ways to save money. But they also avoid hiring in Germany by expanding operations abroad or using more machinery to automate production."[14]

This kind of response to the problems of labor rigidity always has unhappy economic consequences. In the 1990s, for example, Volkswagen

AG, in deference to job protection demands pushed by labor unions, agreed to lay off no one, but cut back to a four-day work week. This was not a business decision dictated by the marketplace. It was a political decision forced on the company by labor, with the tacit concurrence of political leaders. One consequence was job preservation, but less income and slower growth. A second was an agreement in 2006 between the company and its most important union, IG Metall, that permitted Volkswagen to increase working hours without extra pay in exchange for additional corporate investment, on the uncertain assumption that growth and production would significantly increase by 2009.[15]

Justification of antifree and anti–single market policies produces creative explanations. Politicians and labor leaders cite allegedly exploitative American "hire and fire" practices as the reason for their opposition to reform and in so doing perpetuate the life of the straw man, *the American model.* The practice has been to criticize America's labor market as both morally insensitive and socially unjust. Labor unions, together with most of Europe's socialist leaders—with the notable exception of British prime minister Tony Blair—have opposed less regulation and taxation because they see their hold on political and economic power threatened by free and open competition. European politicians, however, are seldom this direct when justifying such policies, and practice instead the clever turn of phrase. French prime minister Lionel Jospin created a masterpiece during a visit to America in 1998. "Yes to a market economy," he said, "but no to a market society." He did not explain how one was possible without the other.

Jospin's views are not isolated ones. In their public statements most of Europe's leaders have been consistent in their criticism of the American straw man. In 2002, for example, Germany's socialist chancellor Gerhard Schröder condemned America's so-called economic model as wrong for Europe: "Anglo-Saxon, and especially American, standards of job security are different from Germany's because of our history of war and economic upheaval." Three years later, in the spring of 2005, when the Social Democratic Party faced a fierce election campaign in the state of North Rhine-

Westphalia, the old rhetoric of the class struggle reappeared. Party chair-man Franz Müntefering attacked American and British corporations for practicing corporate greed, plundering German assets, and arbitrarily lay-ing off workers, and accused them of falling "upon companies like locusts, [to] devour them and move on."[16]

Jospin, Schröder, and Müntefering shared their viewpoint with another practitioner of rule from the top down, the conservative president of France. In what was described as "a highly emotional attack on Anglo-Saxon-style capitalism"—in other words on free market competition—Jacques Chirac condemned it in March 2005 with the phrase, "Ultra-liberalism is the new Communism of our age."[17]

෴

These examples are an illustration of what might be called *the rulers' di-lemma*—how to create a dynamic marketplace without changing the con-ditions that prevent it. This dilemma, moreover, is not the sole property of the socialists. It belongs to all of Europe's political parties to one degree or another, with the exception of the continent's classic free market liberal parties. The issue is the same for all the parties of the left, of the center, and of the right, who rule from the top down. The struggle is between whom, as in which political parties, and what, as in competition in a sin-gle market, wields political influence and economic power. Those who have it do not want to give it up, so they have introduced policies de-signed to preserve their control. This logic was what motivated the French socialists just five years after the Maastricht Treaty took effect in 1993.

In 1998 the party passed a labor law in the French National Assembly which abolished the 39-hour work week and replaced it with a 35-hour one, without a corresponding reduction in salary. In practical terms this represented a government imposed salary increase for all municipal and federal government employees (25 percent of the French workforce), to be paid for by French taxpayers. It also meant an increase in salary for most of those employed by private companies, to be paid for by private employers. The government's justification for what represented, indi-rectly, a new tax, was that less work would create more jobs. The law, which took effect in 2000, allegedly created 350,000 new jobs, according to French Labor Ministry statistics. Each new position, however, also cost 23,000 euros in government subsidies to business to encourage creation of new jobs, financed by French tax revenues.[18] Government statistics notwithstanding, five years later economic growth had stalled and the French unemployment rate stood at a five-year high.[19]

The law had several unintended consequences. French companies were not obligated to hire new employees. The legal limit on how many hours an individual could work on overtime meant that take-home pay dropped. Employers began compensating overtime hours with additional vacation, but not in money. Doing black market work for cash paid under the table, already practiced for decades, became even more attractive, and violated the law. In addition, working less did not produce significant increases in either productivity or employment, but it did reinforce the socialist myth that "working families" are better off if they work less—an effect confirmed in a public opinion poll in January 2005 which reported that 77 percent of the French wanted to keep the 35-hour week and only 18 percent wanted to work more.[20]

The 35-hour work week, described as a measure to improve the quality of life, was a textbook example of rule from the top down. It redistributed income, abolished freedom of choice, and insulted the dignity of labor. In short, it sent a political and economic message, and a social one as well. The political message was that jobs are created by law and not by productivity and profit. The economic message was that growth does not generate jobs, laws do. The social message was that work is demeaning and without value, and the less you have to do of it the better off you are. The socialist decision, taken for political and not economic reasons, also drew attention to differences within the EU, in which the maximum legal working week is currently 48 and the minimum one is 35 hours.[21]

It is beguiling political rhetoric to proclaim support for a market economy, and to reject the inequalities of a market society. But the gears of the marketplace are not oiled by figures of speech. Tax rates, which can stimulate or retard growth, provide another illustration of how state power may be used to encourage or to restrict competition.

The rates differ widely among EU members, as do the kinds of taxes themselves. While employer taxes and charges vary dramatically, they are so high in many cases that employment is stifled as a result. For example, the costs of employee benefits—that is to say various social contract taxes and charges—relative to wages are enormous in much of the EU. In France and Germany the rate is between 60 and 80 percent, so that if the salary is 100 per month the employer is paying between 160 and 180, depending on the circumstances. In Britain the cost is about 35 percent, thanks in large part to the free market reforms led by Margaret Thatcher, and supported by her socialist successor, Tony Blair.[22] In America, by comparison, it is about 34 percent; in other words about half of that in France and Germany whose economies account for more than 60 percent of the EU's gross domestic product. The effect is predictable. French and German employers do not hire until it is absolutely necessary, or they move their production facilities to such EU countries as Ireland, where the mandated level of taxes and charges is lower, thus reflecting the struggle between government control and free competition.

Another illustration is the wealth tax, which does not exist in America. But, at least for the time being (July 2007), it does in three EU countries; namely, France, Greece, and Spain; it exists also in the non-EU countries of Norway and Lichtenstein, and in November of 2005, Germany's new conservative-socialist coalition government announced it would be reintroduced in 2007.[23] The tax, highly controversial, is egalitarian by design, punitive in nature, and confiscatory in effect. It is not a tax on income, but on the value of assets.

By definition, it is reactionary, and penalizes both financial success and wealth. The tax is levied on the total value of an individual's assets, which includes the value of real estate. In this case the tax can become especially onerous if the value is high but the income from which to pay the tax is low (for example, this is often the case with old houses whose adjoining income-producing lands have been sold off in the course of time). In France, for example, it is levied on personal fortunes above 720,000 euros (in January 2007 the minimum was increased to 760,000 euros). In 2004 this affected about 335,525 tax returns and less than 1 percent of France's population of approximately 61 million. It generates a minute percentage of total annual tax revenue, and it has had a predictable consequence. French citizens who have left France to avoid the tax—to live in England and Belgium, for example—have taken an estimated 11 billion euros of capital value with them.[24]

The punitive nature of tax policies in the EU is not only directed at the so-called rich; it is visited on everyone. The average EU individual tax burden is 43.1% compared with 30% in America; in Germany, for example, an unmarried worker without children paid 50.7% of his salary in income and social security taxes in 2001. When high income taxes limit disposable income, tax payers seek ways to avoid them. Because most Europeans cannot easily escape onerous taxation by moving their homes and livelihoods from one country to another, they violate tax laws on a large scale.

This occurs most frequently with the value-added tax (VAT) which does not exist in America either. It is applied at every stage that a good moves along on its way to the marketplace.[25] When the good finally gets to the consumer the VAT is called a tax on consumption that takes the place of a sales tax. In the EU the minimum VAT for the consumer is 15 percent (in Cyprus and Luxembourg) and the maximum is 25 percent (in Denmark, Hungary, and Sweden). The tax is so high that circumvention of value-added taxes occurs everywhere; in 2006 it was estimated that VAT fraud "robbed" European governments of one euro out of every ten.[26] In France, for example, the VAT, set at 19.6 percent, accounted for 45.5 percent of total tax revenues in 2004, while the tax on personal income amounted to just 20.3 percent.[27]

Politicians seldom discuss this effect, and governments do not give wide publicity to statistics on what is a daily part of European life. In Belgium, for example, the normal value-added tax (VAT) is 21 percent of the price of a good or service; although for certain goods and services it can be lower, as is also the case in other EU member countries. Since the value-added tax is generally high and the likelihood of getting caught for evading the VAT is relatively low, large numbers of Europeans cheat their governments. This is done by paying part of the price, plus the legal VAT, by check or credit card, and the other part in cash without the tax. Thus, there is a written record of the former, but not of the latter: in Belgium, if my bill is 100 euros I will write the check for 121 euros, but if I pay the same bill in cash I only need a 100 euro note. The result is to encourage black markets in goods and services, and to pay for them, in both urban and rural areas, in cash or in kind.

By the end of 2006 value-added tax fraud on imported items between EU member states was judged to be so serious that the French finance ministry announced an investigation into the practice. It was estimated by a French financial journal, *Les Echos*, that the amount of the loss could exceed more than one-tenth of annual VAT tax receipts (forecast to be 127 billion euros in 2006 and 133 billion in 2007).[28]

An additional and more significant issue, not yet resolved within the EU, are the differences in corporate taxes. These provide powerful incentives for European corporations, but also for American ones, to invest in EU countries with low rates. Thus, for example, corporations with their headquarters in Ireland enjoy a significant competitive advantage vis-à-vis corporations in other EU countries. Of the original fifteen EU members, Ireland has the lowest corporate tax of 12.5 percent. As a result, its economy is booming. By comparison, Germany's economy, where the corporate rate of almost 40 percent is the highest in the EU, is stagnating.[29] This explains why Germany's largest bank, Deutsche Bank, following significant expansion abroad, had less than 44 percent of its workforce in Germany at the end of 2002 in comparison to 67 percent in 1996.

Before the EU was expanded from fifteen to twenty-seven members in May 2004 the average was about 32 percent. Since then the problem has become even more complex because the ten new members had an average rate of about 21 percent, and one of them, Estonia, levied no corporate tax at all. Europe's socialists condemn the result, which is greater competition, as unfair competition, and are therefore calling for creation of one rate for all members. From their perspective, the aim is a logical one and they describe their proposed remedy as "tax harmonization." But this seemingly innocuous phrase contains a hidden objective. The word "harmonization" is used to describe an effort to establish a common corporate tax rate which would be significantly higher than those which currently exist, for example, in Ireland or Estonia. If the attempt succeeds it will have major consequences: (1) investment, employment, productivity, and growth will be adversely affected, (2) the revenue bases of the high-corporate-taxing countries will be protected, and (3) the income will be used to perpetuate rule from the top down.

How the debate over tax harmonization is resolved will create new realities for the EU marketplace. The outcome will affect everything, which is why the issue is so contentious, and why the answers to the following questions are so important. Does a single market require a single tax code? And, if so, who will write it? If a common set of corporate tax rates is not established how can a single market work?

Transforming the Lisbon Agenda into policy is complicated by a widespread and uniquely European attitude toward money and profit, which offers still another contrast with America. It is not a secret that Europeans, and especially intellectual elites, observe with condescension that America is the quintessence of greed, a materialistic society in which Americans are consumed by thoughts of how much money they can make and preoccupied with how much things cost. There is, of course, some truth to this superficial description, because Americans do talk about money; after all, one of the purposes of a marketplace is to make a profit. But this negative conclusion does not apply to all Americans any more than does the reference to all Germans as "Hitler's willing executioners."

It is also true, however, that there is a difference here between Europeans and Americans. Europeans generally do not talk about money and profit. Seldom do American visitors hear Europeans equating "the best" with "the most expensive." If Europeans do measure the stature of someone or the quality of something according to how much it costs, they seldom say so publicly. This behavior is the other half of the difference; namely, it is what many Europeans do not say, but do think.

The contrast is significant because attitudes about money affect how many Europeans judge the utility of work, and how they measure the importance of the state's social contract vis-à-vis individual freedom to make a fortune. Americans who know Europe well are familiar with the attitude, but generally little attention has been paid to it. Nonetheless the point is more significant than Americans, as well as some Europeans, may assume. It was made effectively in an unpublished letter from Burkhard Koch, a former member of the East German communist party who today heads an international consulting firm located in Berlin.

You can take this with a grain of salt if you wish, but I am going to tell you the truth, this is what I believe. We envy the fact that you can make money, because we can't. We don't like to admit it. But it is so much more difficult for us to become rich, even if we work hard and have some luck.

Why? Because our governments don't let us keep very much of the money we earn. You believe that the money you make belongs to you and your family, but in Europe the attitude is opposite. Government needs a lot of our money to pay for all of our public and welfare services, many of which are individual responsibilities in your country. So it has the right to tell us how much of our money we can keep. That is what our governments do. That is why so many of us do business on the black market, why corruption is widespread, and why most of us try to avoid paying taxes by violating the law. This is how we survive. We hide our wealth and preach equality and social justice. We recognize this is dishonest, because we know that by nature people are not equal even though our governments tell us they can make us so.

Unlike you there is no reason for most of us to hope that we can become rich. Unless, of course, we go to America. There aren't very many "European captains of industry" in comparison to yours. The rise from rags to riches—"the American success story"—isn't told often in Europe, because it doesn't happen often. We envy those who have money, but we never admit it. Some of us, who get tired of pretending we aren't jealous, leave, and go to America. And others of us say "no" to a market economy, but "yes" to a market society, and don't understand that you cannot have one without the other.

So what do most of us do? We don't work very hard. A 35-hour work week sounds great for most of us. We depend on the state. Some of us say we prefer our qualities of life, a claim that is often repeated by American journalists. But is that really true? The fact is why should we work 39 or 40 hours a week, if the government can force our employers to pay us the same amount of money for less work? So it shouldn't surprise you that many people like the 35-hour work week. They work enough to get by, and get the rest from the government. That is not my dream of freedom and independence.[30]

Burkhard's view does not fit very well with the idea that the single market is going to be wonderful. It is one thing to declare in Lisbon the intention to create the most competitive marketplace in the world by 2010, but it is the individuals who labor in the marketplace who must make it succeed. If Burkhard is right Europeans are not given a great deal of incentive to work hard, and without hard work there is no such thing as productivity and growth. So unless they are given a reason to change their attitudes, the future of the single market is not a rosy one.

In my message thanking Burkhard I wondered if the European attitude about money was what prompted the American author, Mary McCarthy, to write, "When an American heiress wants to buy a man, she at once crosses the Atlantic. The only really materialistic people I have ever met have been Europeans." Her sarcastic observation stands in curious juxtaposition to Tocqueville's remark in *Democracy in America*, ". . . I know of no other country where love of money has such a grip on men's hearts or where stronger scorn is expressed for the theory of permanent equality of property."

Tocqueville's comment aside, however, the view of 2010 from the perspective of 2007 is a combination of pessimistic observations and overly optimistic conclusions. In the long run the Europeans may find a way to come to terms with the economic and political realities of a free market. But in the short run existence of the following three problems is the outline of a Lisbon strategy which is more battle than agenda.

The first problem is how European governments will finance their budgets. The old way to satisfy this need was through regulation, taxation, and the printing of money. The new way, within the context of the Lisbon Agenda and the Growth and Stability Pact of the EMU, is to reduce public spending so European governments need less money. Thus far, this problem has not been resolved, which is why the second problem exists.

About half of the EMU member governments are spending more money than they receive. The result is that they have violated the deficit spending limit of 3% set by the Growth and Stability Pact and the EMU has been unwilling to levy fines or enforce sanctions. In 2005, for example, France and Germany did so for the fourth year in a row. They were projected to do so in 2006 and possibly beyond, as well. Rather than adhering to the pact, these two governments of the EU's two largest economies proposed, during the summer of 2003, a temporary suspension of the budget rule, which prompted the Austrian finance minister to comment that merely discussion of the idea "damages the credibility of our finance and economic policy."[31]

By the end of the year, even though Austria, Finland, the Netherlands, and Spain argued that the logic was unsound, France and Germany persuaded the EMU members to suspend the Growth and Stability Pact altogether.[32] At the beginning of 2005 a further step was taken with the decision to renegotiate the terms of the pact. The "coup de grâce" arrived three months later with changes pushed primarily by France and Germany which, in effect, destroyed the pact's efficacy. The "remarkable compromise" allowed the members much greater freedom to run up budget deficits by creating exemptions from the 3 percent rule for such expense categories as "increased aid spending in the third world," "research and development," and the costs of European and German unification.[33] The exceptions, in other words, amounted to a blank check.

Changing the terms is not, in the long term, a viable alternative to reducing expenditures. Weakening the rules of the pact amounted to standing logic on its head, by contending that greater government spending would produce growth rather than free and open competition in a single market. No one recognized this more clearly in the EU than its leaders, but they also understood that cutting budgets and government programs is seldom a popular political choice. The dilemma was easily defined, and Luxembourg's prime minister did so in early 2005: "We all know what we need to do, but we don't know how to win elections after we have done it."[34]

The third problem, of both a short- and a long-term nature, is the old conundrum of rule from the top down. Some Europeans argue that paternalistic Europe is living on borrowed time because the forces of the free marketplace will eventually destroy it. At the beginning of 2003 French social commentator Guy Sorman essentially drew this conclusion, but also acknowledged the continuing duel of the political class versus the individual:

> Europe's free-market liberals have won the intellectual battle but not yet the political war. We still have to demonstrate that the market is not an American invention but a universal concept. We have to explain that individualism is not a social evil but a product of human nature; that the market is not an end in itself but a means to an end called freedom.[35]

The end of the year 2005 marked the halfway point on the road to achieving the Lisbon Agenda, and the "political war" described by Sorman was in full swing in the European Union. But small signs of an independent spirit had become evident as well, and one of them had been sighted in France during the summer of 2003.

In opposition to government efforts to reform the generous state pension system and to reduce equally indulgent unemployment benefits for actors, French labor unions carried out a series of disruptive and expensive strikes during the summer, which forced many French music and theatrical festivals to close. By July thousands of French men and women had taken to the streets, but this time in support of change. Marching under the motto, "Freedom, I write your name"—a choice filled with irony since it comes from the title of a poem written during the German occupation of France by Paul Eluard, who belonged to the French Communist Party—thousands paraded through French towns to oppose the strikes. They were led by a 21-year-old student, Sabine Herold of Reims; as one journalist put it, she sounded more like Margaret Thatcher than Joan of Arc. And, in fact, reform of the pension system, although significantly watered down, was approved by the French National Assembly at the end of July.[36]

Great Expectations

Great expectations have always been associated with the prospect of deliberate change, and this was the case with the Lisbon Agenda of 2000. Americans, in implementing such a program, would more than likely do so directly. They would set forth policy alternatives, develop persuasive arguments, debate which are black and which are white, determine which make sense and which do not, and finally select one. Europeans, in pursuing the goals set in Lisbon, have followed a different path marked by the influences of rule from the top down. This is why the European debate is so contentious.

The expectations are equally great for those who want to regulate competition and impose high taxes on the marketplace to finance Europe's welfare states, as they are for those who want to create greater competition so Europeans can broaden their choices, keep more of the money they earn, and decide themselves how to spend it. The decision to be taken is not between two rational alternatives. In fact, a specific choice will not be made. Whatever emerges will be a result of evolution, which is why the path to the single market is indirect.

❦

The course of European history tells us that the path will continue to take contradictory twists and turns. Thus, the words and actions of French prime minister Lionel Jospin reflected the ebb and flow of political sentiment as well as political opportunism. There was every reason to assume that his derogatory comparison of a market economy with a market society in 1998 meant that his government would retain its ownership in numerous business enterprises. But by early 2002 none other than Jospin, heading a Socialist-Communist-Green coalition, had privatized more than 36 billion euros of state-owned corporations; it was more, some reports assert, than the past six French governments combined. Doing so was not an embrace of free market capitalism. On the contrary, it was a tactical decision. He, as other European leaders, was beginning to sense that the political tide was somehow turning in favor of the marketplace. Parenthetically, they all understood that the sale of government-owned assets could generate large revenues for the state.[37]

It is debatable whether French voters interpreted privatization as a portent of things to come, but they sent the message that they wanted more than the French left was prepared to give. In June 2002 they replaced Jospin in national elections with a new and free market–oriented government headed by Jean-Pierre Raffarin, who thereafter embarked on a path of economic and social reform. The new government began to withdraw and tighten the social safety net; for example, by reviewing the terms of the 35-hour work week and limiting increases in wages and benefits.

This path, as past and future ones, was full of curves. If efforts at reform widened differences of opinion between those who want the jam today and those who want to be able to keep more of the jam they make in the future, labor unions would surely call for strikes and "manifestations" in the streets, and in fact did so. Nonetheless, Raffarin's government recognized that French voters had provided a mandate to try, and that success, for better or for worse, would ultimately be measured at the ballot box. In March 2005 the National Assembly, in effect, abolished the 35-hour work week. The response was predictable. French business leaders welcomed the legislation and France's largest labor union, the CFDT, called it "a political, economic and social mistake."[38]

The noncommunist CFDT (Confédération Française Démocratique du Travail) subsequently brought a suit against the French government alleging that abolishing the 35-hour work week was illegal. The union won the suit in the autumn of 2006 when the French Conseil d'Etat (the equivalent of the U.S. Supreme Court) ruled that the 35-hour work week in the transport, hotel and restaurant industries must be reinstated with back pay for overtime. The suit was welcomed by French Socialists, some of whom argued that should they win the French presidential elections scheduled for April 2007, the 35-hour week should become mandatory throughout the country.[39]

Another illustration was seen in Germany in the spring of 2003. Socialist chancellor Gerhard Schröder changed course before the voters forced him to do so. With social spending at almost 30% of GDP—larger than any county in the world except Sweden, and twice that of America—he announced labor market, health care, and tax reforms in an effort to stimulate growth and create jobs. With deficit spending far above the limit set by the Growth and Stability Pact, with unemployment at almost 11 percent, and with labor union strength at a postwar low—between 1991 and 2003 blue- and white-collar membership in Germany's labor unions declined from 39 percent to 22 percent—he, like Jospin, was reading the handwriting on the wall.

If Schröder needed confirmation that change was in the wind, it was given to him in June when the most powerful labor union in Germany, IG Metall, called off a strike for a 35-hour work week in the eastern part of Germany. It was the first time since 1954—almost fifty years—that the union had failed to win a strike. His views must have seemed close to revolutionary to the members of his party when he told the German Bundestag in early July 2003 that what Germany needed was "a new mentality—away from protecting what we have and toward creating new chances for the future."[40] But whether it was revolutionary or opportunistic was a moot point for the members of IG Metall. The union accepted an agreement with one of Germany's largest firms, Siemens, to restore the forty-hour work week without an increase in salary.[41]

Was it reasonable to conclude that these examples foreshadowed others, and on balance, pointed in one direction? The question cannot yet be answered because the struggle over having less of the jam today or more of it tomorrow is not yet over. Continental socialists have not given up their political and economic vision of a just society in which equality is first and freedom is second. They have, however, changed their tactics. On the one hand, they have challenged selected sacred cows of the old order, as Schröder did in the German Bundestag in 2003. On the other hand, they are trying to have their ideological cake and eat it too, as German Socialist Party chairman Müntefering demonstrated in 2005 when he accused American and British companies of devouring German assets "like locusts." In May 2007 IG Metall had its cake and ate it too when, following threats of a major strike, it negotiated a significant wage increase on behalf of 800,000 laborers in the southwest state of Baden-Wuerttemberg.

As was the case in France and Germany, so also was the struggle actively waged between the Italian left and the center-right coalition of Prime

Minister Silvio Berlusconi, who assumed the rotating presidency of the
European Union in July of 2003. Berlusconi was publicly attacked in Europe for a variety of alleged business crimes, or successes, depending on
how it was interpreted. But criticism of him detracted from the fact that
he, as other European leaders of both the left and the right, was very much
aware of what was at stake. In a paraphrase of Machiavelli in early July,
he told an editor of the *Wall Street Journal* that "the person who has ideas
and carries out reforms is fought by those whose privileges will be threatened by those reforms. But those who will stand to gain from those reforms will sit on the fence."[42]

Berlusconi understood that to build a single market, equality of opportunity must supersede equality of result, and European economic life
must become much less *dirigist*. This explains why European supporters
of free markets, such as Berlusconi, want to place strict limits on centralized power. But they also are aware that political survival requires them
to pay allegiance to *the European socioeconomic model*. They therefore tout
the appeal of equalized social outcomes, even though they understand that
such outcomes are not possible.

Some part of the European populace will always believe that the conduct of business in the marketplace must serve, and should serve, political
and social purposes. Another part, however, will move closer to the American practice. This means that no matter how the Lisbon Agenda is implemented the effort is full of danger. The intangible allure of future
promises is not one all Europeans are prepared to accept, if it means reducing the largesse of the social contract in the present. But those who do
recognize what the promise offers can be eloquent in their endorsement
of it, in just a few words. This was the case in early 2005 when the EU's
Irish commissioner for the internal market and services delivered a speech
in London entitled "The Lisbon Strategy: Why Less Is More."[43]

In the early spring of 2005 the direction was positive and movement slow.
EU governments were continuing to privatize those companies still nationalized, and to reduce significantly their holdings in others. Little by
little, everything is or will be affected, such as financial services and finan-

cial markets, the banking and insurance industries, corporate mergers and acquisitions, stock and bond markets, energy and utility markets, health and education, media and telecommunication industries, tourism, trade, transportation, and the aerospace and defense industries.

The EU, however, also remains a landscape of social contrast and potential unrest. Europe's leaders recognize that their political survival depends on avoiding strikes and demonstrations and on winning elections. They also understand that the ferment accompanying the birth of the free market will claim victims and that they, sooner or later, will be among them. They will encounter public protests and they will lose elections, as was the fate of Germany's chancellor Schröder in September 2005. But they are aware that there is no alternative to continuing on the path to union, just as their successors will learn in due course. Out of each lost election will emerge new debate over the future of *the European socioeconomic model.*

In the last analysis Europe's leaders know, as well, that state monopolies, confiscatory taxes, and burdensome regulation must change, because they are obstacles to growth and stability, to efficiency and innovation, and to job creation and wealth. They also understand that the key to the success of the Lisbon Agenda is creation of a single market that works—to permit "the full force of competition to forge an economy that can compete globally."[44] Just as Benjamin Disraeli observed that time is the best physician, change in the European Union appears to be gathering, slowly, its own momentum. But if it is too late to turn back the clock, it is not yet clear for whom its bells toll.

Competition

A habit of American life is the game, any game—whether it is athletic, commercial, cultural, economic, legal, political, or social. Americans play their games according to rules which give all competitors an equal opportunity at the starting line and which assure that the game itself is played fairly. When the contest is over, normally there is a winner—an individual, or a team, or a product, or a political party, as the case may be. The result, in every instance, is a product of competition.

An athletic contest, such as the game of football, is one illustration of the competitive American spirit. If a team is behind at the end of the first half, there is still a chance to win the game in the second half. If the game is lost today, there is another one next Saturday. And if a team has a losing season, it still has the hope for a better one next year. Competition means that there is never a final result. "Just wait 'til next time," Americans say. Or they announce, "You may have won this one, but you won't beat us again. We'll change our plays, practice harder, and come back with a better team." In playing the game, defeat is never permanent. There is always another day; it is part and parcel of being American. The game goes on, uninterrupted, because in America competition takes place in one arena or another, all year long.

American businessmen and -women thrive on competition. They are also very good at it, as long as the game is played by rules which are both fair and followed. This is why the single, free, and open market proposed by the European Union presents a playing field of great expectations, a field for energetic competition between America and Europe.

Healthy competition in an arena of great expectations, however, will not occur soon. Thus far, concludes the French Institut Montaigne, the Lisbon Agenda is "a great battle plan without an army" and is likely to remain that way as long as "vested interests and rivalries . . . among member states and the different European institutions persist."[45] The idea and spirit of the game, as these are understood in America, are largely absent in European conversations. The essential difference that separates Americans and Europeans in so many ways, also separates them here.

European governments, to varying degrees, view the basic functions of the marketplace to be the generation of revenue for the state, the guarantee of employment, and the maintenance of political stability, but not the arena in which to cultivate a competitive spirit. In turn it is business that is charged with these responsibilities, but not with making the rules. Governments of both the left and the right want to take credit for distribution of the fruits and rewards produced in the marketplace, without taking any of the entrepreneurial risk. Thus, they promote growth, support employment, praise stability, and extol equality of result via regulation and taxation, but they do not encourage equality of economic opportunity or the creation of wealth.

Americans, in general, do not view competition as a tool of social engineering, but as an instrument of economic good, which is used to make a profit so that companies stay in business and employees keep their jobs.[46] Americans believe, also, that inequitable results from competition in free and open markets and the inequalities in income that are produced, are not, by definition, wrong. On the contrary, if marketplaces are really open and competition operates freely, such differences generate incentives. It is free markets that offer choices to the individual. In the American mind choice means social and economic mobility, the chance to move up, to earn greater economic freedom. It is this dream of the possibility that gives American businessmen and -women their competitive spirit. It embraces hope, risk, incentive, initiative, and invention.

This attitude is not an example of the wish being father to the thought. Observers on farther shores have noticed it as well. In the mid-1970s, apropos of this conclusion, French journalist and politician Jean-Jacques Servan-Schreiber compared Europe with America: "We Europeans continue to suffer progress . . . Americans pursue it, welcome it, adapt to it."[47] Thirty years later a corollary to this observation was drawn, again by a Frenchman—Jacques Chirac, the president of France—who, speaking about France and Germany, concluded that "there is a sort of culture of pessimism in our countries." Noting that America is a land of many contrasts, including poverty and income inequality, he observed in April 2005 that "our American friends speak about their successes but never their difficulties. . . . When you have this cult of pessimism, naturally it does not foster creativity."[48]

The American spirit of competition, in practice, does not include the idea of equality of result because it is impossible to achieve. Americans, as well as Europeans, know that those who have tried to force the result in Europe have always failed. American business practices, served by the common law, serve the purpose of assuring a level playing field for companies in competition with one another. In real life, of course, it does not always work this way. Some competitors cheat, some lie and some steal, and some profit at the expense of others by tricking them, or by deliberately producing products of inferior quality. For such cases laws exist in America, as they do in Europe, to punish those who violate the rules. But when American businesses encounter problems, like deceptive advertising, predatory pricing and monopoly practices, they are dealt with differently: "instead of regulating business practices up front, the way Europe does—at great cost—the United States cedes much of the work to the legal system, which dangles the threat of financial ruin for companies that fail to protect the consumer."[49]

There is also another consequence which comes from how competition is practiced in Europe and America. In Europe the primary beneficiary is the government, and producers and consumers are secondary. In America the primary beneficiaries of competition are both producers and consumers. Americans create wealth, keep it, and decide how to spend it, which is part of the explanation for widespread philanthropy in America as compared to Europe.

In fact, the practice of philanthropy and volunteering is almost twice as common in America as it is on the continent.[50] In America, both are the exercise of private initiative to benefit the public good, also defined as "the organized expression of the highest of American ideals: the belief that Americans can create wealth, and then use it generously to establish organizations that act in good faith and have the wisdom, compassion and initiative to help others, without undue reliance on government."[51]

Americans decide, individually, how, what and whom they can and wish to help. Much of the achievement of social goals in America is accomplished by Americans helping each other, as a consequence of wealth created in the marketplace. Americans assume that success in the marketplace will give them, individually, the economic freedom to define and set their social priorities themselves. This approach helps explain why philanthropic contributions make up about 1 percent of America's gross domestic product, compared with 0.2 to 0.8 percent in European countries.[52]

As the European Union advanced into the twenty-first century the reaction among those following the progress from America was mixed. Some welcomed the EU as an unqualified opportunity. Those who believed in the inherent strength of free markets recognized that competition would make Europe and America both stronger, and neither weaker. This conviction rested on the assumption that the members of the EU would, in fact, realize their three objectives: (1) an operating single market in all areas of capital, goods, and services, (2) an EU budget that would become "the most important lever for making national budgets better geared to foster growth and employment,"[53] and (3) unanimous observance of a growth and stability pact that "guarantees the cohesion of the single currency area in the absence of a fully-fledged political federation."[54]

If these goals were achieved competition with America would intensify. It would involve competition in trade and commerce, competition for productivity and growth, and competition between the euro and the dollar for investment capital. From a European viewpoint a thriving single market would generate jobs and productivity. From an American viewpoint the operation of a free marketplace produces better products, at lower prices, for more people, and in so doing contributes to prosperity and peace. The concerns represented by these two viewpoints were not entirely alike, but creation of a true single market in Europe was welcomed by Americans who had confidence in the principle and practice of competition.

There were also Americans, however, who looked at the EU and saw a potential new rival. Critics called competition between the euro and the dollar an inevitable clash for "control of the international monetary system." They interpreted the differences between European supporters and opponents of a true single market as irreconcilable. They missed the existence of a strong EU military force and saw no prospect that one would appear in the foreseeable future. They anticipated that the great disparity between American defense expenditures and those of individual European countries would stir controversy over the purpose of NATO, over the responsibility for peacekeeping operations, and over the appropriate use of military power versus negotiation and diplomacy. In the absence of the Cold War threat to European security, they argued that promises of opportunity alone could not be translated into common interests with which to frame a new economic, political and military relationship. In short, to some Americans, the rancor signaled that "a once united West appears well on its way to separating into competing halves."[55]

What received much less attention was whether competition could take the European-American relationship in a positive direction. Creation of the EU, as the centerpiece of post–Cold War Europe, was not inherently divisive, nor was it designed to be used as a weapon against an American rival. Americans who respected the independent spirit of the initiative awaited a strong competitor who understood that the rules of the marketplace had to be the same for everyone, that the game, as it were, had to be played fairly. From the American backyard the single market would represent a positive, competitive challenge that in the long run would sustain Europe and America.

A majority of Americans saw it that way. In a survey published by the German Marshall Fund in November 2004, almost seven out of ten Americans described strong EU leadership in the world as desirable.[56] Their support, however, rested on the tacit assumptions that, (1) strong leadership in both America and in Europe is complementary, and (2) that Europeans and Americans define the practice of competition the same way.

If there is a realistic possibility that European governments will moderate their vested interests, it will only come via the institutions of the European Union. Most European politicians do not have the confidence to attempt the changes by themselves. So they are using the institutions of the EU both as the means to create what amounts to the new *European socioeconomic model* of the Lisbon Agenda, and as the straw man to blame for the changes.

In the mid-1980s Margaret Thatcher considered the EU Commission a threat to creation of a free market. But just twenty years later, in 2005, it was the un-elected commissioners who were playing the leading roles in the effort to make the Lisbon Agenda a reality. They were attempting to transform the nature and practice of top-down politics and economics in Europe, and to prevent the socialization of Europe via the backdoor. If there is a Lisbon battle plan, it comes from the commissioners, but their influence is limited by national interests. So it was in 2005 during the circuitous course of discussion and debate over creating a single market for services.

The potential impact of this market is enormous because services comprise 70 percent of the EU's economy, and would allow a multitude of blue-collar professions, such as carpentry or plumbing, and hundreds of others, such as architects, management consultants, doctors and nurses, insurance and transportation companies, investment advisers, bankers, caterers, professors and lawyers, to compete in any and all of the EU's twenty-seven member countries. As is already the case with the disappearance of customs duties on goods shipped from one EU country to another—this affects all consumer products, including food and clothing—increased competition will be the result. The beneficiaries will be consumers.

This EU initiative dates from 2003, when the Dutch commissioner for the internal market and services, Frits Bolkestein, proposed eliminating national barriers to services. Bolkestein, who is a member of the Mont Pèlerin Society, was taking another and logical step down the path endorsed in Lisbon by the EU's members, including France and Germany. The directive represented the continuing effort of the European Commission to expand cross-border competition.

Fierce opposition to this measure, however, emerged in 2005, when the president of the European Commission, former prime minister of Portugal Manuel Barroso, recommended implementation of Bolkestein's proposal. While it was welcomed by those Europeans who believed in the single market, it was criticized by selected politicians on the left, the center, and the right within the EU, and particularly by the governments of France and Germany. Were conservative Jean-Pierre Raffarin and socialist Gerhard Schröder opposed in principle? Were they really unwilling to give up control over "their markets of services"? Or did their opposition reflect the normal conduct of contradictory politics in Europe?[57]

The change in political weather highlighted, once again in the short history of the EU, the attachment of European political leaders to contradictory realities. To make their countries competitive in an expanding world of global trade, they extolled the idea of the free market, but even as they championed reforms, they proclaimed a state responsibility to protect their citizens against the short-term effects.[58] What they feared, or so they said, was "that new rules could allow cheap providers of services from new EU states like Poland and the Czech Republic to undercut local firms, thus destroying jobs."[59] To justify their opposition they invented the specter of "the Polish plumber," lurking about on French and German borders, waiting to seize opportunities for work at below-market wages. What was really at stake, however, were the political jobs of EU leaders.

In March 2005, in response to what had become a quarrelsome political fight, Bolkestein's successor Charlie McCreevy, a strong advocate of the directive, reversed his earlier position and withdrew his support for those providing health care services who wished to work across national borders. Socialists in the EU and in the European Parliament publicly claimed a political victory, while the commissioner announced that a new effort to create an acceptable plan would follow.[60] His overriding concern was that, in his estimation, 600,000 jobs could be created in this single market for services: "If . . . 70 percent of the EU's GDP is tied up in services, you don't have to have a Ph.D. in economics to realize that it is in the services area that you must do something to galvanize Europe's economic activity."[61]

This short episode in a continuing story illustrates the EU's single market paradox. Two, countervailing forces are in constant conflict—opposition to reforms and support for their implementation. As a result the picture we see, as spectators, is full of disorder. But we should be cautious in how we pass judgment, because beneath the surface, supporters of a single market know where they are going. To get there they know they cannot take a direct path, so they are taking a European one. It is indirect, but it will eventually end at the doors of the European Commission.

Will they arrive? If not, great expectations will remain just a dream, the gossamer of a benevolent fiction called *the European socioeconomic model*. By the same token, is it possible that those Europeans who hear the drumbeat of the single market, have recognized something in *the American model* they admire, and have decided to adopt the rules of the American game? An indication of what the answer may be appeared in March 2004, when EU enterprise commissioner Erkki Liikanen announced an "Action Plan for Entrepreneurship." He pointed out that in America almost three times as many people are involved with new entrepreneurial initiatives as in the EU, and that, therefore, the focus of his plan would be on changing the mind set of Europeans, to encourage them to take risks and "to see self-employment as a preferred route, rather than a last resort."[62]

Critics may argue that Liikanen's proposal had all the earmarks of rule from the top down; but if it did, it was one with a difference. The proposal, indeed, came from the top, but the content was all about rule from the bottom up. Liikanen's idea had little in common with French and German *dirigist* rhetoric about creating "European industrial champions," as though champions are made by state decree and clothed in national uniforms rather than by hard work and competition. The EU's commissioner for competition, Neelie Kroes, was well aware of this distinction, and was supported in her skepticism by the president of the European Commission in early 2005: "There is a tendency in Europe, faced with increased competition from other parts of the world, to go for interventionist policies . . . I'm not against European champions, but they must come out of competition."[63]

While a glance still finds the path to the single market strewn with economic and political boulders, the nature of the European marketplace is changing. Visa controls are disappearing, customs duties have been abolished, and national telephone monopolies have been privatized, one by one. The result has been the emergence of new companies. Competition in the telecommunication market has produced broader choice, improved service, and lower prices; the best examples are found in France and Germany. But the decisive change, thus far, has been introduction of the euro. Euro-bonds, coins and paper money have transformed Europe's commercial landscape, and have given as well an enormous symbolic push to the legitimacy of the competitive spirit.

More Europeans own stock today than at any previous time in European history. For the first time since creation of the Common Market in 1957, stifling tax policies and constricting regulation are under major attack by private businessmen and -women, and by some political leaders of both the left and the right. Those who believe in free markets may ultimately get what they wish for, and those who do not may get it in spite of themselves.

For decades Europeans have criticized Americans for being consumed with making money. But today, thanks to the end of Europe's division, to formation of the European Union, and to the Internet revolution, new generations take pride in making a profit, reject the socialist idea that work is bad, and believe that stock options are not the invention of selfish capitalists, but a positive incentive to create wealth while building something productive and progressive. The Old World has begun the laborious task of reinventing itself.

Both the euro and the Lisbon Agenda are stages along that path of reinvention. For members of younger generations, traveling down the path is becoming part of their daily lives. Those born after 1989 do not have a long memory of anything else, nor are their sentiments emotionally touched by a photograph of the president of France and the chancellor of Germany standing side by side at a military graveyard. This generation does not think of the European Union just as an antidote to war. They think of the EU as part of their economic future, and they want it to succeed.

How they will play their roles in making the single market a reality still lies ahead because it is not yet time for them to take the political stage. It is safe to say, however, that when they do—and it will be soon—fewer of them will share the predilection for rule from the top down as practiced by today's political leaders, who, for the most part, are products of a post-war era that is disappearing.

Members of Europe's younger generations will not be unreserved believers in the old *European socioeconomic model*, because they know that the adversarial concept of the public good versus the private interest is out of step with their modern world. The old approach is living on borrowed time. Class conflict no longer exists in Europe, except in political speeches and history books. European society has become bourgeois, while the size of the so-called working class has relentlessly grown smaller since 1945. Although the social contract is still the common practice and not the exception, continental rule from the top down is under attack everywhere in the European Union.

As Frits Bolkestein asked rhetorically in mid-2005: "How social is an economic model that throws up 12 percent unemployment as in Germany, or 10 percent as in France?"[64] And, as other Europeans have pointed out, it is neither a model nor is it social; and no one wants to emulate it. But if its future is still uncertain, the passage of time tells us that a new generation is preparing to inherit the legacies created by Europe's leaders since 1945. Just as Europe was a very different place at the end of the Fifty Years' War in 1989–1990 from what it had been in 1939, it will be profoundly different fifty years from now. Will Europe's future leaders, now in their twenties and thirties, agree with German chancellor Schröder's prediction, made at the end of June 2005, that "those who want to destroy this model due to national egoism or populist motives do a terrible disservice to the desires and rights of the next generation"?[65] Two years later the verdict was still out: not only had IG Metall forced a substantial wage increase in the spring of 2007, but Germany's unemployment rate had dipped below four million for the first time since 2002; the EU rate as a whole had dropped to its lowest point since 1993. In addition, in May 2007 the Socialist Party of France was soundly defeated in national elections for the French presidency.

PART THREE

Freedom and Order

Preface

The essential difference between the New World and the Old is not a hypothesis by social scientists, but a legacy with which we have been endowed. It establishes the priority we place on freedom versus order. It is the idea of individual liberty from the bottom up that gives America its identity in contrast to the identity of Europe as a tree of rule from the top down.

We see the contrast everywhere, in how we describe who we are, the qualities of life we prize, the leadership we admire, and the societies we respect. The contrast is made bolder by the lessons we draw from our respective historical experiences, and therefore by our descriptions of the paths that lead to freedom and peace. The contrast is found in how we explain who we are, in how we lead, in how we address one another with words of condescension (Europeans speaking to Americans) or incredulity (Americans addressing Europeans) when we disagree, and in the different priorities we place on freedom and order.

All these things, in the current context, become the yeast for acerbic disputes on all manner of concerns: free trade and protectionism, agricultural policy, environmental protection and global warming, governance of the Internet, acceptable tools of diplomacy, cultural diversity and globalization, the international criminal court, the death penalty, how to alleviate poverty and combat the spread of AIDS, the advantages of "soft" versus "hard" power, how to promote peace in the Middle East, the use of military force, how to control the proliferation of weapons of mass destruction, how to address the causes of terrorism, the role and authority of UNESCO and the United Nations, and finally, how to define what constitutes threats to freedom and peace and how to employ the means to preserve both.

The most colorful illustrations of how we have conversed with each other recently, and also the most lamentable, are not yet bold examples in history textbooks. Since 2002, however, they have been cited with relish and documented ad infinitum in the European and American press. For the multitude of examples we have ourselves to thank. It has been with our own words that we have provided future historians ample proof that the essential difference is still alive, well, and very much with us.

The references and citations presented in the three essays which follow should not be dismissed as simply a collection of excerpts from press clippings. That is not what they are. Rather, they are the evidence of how we, Americans and Europeans, have more recently chosen to unravel and analyze the complexities of the world around us. The object is not to resolve arguments nor to pass judgment on who is right and who is wrong, but to shed light on why we do not always agree on the meaning of what we see.

There is also a specific purpose. How we consort together warrants our reflection because new crossroads await Europeans and Americans. Sooner, rather than later, we will have to decide where the crossroads lead and which way we want to go. Will we act as rivals, or to recall the words of Benjamin Franklin, will we hang together? Will it be the force of things that determines our choice, or will it be obligations written in our hearts?

CHAPTER V

Legacies, Ancient and Modern

The Idea and the Tree

THE HISTORIES OF Europe and America have bequeathed to us different legacies. In Europe economic and political power begins with the state. In America it begins with the individual. But, although we are both products of our cultures, do we see clearly who we are, or, perhaps more accurately, what we have become? There is no right answer to this question, but I received an unusual response to it from a German colleague in Hamburg. He began his explanation with a quotation:

> America, you've got it better
> than our old continent. Exult!
> You have no decaying castles and no basalt.
>
> Your heart is not troubled,
> in lively pursuits,
> by useless old remembrance
> and empty disputes.
>
> So use the present day with luck!
> And, when your children a poem write,
> protect them with skill and pluck,
> from tales of bandits, ghosts, and knights.[1]

That quotation comes from Johann Wolfgang von Goethe's poem "To The United States," written in 1827—for us that is not very long ago. It puts the differences between Europe and America, that you have been telling me about, into another kind of context. It is one in which age and time play the decisive roles. Goethe was saying that the youthful history of the US allowed America to go forward without any of the quarrels that so typified "Old" Europe, that you should make the most of it, and that yours is the land of the future. In other words, you were without the weight of ancient legacies symbolized by decaying castles and recounted in stories of knights, robbers, and ghosts. Americans consider castles and knights part of their romantic image of Europe, and in truth they are. For us, however, they are images of our European background.

Europe is a region, a historical fact, like a tree, with European countries representing branches of the same tree. At one time Europe was the name for central Greece and perhaps you could say, as Roman armies explored the land mass of Europe, it later became an idea associated with the relationship of Romans with their government. But that point is always subject to different interpretations. So let us just say that at least during the Roman Empire the relationship was symbolized by an acronym that appeared on public buildings everywhere: S.P.Q.R. In Latin it was written *Senatus populusque Romanus,* and stood for *The Senate and the People of Rome.* And of course to be a citizen of Rome—*Civis Romanus Sum*—that is to say of the Roman empire, was to take pride in being Roman and subject to Roman law; in a manner of speaking it was the Roman dream.

But fifteen hundred years have gone by in the meantime, and that idea has long since been forgotten, although Roman law still provides the basis for much of Europe's legal system. Europe today is the result of its history of rule, both ancient and modern, a history of war and conquest, of victory and defeat, of destruction and reconstruction, of dark ages and enlightenment. In this sense Europe's history very much influences its present. Europe's past does not become more distant as time goes by, but forms an ever larger part of its future, as Europe grows older.

America was never a historical fact. It was an idea, a symbol of hope. And today it still is, in spite of your many differences of opinion or perhaps because you express them so freely. To be sure, America is a distant relative of the European tree. But it is an idea of freedom, independence, and opportunity that you, of all ethnic backgrounds, rediscover and renew with each passing day. That is why you still remind yourselves, constantly, that you are Americans. The symbol is your flag, but the substance is your idea. As America grows older this idea of freedom is a living part of your present, and continues to beckon. It is, almost, as though you hold time in contempt.

⌒❧⌒

The idea of Europe as a nation, whose citizens have real European hopes and concrete dreams, is still a wish very much father to the thought. To paraphrase André Malraux's observation from the early 1970s, that is what it will remain, a wish:

> There is no such thing as Europe, there never was. It is the last of the great myths. There's a pink spot on the map and then it was decided that there is a Europe because there was a Christianity. Christianity! That was something important. Europe is a dream.[2]

Malraux notwithstanding, it was true in early 2005, according to a study by the Royal Elcano Institute in Madrid, that about 45 percent of Europeans considered their European identity to be as significant as their nationality.[3] Their identity, however, is no longer associated with Christianity, but without it what is it? What do they believe in? Those who live in Europe are Europeans in the sense that they share Europe's past, present, and future, but they are not Europeans in the same sense as Americans in America. Rather, they are nationalities, such as Swedes, Italians, Spaniards, Poles, Germans, and French, all speaking different languages. They are part of, and equally proud of, their respective national pasts and are very much committed to their different customs and traditions. In some cases they have existed as nations well over a thousand years. Europeans may travel as citizens of the EU with an EU driver's license or with an EU passport (on which is written the name of the country of which they are a citizen), and businesses in Europe can give their Internet addresses a European Union identity with a ".eu" extension, but these contrivances do not create loyalty to a European identity.

To speak of the idea of Europe in the same way that Americans define the idea of America is a fiction. As a grand European concept the vision of building one nation may stimulate the imagination, but it does not create a union or a nation, because Europeans are not committed to the idea of Europe as Americans are to the idea of America. The European Union, writes Imre Kertesz, the 2002 Hungarian Nobel laureate in literature, may be a web "of financial and economic ties, but a European spirit, an identity that binds us together beyond our individual nationalisms, has yet to be born."[4] In fact, one of Kertesz's neighbors, the former Romanian foreign minister Andrei Plesu, has taken the opposite view by describing Europe as "something in an old faded photograph, the world between the two world wars, a nostalgia, a longing. In the West, Europe is a project. In the East, it's a memory."[5]

The other side of the argument, however, is that the Europeans have intentionally established common institutions. It might well have been pointed out to Malraux, as Jean Monnet did to a British audience in 1962, that "European unity is not a blueprint—it is a process. Human nature does not change. But when nations and men accept the same rules and the same institutions, their behavior towards each other changes. This is the process of civilisation itself."

How would Malraux have responded? Would he have questioned whether rules and institutions suffice? And if so, what kind of institutions? What of the importance of the institution of Christianity, and of the significance of its decline on the continent? Would he have said that the concept of unity needs something more than just pacts and regulations in order to become real and lasting? Would he have argued that the American experience cannot be duplicated in Europe? Are the idea and the tree really the same thing?

We know that Europeans and Americans share an appreciation for much that unites; the genius and imagination which have produced the artistic, literary, musical, philosophical and scientific masterpieces of Western civilization. But the similarities do not go further, because political and economic events have ordered American and European society in fundamentally different ways. History has not yet destroyed the continuity of America's trust in freedom; Americans believe in it. Europeans, on the other hand, have no order given to them by one declaration of independence, and by one constitution of liberty. So they do not focus on a belief in freedom and opportunity, because it does not exist. That is what separates the idea from the tree.

An inelegant contrast between the American and European concepts of identity is the comparison of America's Constitutional Convention with creation of the European Constitution between 2002 and 2004: citizens as opposed to bureaucrats, inspiring prose versus Eurocratic jargon. My European friends would point out that the comparison is unfair, because more than two centuries separate the two events and because the former was born of revolution and the latter is the child of government. But they would also tell me that the centuries-old European approach of rule from the top down continues today and assures that united Europe will never exist in the same sense that Americans use the phrase "the United States."

As an illustration they cite a project which began in the summer of 2002. At that time a 105-person assembly of European politicians from 28 member and candidate EU countries, headed by former French president Valéry Giscard d'Estaing, began to draft a constitution for the EU. This effort was called the Convention on the Future of Europe and had the goal of producing a "blueprint for a streamlined system of EU policy-making." It was completed and signed by EU leaders in Rome in October 2004 as a constitutional treaty of 465 articles, 80 percent of which had been taken from previous treaties and rearranged. The constitution was to be presented for ratification as a treaty by EU parliaments or as a referendum for voter approval. That is to say, the choice was up to the individual country but unanimity would have to prevail. In other words, for it to take effect on November 1, 2006, all 27 members of the EU and the 732-member European Parliament would have to approve it.

The constitution restated the concepts on which the EU's legal, political, and economic order are based in accordance with existing treaties, introduced a Charter of Fundamental Rights, created the positions of European president and European foreign minister, designed a new system for majority rule within the EU, set forth how the EU's policies are to be formulated and implemented and how the provisions governing operation of its institutions apply. If adopted, the EU would exist as a legal entity whose president and foreign minister could sign treaties and agreements on behalf of its members, and the constitution itself would become "the first statement of EU values."[6]

Following Spanish approval in a referendum in early spring 2005, the constitution was voted down by French voters on May 29, 2005, by a margin of 55 to 45 percent, and by Dutch voters several days later, with a still larger margin of almost two to one. Rejection by two of the EU's six original founding members greatly agitated Europe's politicians, resulted in the appointment of a new French government by President Jacques Chirac, and caused a drop in the value of the euro of close to 5 percent.

The short-term consequence of failure was made immediately clear by the new French prime minister, Dominique de Villepin. Mixed messages would be the order of the French day, which was exactly what the country's majority had voted against.[7]

In a classic example of political contradiction, Villepin announced that his government would (1) pump 4.5 billion € into the French economy to create jobs, (2) cancel President Chirac's 2002 promise to cut income taxes, (3) pass legislation to make hiring new employees financially more attractive, (4) proceed with the long-anticipated partial privatization of Electricité de France and Gaz de France, (5) oppose EU free market reforms that would reduce welfare benefits and weaken labor protections for French citizens, and (6) endorse the message delivered by French voters: "Globalization is not an ideal; it cannot be our destiny." He then blamed creation of most of France's problems on "15 years of socialism."[8]

In some ways, the long-term effects also became apparent quickly. The European Union would go on. The EU commissioner for enterprise and industry, German socialist Günter Verheugen, announced that the Lisbon Agenda would continue, that plans to increase competition would not be modified, and that "more integration is not the problem; it is the solution."[9]

The rejection would not stop the EU from moving forward, but it would focus renewed attention on the reasons why the EU was created in the first place, on the debate between central planning versus the free market, on the economic viability of *the old European socioeconomic model*, and on the clash between the forces of rule from the top down and from the bottom up—in other words on the inevitable conflict that emerges when the burdens of historical legacies confront the aspirations of historical undertakings.

As a symbol the constitution did, indeed, mirror a European dream, because its purpose was to codify what the EU should become, under a single umbrella of "rights." Its length and contents were not the epitome of clarity and proud principles, but the constitution did provide a canopy for the different branches of the European tree. This was the gist of the argument made by the EU's high representative for common foreign and security policy, Javier Solana, in October 2004:

> What the Maastricht Treaty did for the euro, the constitution could do for Europe's role in the world. . . . A continent that was shattered by war and divided by ideology has been transformed into an attractive and prosperous model of co-operation and a net exporter of stability. . . . The international constitution of the European Union can be a substantial one in a century that will be characterized by global interdependence. We want to work with our friends and partners to help deliver solutions for the many contemporary problems that defy borders. . . . With the constitution, we do not just open a new chapter in European history, we also hope to renew our partnership with the United States.[10]

Solana's declaration of hope, admirable and dignified, was based nonetheless on a contradiction. On the one hand he was equating identity with stability, but on the other he was describing a postwar identity for which the majority of the EU's 450 million citizens would never be called upon to vote. Perhaps in the expectation that it would become more attractive to European voters, Solana too, as all of Europe's leaders, labeled the treaty a constitution. But the document was nothing of the kind, nor did it draw "on centuries of political experience . . . informed by tragic wisdom borne of millenniums of wars . . . influenced by European philosophers like Hobbes and Rousseau, Hume and Kant, Machiavelli and

Montesquieu, who addressed fundamental questions about government and human nature."[11]

It was, however, another step very much in keeping with the effort to transform, from the top down, the dream of Europe into reality. In this regard the work of d'Estaing's committee was more than just a noble gesture. It was the crown on the commitment to change the postwar face of Europe, to create a different European inheritance for the future. Thus, a 54-year-old retired Spanish bank employee explained in February 2005 why he would vote to approve the "constitution":

> In 2,000 years we've never agreed on anything. The European Union is the only way to mix European cultures and to overcome nationalisms. . . . The constitution treaty is Europe's salvation.[12]

The middle-aged Spaniard was far from alone with his conviction. Similar views were ardently expressed throughout the union, including in France and the Netherlands, but they were not the only strongly held opinions. In the days and weeks preceding the referendum in France the arguments used to justify voting yes or no transformed the vote into a French plebiscite on everything the French liked, and disliked.

The election results reflected suspicions about the financial and political cost of enlarging the EU, frustration with the high French unemployment rate, ignorance of how free markets work, fears of immigration and globalization, doubts about giving up sovereignty to Brussels, and general pessimism concerning the future of a union that lacked identity.

Proponents and critics of the constitution argued both for and against a whole host of issues: Muslim influence in general and Turkish membership in the EU in particular; elitism and social engineering; free markets and stability; "the Polish plumber" and social dumping;[13] competition and the proposed single market for services; protection of jobs and greater labor mobility; nationalism and leadership of the European Union; and interventionism and European security.

The differences of opinion did not mirror a clash of conventional political classes, because many of the same positions were argued by conservatives and socialists alike. The differentiation lay in who among them would vote "yes" and who "no," and of this there were hundreds of examples.

The contrast was dramatic among French socialists, whose leader, François Hollande, was strongly pro-constitution while his deputy chairman and former prime minister, Laurent Fabius, spearheaded the no vote. The widow of deceased French socialist president François Mitterrand was in the no camp while her son urged a yes vote, and Mitterrand's daughter was reluctant to commit on either position.

On the other end of the political spectrum, confusing behavior was also the order of the day. A majority of the conservative members of the French Senate and the National Assembly strongly supported the constitution, but there were also those who opposed it with a mixture of xenophobia and nationalist pride in the role France could, or should play in the EU. Less than one week before the vote, a former conservative member of the French Senate proclaimed privately that the future of France lay in the hands of Laurent Fabius, whose leadership and courage of conviction were exemplary.[14]

In short, in the camps of both yes and no the coalitions were patchwork political quilts made up of those on the left, in the center, and on the right. They had nothing in common, with one exception. They all focused only marginally on the contents of the constitution itself.

There was truth to be found in all of the numerous sentiments expressed; but in reality the vote was about confidence, or the lack of it, in the idea of Europe pedagogically described in a draft constitution of almost 500 pages—a trifle too large, some Europeans noted, to carry around in one's pocket. In this sense the debates in France and in the Netherlands reflected a much wider and significant uncertainty in the EU about the identity of Europe itself. Would Europe remain a continent, as Frenchman Guy Sorman had argued in early 2003, where the marketplace is considered to be a means to finance the social contract, or to be an end called freedom?

Laurent Fabius understood the significance of the challenge and the ultimate outcome. This is why he had begun calling for modifications in the constitution in the autumn of 2004. He argued that the treaty should "include provisions that protect wealthier West European countries from losing jobs to the east, where labor costs and taxes are lower." He accused the constitution's framers of "paving the way to a European Union 'where competition reigns above all else,'" and noted that the word "market" appeared in 78 different places in the text while the phrase "social progress" was used only three times.[15]

To couch his objections in another way, the concept of equality of result had a new rival called *the demand for equality of opportunity*, a life-threatening challenge to the legitimacy of the socialist idea at the beginning of the twenty-first century. Even though socialism in Europe was still an enormously powerful political force in 2005, it was also in danger of becoming obsolete in an increasingly competitive economic environment. The fear of irrelevancy may explain why Fabius sought to polarize the political landscape by distorting his references to the words "social," and "market." A review of the draft constitution in March 2005 did show that the word "market" appeared at least 65 times, but it also showed that the word "social" appeared in the document more than 125 times.

Fabius' objections, as well as those of his conservative counterparts, were understandable. Both wanted to slow down the movement toward unity, toward creating a European identity in a European marketplace, because both had much to lose. A strong European Union, based on a vibrant free market competing successfully on the stage of world trade and commerce, would undermine rule from the top down, whether of the left or of the right.[16]

Was it possible to tell from the results of the referenda in France and in the Netherlands what the purpose of the constitution really was? Was there a hidden agenda to make rivals of the EU and America—a rivalry in which Europeans would view themselves as "a net exporter of stability" and Americans would consider themselves a committed exporter of freedom? Or was this too simplistic an explanation? Was it more accurate to ask whether the convention's intent was to produce a constitution of liberty and opportunity; or a constitution of entitlements and equality? For these questions there were no direct answers, but one of the convention's members noted that "it was the Bill of Rights that created American identity. They were Americans and so they had rights. It will be the same with Europeans."[17]

Many Americans, and some Europeans as well, would take exception to the latter conclusion. They would argue that it was because Americans knew exactly who they were and what they believed in that they created the Bill of Rights, and not vice versa. The Bill of Rights did not give them their identity it was a mirror image of it, transformed into law. This is why, for some Europeans, the interpretation of "rights" as the definition of their identity was more than just disturbing. They were apprehensive that the identity as set forth in the constitution was not made of who they were, but was being imposed on them.

From an observer's viewpoint there was reason for unease. Between 2002 and 2004 the convention had focused on what powers should be given to government and on how much political and economic control government should exercise. There were no formal meetings to consider how much freedom the individual might lose as a result. To some it appeared as though the constitution's writers were more intent on symbolism and compromise than they were on writing a constitution of liberty. The draft contained an official motto, "United in Diversity," and designated Schiller's "Ode to Joy," set to the music of Beethoven's Ninth Symphony, as the European anthem, the euro as the official currency, and May 9 as Europe Day.[18] It did not contain a single reference to God, to Christianity, or to Europe's Christian heritage, or to the fact that those who had formed the Common Market in 1957 welcomed specifically, one year later, the proclamation by Pope Pius XII naming Saint Benedict as the "Father of Europe."[19]

The constitution's preamble acknowledged "the cultural, religious and humanist inheritance of Europe, from which have developed the universal values of the inviolable and inalienable rights of the human person, democracy, equality, freedom and the rule of law." This insipid description, far from elevating, prompted the Roman Catholic primate in Hungary to remind the drafters that "without Christianity, the heart of Europe would be missing." Where, wondered not only clerics, did respect for human rights come from, if not from Christianity? What kind of risks did denial of Christian heritage entail?

Indeed, if the European Union's heart was not a Christian one, what was it made of? The aim of the union, as defined in the treaty, was "to promote peace." The union shall work for "sustainable development . . . based on balanced economic growth . . . a social market economy . . . [and] full employment and social progress." This ambition was bolstered by a 50-article charter of fundamental rights. The charter contained no references to responsibility, but an almost inexhaustible recitation of concerns at least one of which would appeal to every man: a right to life, integrity of the person, collective bargaining, fair working conditions, prohibition of slavery and forced labor, shelter, liberty and security, respect for private and family life, marriage, freedom of thought, freedom of the arts and sciences, free compulsory education, the rights of the child and of the elderly to lead a life of dignity and independence, social security and social assistance, health care, environmental protection, and a right to good administration. As Giscard d'Estaing described it in June 2003, "of all the men and women in the world, it is the citizens of Europe who will have the most extensive rights."[20]

As a commentary on this observation it should be noted that the convention's chairman was trying to sell the constitution's virtues, as was Javier Solana one year later. Some Europeans, however, questioned the real value of having more rights than anyone else when so little attention was focused on where they came from, or on the obligation to protect them. Others did not understand why Solana praised the EU as "a net exporter of stability." The words were unquestionably reassuring, but it was unclear what they meant. Still others were concerned with the "disappearance" of Christianity. If Europe's leaders no longer believed in the value of the Christian commitment, what did they believe in?

Had the leaders of "Old Europe" forgotten, so soon after the fall of the Berlin Wall, that the best guarantee for stability is an unequivocal commitment to human freedom, backed up by the means to defend both?

If they needed a reminder the leaders of "New Europe" in Budapest, War-saw, and Prague and in Estonia, Latvia, and Lithuania were well qualified to teach this lesson learned from their history of the twentieth century. But they were not asked, nor were they the architects of the European Union.[21] Neither, of course, was American journalist William Pfaff. But at mid-year, 2005, following the treaty's rejection, he drew some troubling conclusions:

> People become uneasy when religion is brought up as a basis of civilization, but historically that has been the case. Europe now is deeply secular, but Europe's secular civilization itself is Christian. That's what makes it different from secular civilization in Japan. . . . People say Europe can't stay a Christian club. This is considered illiberal or discriminatory, or even 'racist.' But Europe is what it is, and well-intentioned meddling with the values, perceptions and assumptions responsible for a society's deep sense of individual and national identity is very dangerous. . . . The EU's crisis is due in part to its leaders' efforts to de-Europeanize Europe in the name of internationalist abstractions. The French and Dutch have rebelled against this. Europe's leaders, I think, should reflect more on the significance of what happened three weeks ago.[22]

The draft constitutional treaty was a reflection of the views of those who drew it and thus a symbol of the European experience, just as the American experience "is completely alien to the European mind, as exemplified by the remark attributed to Georges Clemenceau[23] that Americans have no capacity for abstract thought, and make bad coffee." In a book entitled *The Age of Reagan*, Steven Hayward continues that "the maxim for European foreign relations is *raison d'état*—reasons of state, that is, self-interest. There is no shorthand maxim for America's foreign outlook, but it might be—if we spoke French—*raison droit* [sic] or perhaps *état de droit*, that is, reasons of morality or a state based on right." And he concludes that "this turns Clemenceau on his head, for the basis of America's moral outlook on the world was what Lincoln called an abstract truth, applicable to all men at all times."[24]

The differences Hayward writes about apply not only to the foreign relations of the EU, as Solana outlined them, but also to domestic pursuits. If Americans think of freedom in terms of rights and responsibilities, Europeans think of freedom in terms of stability and order. Because of the continent's history, Europeans are preoccupied with keeping their glass no less than half empty, and stable so it does not spill, with balanced economic growth, full employment, social markets and social progress, and sustainable development as the desirable alternative to the continent's history of endless conflict.

The European preoccupation with equilibrium and order—what Americans might describe as "don't rock the boat"—is another lesson taken from history, a lesson which was described for me by a French friend of many years, educated in California, who lives with her husband in Brussels.

We like to talk about the traps, not about the opportunities. We are reluctant to take a chance. We're suspicious, so we always question the motive, and ask "what is your self-interest?" We do that because that's how we look at the world; we call it being realistic. Our teacher is our history. So is yours, of course, but your history is different. When you focus on a concern—foreign or domestic—there is always an idealistic or moral element to the consideration. That element makes you want to state your case in terms of what is "fair" and "just." You do that because you don't think about acquiring "interests" as though they were pieces of property. You talk in terms of defending principles, and the definition always has a portion of "freedom" attached to it. In other words, Americans may support opposition to tyranny because they believe it is in the national interest. But you also do it because you believe it is morally "right." And maybe, for you, the two are one and the same.

I would say, as a European—and my husband and I have talked about it for almost forty years—that this difference explains why you became involved in Europe during World Wars I and II, why you defended Berlin after 1945, why you went to Korea, to Vietnam, to former Yugoslavia, and why you fought against a dictator in Iraq twice. In all those cases most Americans felt something wrong was happening and that something had to be done about it.

Many of us, of course, roll our eyes at all this because we're made differently. We can't imagine that you're serious when you talk about national interests and morality in the same breath. It's not part of our political and economic culture to think this way. We believe in order, in protecting what we have acquired, not in waging crusades for freedom. What we think today was said long ago by Lord Palmerston, England's prime minister in the late 1850s and early 1860s. You have to agree that he put it memorably, and maybe a little indelicately—"We have no eternal allies and we have no perpetual enemies. Our interests are eternal and perpetual, and those interests it is our duty to follow."

History Lessons

Much of what America and Europe have accomplished separately has reinforced nonetheless our faith in the values we have in common. That confidence is just as strong today as it has ever been. When we do have disagreements they are not about the values, but about the most effective way to re-enforce and defend them in a world in which Americans and Europeans have learned different lessons about freedom and peace. It is in the realm of interpreting the meaning of history that our vision is not always the same. Understanding why this is so is of crucial importance to us both.

In 1945 the smoking ruins of continental cities sent an impressive message about war to Europeans which contained an immediate problem and a long-term challenge. The problem was how to deal with the urgent demands of political and economic recovery and reconstruction. The challenge was how to assure that war would never again ravage the continent. The answer chosen lay in the concepts of defense and prevention. The creation of the North Atlantic Treaty Organization (NATO) in 1949 became the means of defense, and European economic integration became the means to prevent war.

As Europeans began to rebuild their continent, the rubble in the streets of Germany, but also the cemeteries above the beaches of Normandy, were a constant reminder of the unholy heritage of war. Some of Europe's great cities, such as Paris, Prague, and Vienna, had been spared destruction, but most of them were as dead as their inhabitants. All the Europeans, from Finland to Spain, from Ireland to Greece, from England to Germany, from France to Russia, were affected by so many lives gone—for example, almost 500,000 in England, about 250,000 in Denmark, almost 600,000 in France, more than 530,000 in Italy, around 6 million Germans, and millions more in Russia.

The total loss approached 50 million, which does not include the murder of more than six million Jews. Whether the number is 50 or 56 million, however, it is a statistic more of shame than of substance, because it is impossible to imagine that many dead on a field before you, stretching as far as the eye can see. But the painful meaning of death and devastation was much easier to grasp for the families affected—the loss of husbands and wives, children without parents, hunger, disease, streams of refugees fleeing from the violence of the "Red Army" into Western Europe. The Europeans all had to put their lives back together again.

This point applied as well to thousands of American families that had also been torn apart by the tragedy of warfare. They, too, had lost fathers and mothers, brothers and sisters, sons and daughters, and they had been touched by something else that many Europeans tend to ignore today. During the war Americans suffered in a different way. On the other side of the Atlantic they sat helpless in their living rooms, listening to their radios or reading letters from Europe with no return addresses – it was news about war, about the deportation, arrest and murder of their European relatives across the continent, from London to Paris to Berlin to Moscow.

It is true that once the war was over Americans did not have to rebuild their towns and cities, nor did they have to worry about how to find medicine, if there were enough to eat, and where they were going to sleep. In America postwar generations grew up in comparative plenty without daily reminders of loss and privation, while European postwar generations grew up haunted by the silhouettes of bombed-out buildings. These two circumstances did not make Americans less sensitive and the Europeans more so. But the war, and its aftermath, did mold American and European perceptions of what was important in the world, and did so differently.

The values of freedom and peace were recognized and understood by Americans who had fought in Europe to defend the one and achieve the other. That is why American soldiers went across the Atlantic. But on the continent the idea of freedom was of less importance to Europeans than the assurance that war would never take place again, under any circumstances. That the Europeans had brought the plague of war upon themselves, twice within three decades, was exactly the point. A phrase was coined for it in Germany almost immediately after 1945, *nie wieder Krieg* (never again war). It became the rallying cry of the peace movement, and although the political orientation was left wing, the plea was one to which millions of Germans, of all political persuasions, subscribed. One of the consequences was major opposition to the rearmament of Germany, not only among Germans but among Europeans as well. When it did begin in the mid-1950s it took place very slowly, and when, almost forty years later, newly unified Germany became a member of NATO, it renounced the manufacture, possession, and control over nuclear, biological, and chemical weapons.

It was not only in Germany that the European experience with the horrors of war had many consequences. Preservation of peace was not a joint American-European effort of equal proportion. After 1945 America assumed the primary burden for the defense of Western Europe, because the government was in the position to do so, and because American citizens favored it. European governments were not in that position and hundreds of thousands of European soldiers were dead.

Initially, disproportionate sharing of burdens did not pose major problems. But it meant that Western European security was dependent on American armed forces and on America's willingness to maintain them. As long as Europe remained divided, and as long as America assumed the major role, there was little incentive for European governments to improve their own military capabilities. With the notable exceptions of

England and France, the rest did not. The eventual result was a gap between the relative strength of European and American military power. The larger the chasm grew, the more acrimonious became transatlantic conversations about sharing the economic and military responsibilities for preserving freedom and peace.

By the end of the 1970s America was informing Europeans that they "needed" to understand that they "must" spend more on defense. Unless the Europeans devoted more of their gross domestic product to national security, so it was argued, the already "troubled partnership" would become more stormy. This, indeed, is exactly what occurred during the decade of the 1980s, until three things unexpectedly occurred: (1) Communist governments collapsed in 1989–1990, (2) the military threat from the East disappeared at the same time, and (3) in the absence of the threat the rationale for developing greater European military power seemed to vanish, for many.

Everywhere on the continent the reaction to "the velvet revolution"—the phrase coined to describe the collapse of Czechoslovakia without a shot being fired—was jubilation, because the Cold War was over. It was also a relief, because Europe was no longer divided. Many Europeans believed that the peaceful end to "history hung in chains" presented an unprecedented opportunity to unite Europe. Others were quick to point out that there were not just one, but two intimately related opportunities. The second was the chance to modernize Western Europe's defense forces and integrate them into a strong security framework for all of Europe. To accomplish both would require visionary leadership on the continent and strong support from America.

Few Western European governments, however, saw any reason to close the gap between European and American military power. Nor did European leaders take any significant steps toward creation of a strong security framework for all of Europe. In addition, little encouragement was sent across the Atlantic by American leaders. The consequence was threefold. European leaders developed a post–Cold War identity, a security framework for all of Europe remained unbuilt, and the American-European partnership drifted.

European politicians were not prepared to justify spending money on defense against a threat that no longer existed, and be accused of squandering "the peace dividend." Neither were they anxious to increase their defense budgets and risk being voted out of office. In addition, they were unwilling to decrease expenditures for their respective social contracts. But they were eager to declare that all Europeans, free from dictatorship for the first time in more than fifty years, shared as their first priority elimination of the causes for future war on the continent. This is why European leaders, in 1991, turned to transforming the Western European economic community into a European Union.

On the subject of war and peace there is a major difference between Americans and Europeans. Today, a majority of Europeans of both socialist and conservative persuasions discuss peace as though it were black and white; that is to say, one is *for* peace and *against* war, or *for* war and *against* peace. On this subject Europeans notice very few shades of gray, which is ironic, because Europeans normally see shades of gray everywhere. When European leaders refer to peace it is as though the word were not just a vision, but an inventive tool of diplomacy. Another way to express this thought has been found by French novelist Pascal Bruckner, who argues that "our great problem as Europeans is that we want to exit from history. Sometime after 1989 we developed the belief that barbarians could be refuted intellectually."[25]

In contrast to Europeans, Americans talk about freedom as a principle of diplomacy, genuinely believe it, and consider it the indispensable ingredient for a just and viable peace. They have learned from their experience, and from the Europeans themselves, that freedom has enemies, and that sometimes it is necessary to fight for freedom in order to preserve it. Europe's long and tragic history of anti-Semitism has also taught Americans that if a disaster such as the Nazi Holocaust—that began in Germany in the 1930s and ended in Germany in 1945—is to be avoided in the future, there can be no appeasement of dictators, wherever they may be.

European history has also taught Americans another lesson. German political scientist Christian Hacke defined it in April 2003, when he wrote that the experience of World War II should have produced the conviction in Germany of "never again dictatorship and aggression" rather than "never again war."[26] He also expressed the view, shared by many Americans, that "whoever wants to prevent war, must in the last analysis be prepared to fight one." For Americans the lesson of World War II was that military weakness is no substitute for military power, and some Americans would argue they were reminded of it brutally, again, on September 11, 2001.

In reference to Europe's "catastrophic loss of status" since World War II Henri Astier, in a brilliant review of Jean-François Revel's book on anti-Americanism in France, summarized his conclusions on the legacy of twentieth century conflagrations in Europe:

> Europe virtually tried to commit suicide in the twentieth century, and American preponderance is a direct consequence of its self-inflicted wounds. In the space of thirty years, the Europeans triggered two World Wars from which the Americans had to come and rescue them. But rather than face up to this sorry history, Europeans prefer to pose as victims of America's drive for world domination. American 'unilateralism . . . is the consequence, not the cause, of power failures in the rest of the world.'[27]

Another consequence of power failures, as Ravel names them, is the attempt to transform the vision of peace into an effective weapon, in the absence of real military strength. By definition such an attempt is condemned to failure, unless all support the vision of peace in the same way. In the last decade of the twentieth century the failure was nowhere more evident than in Europe where, to cite French commentator Dominique Moïsi, "the seeds of intolerant nationalism" and violence were still alive and well.[28] The decade of the 1990s was full of both in provinces of the former Iron Curtain countries, from the former Soviet Union to former Yugoslavia, but also in Ireland and Spain.

Members of the newly created European Union urged restraint, condemned violence, and counseled peace, but they were unwilling and unprepared to stop the bloodshed while thousands of people were murdered during the mid-1990s. Intolerant nationalism continued to express itself in internecine warfare, euphemistically baptized ethnic cleansing by journalists covering events in former Yugoslavia. In those countries no one knows what the Europeans might have done, eventually, because America finally intervened to stop the killing. Under the circumstances the American conclusion that the Europeans may have learned that war is terrible is hardly surprising, but they have neither the will to preserve peace nor the power to protect freedom.[29]

In wealthy Western Europe, to which some Americans derisively refer as "paradise," the Europeans are reminded every day of the consequences of war, and therefore of what they do not want to lose again. They recognize the signs in the streams of refugees arriving in the countries of the EU from different parts of central and Eastern Europe and from Russia, escaping both poverty and strife. They see the reminders also in the monuments to those who have been killed, on the lists of those who have died in war and revolution, carved into the stone of their church walls, and in the inscriptions on the tombstones of their cemeteries. Most Europeans recoil at the prospect of war, and when asked to describe it, call it immoral and catastrophic.

European leaders talk about peace as often as Americans talk about freedom. There are two, predictable, results. Americans wonder if Europeans have had the desire to defend themselves bred out of them, and Europeans wonder if Americans are so preoccupied with freedom that they are unable to see that without peace, freedom is not very useful.

Even if Americans and Europeans do not agree, this difference in approach has been put in terms they both can understand:

> Europeans think that Americans are on their way to betraying some of the elementary tenets of the Enlightenment, establishing a new principle in which they are 'first among unequals.'
>
> And Washington accuses Europe of shirking its international responsibilities, and thus its own human rights inheritance.
>
> After all, what is the point of international law if it prevents intervening

in the affairs of a brutal regime to stay the hand of a tyrant? Who is the true advocate of human rights: the one who cites international law to justify standing by while genocide is being committed or the one who puts an end to the genocide, even if it means violating international law?[30]

This fascinating and frustrating difference in attitude, presented by German writer Peter Schneider, can be reduced to a straightforward conclusion: Americans see peace without freedom as bondage, and Europeans see freedom without peace as war. This simplistic logic, however, begins and ends here.

The lessons Europeans have learned from the struggles to wage war, to protect freedom, and to preserve peace are not all black and white, they reflect shades of grey as well. When comparing themselves to Americans, some Europeans observe sarcastically that defending freedom and preserving peace is not like conquering the American west; namely, it is done once and it is over with. Their history has taught them that nothing is ever final, that little is ever what it seems to be, and that the use of force always has unintended consequences. That is why war frightens many Europeans, and why so many of them are willing to go to any length to avoid it, as though a state of peace were an Eleventh Commandment.

Europeans often dismiss the American commitment to "the defense of freedom" as arbitrary and naive, and assert that Americans are ignorant of the consequences of warfare, and therefore foolishly rush into it. They condescendingly explain that wars in which Americans have fought during the last one hundred years have always taken place somewhere else, which by insinuation, makes Americans insensitive to the real horror of warfare. It is true that, with the exceptions of War of 1812, the Civil War, the bombing of Pearl Harbor, and the attack on the World Trade Center, Americans have been spared the tragedies of death and destruction at home. It is also true, however, that when Americans look at their flag they do not see different shades of gray. They see freedom, as trite as it may sound, in the colors of red, white, and blue. They know what they are for, which is why their elected representatives spend a significant portion of American taxes on maintaining the military means to defend America's freedom, and also to defend that of others. This is why it is difficult for Americans to be patient with European condemnation of America's willingness to defend freedom against threat, as though Americans love violence.

Like Americans, Europeans also think in terms of historical experience, but unlike Americans that experience has taught Europeans what they are against, not what they are for. Europeans do not have a Declaration of Independence, or a constitution of liberty, in the sense that American culture and tradition is the idea of freedom. What Europeans do have is a collective memory of war's atrocity, punishment, and sorrow. For ordinary Europeans war means tanks in the streets, and they fear them more than the threat of an asserted axis of evil formed by countries on other continents.

If the foregoing applies to America, what does Europe stand for? The formation of the European Union is one answer to the question. In the spring of 2001 Heide Simonis, then minister-president of the *Land* Schleswig-Holstein in Germany, urged an American audience in New York City to recall Europe's past:

> We have to remember that for 1,500 years, up to 1945, no period of peace in central Europe lasted longer than 30 years. The nations that have now come together in the European Community were constantly at war with one another in various constellations. Then, for 40 years, [the reference is to the period 1949–1989] we had no war in central Europe, but some 500 million people on the Old Continent lived under the threat of a global nuclear confrontation. We were dead certain we would be the battlefield of a potential worldwide conflict between East and West. In the truest sense of the word: *dead certain.*[31]

Several months later, in July, the president of the EU Council of Ministers, Louis Michel of Belgium, was more specific. "It is high time," he cautioned members of the European Parliament, to acknowledge "that Europe stands for peace. . . . We must trumpet the fact that European integration is all about bringing men and women from different countries together for a common cause, making them aware of what united them and giving them a shared destiny."[32]

Both Simonis and Louis Michel expressed a European conviction honestly held, and particularly so by Germans. To Europeans who recalled World War II there was nothing strange or secret about the purpose of the European Union. It was not created to become a rival to the United States. Its overriding purpose was simple and straightforward: to preserve peace by creating an integrated European economic, political, and military union served by common institutions.

Americans note that the Europeans are making agonizingly slow headway in this direction, and are critical of what even some Europeans call moving "at the pace of the slowest camel in the train." But if the Europeans have learned from their experience as well as they assert, they will continue their efforts; hence, they admonish, don't judge a tortoise by its speed. They may sometimes take two steps backward for each step forward, but they will advance on a circuitous path made of European history lessons, just as Americans travel a direct path made of the American experience with the history of freedom.

In that summer of 2001, as Louis Michel held forth on what Europe stands for, it was unlikely that the leaders of the American republic and the architects of the European Union were aware of a little known message to Americans sent by a European in the 1930s. Had they been familiar with it, they might have found it helpful following the eleventh of September when American and European fervor about freedom, peace and war reached new heights.

J. J. Jusserand was married for almost forty years to Elise Richards, an American, from a New England family. He also served as the French ambassador in Washington, D. C., between 1902 and 1925. Shortly before he died in 1933, he sent a letter of "farewell forever" to his American friends:

The sands in the hour-glass are running low; I must take leave, probably forever. May peace, prosperity, happy homes be the meed of your energy,

good sense and kind hearts. When we judge each other we are not bound
to applaud all that the other does, nor even to avoid expressing our blame
when there is cause; but blame must not be peppered with sarcasm and
irony; the tone should be that of the affectionate reproach to a loved
brother. . . . Remember this also, and be well persuaded of its truth: the
future is not in the hands of Fate, but in ours.[33]

CHAPTER VI

The Fly in the Soup

Changing Relationships

I F THERE IS A fly in the soup—and there always is—it comes from us, members in good standing of the human condition. Sometimes active, and at other times passive, the fly in the soup never plays the same role twice, but it is always there, in one way or another when we converse and consort with each other. Often it can be seen in how we form, interpret, and manage our relationships. It is frequently contained in our opinions, heard in the tone we use to express them, and present in how we listen. And, it is always set forth in the conclusion, drawn by the Duc de La Rochefoucauld in the seventeenth century, that we as human beings seldom meet other people of good sense, unless of course, they share our opinion.

Rochefoucauld's conclusion, as it applies to past flies in the soup, also describes the most recent arrival, known as "globalization"—that is to say, the international arena of trade and commerce, industry and manufacturing, finance and investment, stock markets and banking, knowledge and services, politics and peacekeeping, diplomacy and defense, terrorism and national security. In fact, however, it is not globalization itself that is affecting our relationship, but our different reactions to it. As one French political commentator observed in late 2006, "of all the globalizations it is that of Islamic Fundamentalism that has proved the most successful, at the very time that Europeans and Americans are drifting apart."[1]

In America, globalization is discussed as representing new challenges and new opportunities, as well as new threats. In the EU, the word is used similarly by some Europeans, but not by others. The result is confusion. There is general consensus in America and Europe that national marketplaces are operating today, perforce, in an international arena defined by global competition; but there is not agreement on either its desirability or its significance.

The view endorsed by those Americans and Europeans who believe in the efficacy of free markets was put into words, perfectly, by the president of the European Commission in September 2005, in an article published in the *International Herald Tribune* entitled "Europe must open up to the globalized world":

> In the new, global century, change takes place at a breathtaking speed. We must manage this change, not try to resist it. In order to promote freedom, security and prosperity, we need to reap, not reject, the benefits of globalization. . . .
>
> We can respond more effectively together than apart. The EU has the scale, with 450 million [479 million, as of 2007] people, and the means. We must have the confidence, energy and determination to act, because the world will not stop for Europe.[2]

Barroso's concerns were shared by many other European leaders as well, including the new, conservative chancellor of Germany, Angela Merkel, the socialist prime minister of the U.K., Tony Blair, and the prime minister of Denmark, Anders Fogh Rasmussen. But there are also those who react to the world of the twenty-first century in a different way; to wit, the conclusion drawn by the prime minister of France following defeat of the European constitution at the end of May 2005: "Globalization is not an ideal; it cannot be our destiny."

So employed, globalization is a catchy word for an old fly in the soup; namely, *the essential difference*. However the word may be used, it is nonetheless a twenty-first-century description of a history of discoveries, occurring one after another and often at long intervals, that has been going on for five hundred years. The latest event is the invention of a worldwide web of communication, one of whose incidental casualties is the death of the information monopoly used by European politicians for centuries to manage rule from the top down. In a little-known book[3] published in 2000, globalization's progression was summarized as follows:

> This web represents a further shrinkage of the world's cultures that has been going on since the Age of Discovery, when the seeds of a global economy were sown for both goods and ideas. Since the 1500s the process of amalgamation of the world into one intellectual and commercial enterprise has been rapidly accelerating. This contraction has been made possible by physical and electronic travel via ships and navies, automobiles and airplanes, telegrams and telephones, radio waves and television broadcasting, fax machines and satellites, and today by the convergence of computers with telecommunication.
>
> Before the Age of Discovery the first part of human history was expansion outward, from the original human homeland into every corner of the globe, where unique cultures developed to fit into local environments. Since then the increasingly sophisticated modes of transportation and communication that enable goods and ideas to move across the seas, earth, and sky, have been gradually redefining the human adventure. What is now changing is the speed with which ideas and commerce travel about the world, whether they concern astronomy or physics, fashion or food, engineering or computing, stock markets or financial markets. In the year 2000, ideas and wealth move in real time via the Internet. The Internet gives a quantum leap to this process of acceleration. This is nothing less that a revolutionary change.[4]

What we are witnessing today is a product of evolution, which is always affected by revolution at unpredictable intervals. Taken together the cumulative power is huge. The issue is not whether we wish to accept or reject globalization as our destiny, because the choice is not ours to make. It has already been made for us by the force of things.

American and European efforts to deal with our constantly changing world accent and reinforce our transatlantic differences and affinities in various ways. In this sense globalization does not mean we stop behaving like Americans and Europeans, but it does mean that our relationships become intensely more private, more professional, more public, and more complex. Nor does globalization replace our history, our heritage, or our habits of life, but it does mean we must pay greater attention to protecting our faith in the value of what we have in common, forged not by politicians in time of need, but created by individual Americans and Europeans over the course of centuries.

Our relationship is made of many things. A very public part of it, of course, is about how we deal with each other on diplomatic levels. An equally important but much less visible aspect concerns the private and professional lives of millions of Americans and Europeans bound together in a multitude of ways. Some of these connections come from the ties formed by trade and commerce; others come from educational exchanges, and unexpected ones arrive daily via the continuing revolution in computer and communication technology.

The oldest connections were created by European explorers, and the newest ones are made of millions of electronic messages flying across the Atlantic each day. During the intervening five centuries our universe has become one of accelerated time and shortened distance, and also more complex, as the ties we share have drawn us closer.

☙❧

Communication between America and Europe has never been easier. The great oceanic divide no longer poses the transportation problems it once did, either. A visit to Europe or to America is still an adventure, but it is much easier to get there and it takes a fraction of the time it took before World War II. During 2000–2001 more Europeans and Americans than ever before—twenty-four million traveling back and forth across the Atlantic Ocean—visited one another: approximately thirteen million Americans to Europe, and more than eleven million Europeans to America.

The close nature is reflected in the hundreds of weekly airplane flights between Europe and America, in passenger and freight ship traffic, in thousands of daily telephone calls, and in the number of packages that travel back and forth for anniversaries, birthdays, and holidays. E-mail communication generates more than 1.5 billion messages sent between America and Europe each day, just as thousands of Americans and Europeans exchange information, continuously, on the Internet.

The extent of the European-American commercial relationship is staggering, just as the vastly different kinds of companies involved are fascinating. Most Americans, as well as Europeans, are surely unaware that such well-known European car brands as Aston Martin, Volvo, Jaguar, and Land Rover are actually owned by one of Detroit's "Big Three," the Ford Motor Company, although many Americans know that another of Detroit's "Big Three" is owned by Daimler-Chrysler of Stuttgart.

The famous *American Heritage Dictionary* is a property of the French corporation Vivendi and RCA Records is owned by the German company Bertelsmann. American corporations are just as well represented in Europe via McDonald's hamburgers, Starbucks coffee, and the clothing manufacturer Gap. And that point has a counterpoint. American clothiers Brooks Brothers and Casual Corner are owned by an Italian conglomerate, Burger King belongs to a British firm, and Nestle SA of Switzerland owns Taster's Choice coffee and Dreyer's Ice Cream, a company founded in California. Another example is Holiday Inn, the quintessential American success story of the creation of a motel chain, started in the early 1950s. It takes its name from the 1942 film of the same name, in which Bing Crosby sang "White Christmas" for the first time; but the owner is a British firm.[5]

The interrelationship is also found on college and university campuses, where a major component of European and American academic life consists of visits and exchanges of all kinds. European and American students study at each other's universities and American and European professors teach and conduct research in the humanities and sciences at those same institutions. Of the top ten countries where Americans study abroad, European countries account for six of those places, and the top three are the United Kingdom, Italy, and Spain. Of the nearly 600,000 international students—many of them European—enrolled at approximately 125 American colleges and universities, 70 percent of them pay their own way. During 2003 they contributed over $13 billion to the American economy and made up 4 percent of total enrollment.[6]

Ties are also defined by the impact of trade and investment; that is to say, the American-European business dealings that result in capital expenditures, in jobs, and in the movement of goods back and forth between countries. Each year America sends one-third of its exports to the European Union, 25 percent of the EU's exports arrive in America, and more than thirteen million Europeans and Americans go abroad to work for companies on both continents. In 2000, according to the U.S. Department of Commerce, American direct investment in Europe was about 650 billion dollars, and European investment in America amounted to almost 900 billion dollars. Americans and Europeans share 50 percent of the global economy, and engage in annual trade and investment in excess of 1.5 trillion dollars.[7]

There are numerous observations on the character of this relationship. One of them, made long ago, is the conclusion attributed to John D. Rockefeller that "friendships founded on business work better than businesses founded on friendship." Another, of more recent date, comes from the president of the French American Chamber of Commerce in Paris who noted in February 2003 that the economies of America and Europe are "so closely intertwined that trying to take measures against the other would be equivalent to shooting oneself in the foot."

Our trade and commerce are thriving, in spite of our sometimes differing views on globalization. There is, however, another fly in the soup which may prove more disruptive. American and European memories of what we have in common, and of why it is important, are fading, and for some they do not exist at all. For many in Europe knowledge of the connection between Christian humanism and the continent's cultural identity is imperfect, and for many others it is irrelevant. And, for many in America, the unique tie between Christianity and democracy, so eloquently described by Tocqueville, is all but forgotten.

In the course of the last thirty years it has become popular for some in America to denigrate the impact of Europe on the New World as debatable at best, and as exploitative at worst. Some have chosen to conduct protests against observance of Columbus Day. Others describe the history and philosophy of European civilization as the legacy of "dead, white males," and assert that their contributions are no longer germane to a world of diversity. Indeed, in many textbooks used in American secondary schools, the history of Europe and America is described as one of oppression and invasion, while the history of Islam, for example, is described as one of expansion and social mobility.[8]

As the American melting pot continues to boil, there is less and less attention to European history and culture, and simultaneously more and more criticism of Europeans. Younger Americans have little knowledge of the instrumental role played by the French in the American War of Independence and know equally little about their own history between the eighteenth and twentieth centuries. As a consequence, an increasing number of American students cannot present an intelligible explanation of European influences on the making of America.

The same point applies to younger Europeans as well. During the ceremonies commemorating the sixtieth anniversary of the Allied landing in Normandy, held in France in June 2004, French political analyst Dominique Moïsi was stunned to hear French high school students discuss whether the Battle of Normandy had been an American invasion or an American liberation, as though it were a legitimate question. "It was," he wrote, "the first troubling sign of the deterioration of the knowledge and understanding of the past. . . . What can the future of transatlantic relations be if the past is not taught properly in France, and European history is completely ignored in the United States?"[9]

From the vantage point of our respective backyards Moïsi's question has frightening implications. Without a knowledge of our history, our heritage, and our habits of life, current events have no context. Without a historical context, events have no meaning. They float, aimlessly, on a sea of ignorance, and when they collide the damage can be severe. The appearance of this fly in the soup, whose character is made of disaffection, is recent, and also ironic in the American-European world where the quality of education and enlightenment have always been matters of pride.

The transatlantic community seemed extraordinarily strong in the days following the terrorist attack on America of September 11, 2001. European newspapers assured their readers that, "We are all Americans now," and millions of Europeans genuinely felt that way. That conclusion had a historical context. It was about supporting each other in a time of need.

In the weeks that followed, however, such sentiments were gradually replaced with headlines of criticism; if you will, with the reappearance of an old fly in the soup named "discord." There was less talk about amity, and more about what Americans and Europeans disliked about each other. Many Europeans and Americans watching this transformation, both political leaders and private citizens, began actively to contribute to it. In tone and tenor their sarcastic speeches and ironic letters to the editor suggested a dialogue of the deaf. Were Europeans and Americans really listening to each other? Some drew attention to the values that Europe and America have in common. But few mentioned the obvious point that friends who enjoy each other's respect and trust do not always agree. Was this because our historical memory had become so short? Or, because Americans and Europeans really saw the world so differently?

Some Americans thought the answer was yes to both questions, and one of them, Robert Kagan, wrote a simplistic, but provocative essay about it in the summer of 2002. It was entitled "Power and Weakness" and began with the premise that "it is time to stop pretending that Europeans and Americans share a common view of the world, or even that they occupy the same world." Kagan summed up "today's transatlantic problems" as "a power problem;" namely, that "American military strength has produced a propensity to use that strength. Europe's military weakness has produced a perfectly understandable aversion to the exercise of military power."[10]

The superficial merits of the comparison notwithstanding, American military power is not synonymous with being the indispensable nation. Many Americans and Europeans are well aware that they occupy the same world, and that they have seldom seen it through the same lens. But even though Americans and Europeans have not always shared the same views, and have not always pursued the same goals, they have always recognized that differences of opinion are not the same thing as irreconcilable divides.

Until that is, after September 11, 2001. Since then something new has emerged. It is growing discordance, propelled forward by ignorance, jealousy, arrogance, and mistrust. It has led some to ask whether Americans and Europeans have forgotten why we are partners and friends, and others to observe, from commanding and sometimes neoconservative analytical heights, that the differences cannot be resolved.

Kagan concluded his essay with the observation that, ". . . it is more than a cliché that the United States and Europe share a set of common Western beliefs. Their aspirations for humanity are much the same, even if their vast disparity of power has now put them in very different places. Perhaps it is not too naively optimistic to believe that a little common understanding could still go a long way." Indeed, it is not naively optimistic. But arriving at "a little common understanding" requires a little common knowledge, and the willingness to listen. Both seem to be in short supply in America and Europe.

The European-American relationship is not made of just two elements called power and weakness. It is made of many things which fit together in complicated ways. An accurate measure was taken in a speech in Wilton Park, England in January 2000, well before the acrimony about who is strong and who is weak, and perhaps in response to mounting criticism in Europe that America was becoming a "hyper-power." The measure was offered by then U.S. ambassador to NATO Alexander Vershbow, an American with European ancestors. "Democratic Europe and North America are bound together," he said, "as no other two regions in the world. We are inextricably linked in a fortunate tangle of kinship, society, science, letters and commerce. Our remarkably similar values and world views would inevitably bind us. The relevant reality is this: We and you— North America and Europe—could not extricate ourselves from each other's intellectual, cultural, business and national lives at this point even if we wanted to."

Vershbow's views were, and are shared by many Americans and Europeans. In Europe the "Atlanticists," as they are sometimes known, believe in a European Union with strong political, economic, and military insti-

tutions that complement those of America, rather than serving as a rival
to them. Together, as friends and allies who hold each other in high regard, the Atlanticists argue that Europe and America have both independent and joint roles to play in technological advancement, the promotion
of human rights, the development of free markets, the settlement of international conflicts, in defending freedom against tyranny, and in contributing to the preservation of peace.

On the American side of the Atlantic they believe in a strong America
that leads judiciously and decisively, together with Europe, that earns respect as a consequence of responsible behavior and prudent conduct. Although from today's perspective it may seem like a long time ago,
President George Bush put it very well during his visit to Warsaw in June
2001, shortly before Heidi Simonis was getting ready to deliver her speech
in New York City about peace in Europe. "Our goal," Bush said, "is to
replace the false lines that have divided Europe for too long. . . . My
nation welcomes the consolidation of European unity and the stability it
brings. . . . And all in Europe and America understand the central lesson
of the century past. When Europe and America are divided history tends
to tragedy. When Europe and America are partners, no trouble or tyranny
can stand against us."[11]

If the conclusion has not lost any of its validity—and it was reiterated
by both American and European leaders during President Bush's visit to
Europe in February 2005—what are the reasons for existing unhappiness?

Interpreting September 11, 2001

Following the attack on the World Trade Center and on the Pentagon,
the American government rewrote the rules governing national security.
In the parlance of the defense analyst, this meant an unprecedented re-
evaluation of American threat perceptions, military structures, and strategic doctrine. In the language of the historian, it meant that America's
response to the unprovoked attack was declaration of an unconditional
"war on terrorism," to begin in Afghanistan. It was a response that, initially, found overwhelming support in Europe, part of which included

fighter aircraft sorties flown by Dutch and French pilots.[12] The ensuing consequences for the terrorists of the Al Qaeda network were devastating. But there were also unexpected consequences for the Atlantic alliance.

By December 2001 the Taliban had been defeated in Afghanistan. "As a mirror of the American capacity for reaction to unforeseen crisis," wrote the Paris daily *Le Monde*, "the events of Sept. 11 have provided grounds for astonishment. . . . By comparison, Europe appears to be a giant ensnared in its own rules and procedures."[13] Less clear, however, was whether Europeans had understood how the American government, and millions of Americans, interpreted the assault on their freedom.

Explanations were available in Europe. The majority of them contained the same judgment: Americans were in a state of shock. One such conclusion came from an Englishman with many friends in America, Christopher Patten, who was also EU commissioner for external affairs. In early 2002 he explained that the Europeans did not "fully comprehend the impact of a grand innocence and a sense of magnificent self-confidence and invulnerability being shattered in that appalling way."[14] A year and a half later the same point was still being made by a distinguished professor in Paris, Pierre Hassner. He argued that the new and notable difference between America and Europe was that America now recognized it was no longer a sanctuary, in contrast to Europe, which had long since become accustomed to its vulnerability.[15]

These two, related interpretations made it much easier for Europeans to condemn what they considered to be precipitous and unilateral American behavior, and to criticize America for its naiveté in contrast to Europe's worldly wisdom. Novelist John le Carré did both by writing in *The Times* of London in early 2003 that "America has entered one of its periods of historic madness, but this is the worst I can remember."[16] This conclusion appealed to a great many Europeans, but found little sympathy with Americans.

Not only had American freedom been violated, but so had the freedom of all those who had died in Pennsylvania, in Washington, D.C., and in New York City, men and women from at least seventy different countries.

It is true that many Americans were appalled that anyone, even terrorists, would want to kill innocent people in such a barbaric way, but American reaction was not one of shock.

Americans were furious. Their reaction was an aspect of the American character that few non-Americans have ever understood well.[17] A notable exception was Winston Churchill, whose words captured perfectly that certain trait of the American spirit: "The United States is like a gigantic boiler. Once the fire is lit under it, there's no limit to the power it can generate." The last fire had been started by the unprovoked Japanese attack on Pearl Harbor on December 7, 1941. The attack on September 11, 2001, also ignited a fire, and was similarly a fatal miscalculation. Americans were not prepared to stand idly by and let terrorists strike again. So they took steps to combat it. Americans considered themselves in a war being waged against freedom, and intended to remain at war until they defeated the enemy. In so doing life was given to another American proclivity. John le Carré had called it a period of "historic madness," but those who knew Americans well recognized it as a view of the world in which good is pitted against evil, and expressed in terms of, "either you are with us, or you are against us."

Often critical of Americans for focusing on the short term, many Europeans who had only met Americans via television did not recognize that American outrage also reflected a limitless capacity to right what they see as wrongs against them. Americans began by immediately taking great comfort in publicly supporting each other as one out of many, of which the appearance of millions of American flags throughout the country was a symbol. It was an instinctive reaction and not, as some Europeans suggested, a "politically correct" response or an attempt to restore confidence in Wall Street's financial prowess.

There was, however, misunderstanding in America as well. Some Americans misinterpreted the initial outpouring of sympathy and support from Europe, and assumed that the Europeans were just as angry. That was evident, so it was assumed, in their immediate response. The first

European head of state to visit the twin towers' site, almost at once, was the president of France, Jacques Chirac.

In Germany Chancellor Schröder addressed the Bundestag to express "unconditional solidarity" with America, eulogized New York City as the world's "symbol of refuge," and won parliamentary approval to send German forces to fight with American forces in Afghanistan. It was the first deployment of German troops outside of Europe since the end of World War II—a decision of monumental import for the Germans, but whose significance went unrecognized by the American government and unnoticed by Americans. Moreover, and not unsurprisingly given America's defense of Berlin, thousands of Berliners demonstrated at the Brandenburg Gate to express their support. In addition, German businesses as well as individuals contributed, almost immediately, the enormous sum of $42 million to help survivors and aid families of victims.[18]

Misunderstanding was further complicated by the reaction of the American government to NATO's response. The alliance invoked Article 5 of its treaty for the first time in its history, the article which considers an attack against one member an attack against all. The European members prepared a list of military responsibilities they could confidently undertake during the first phrase of the war against terrorism in Afghanistan. But the American government's gratitude was not as enthusiastic as European leaders may have expected.

Some American national security advisors maligned the offer, explaining that Europe's limited military capabilities would not be much help. Others argued that Europe's offer "was a ruse to tie America down." "The Bush administration," wrote Robert Kagan, "viewed NATO's historic decision to aid the United States under Article V less as a boon than as a booby trap. An opportunity to draw Europe into common battle . . . even in a minor role, was thereby unnecessarily lost."[19] It was a gratuitous and short-sighted policy decision, but a response consistent with a view of the world that is black and white.

In the event, American and European military forces joined together in the effort to destroy the Taliban and the Al Qaeda network in Afghanistan. It began in the late autumn of 2001 and would continue for many years. But European views of how to deal with terrorism's long-term threat to freedom were mixed.

During 2002, as American officials began developing the rationale for an invasion of Iraq, European doubts expressed about the wisdom of going to war in the Middle East were seen by Americans as betrayal. They believed that America's new national security strategy was reasonable, morally just, and deserved unequivocal European support. Produced by the American president's National Security Council, it was made publicly available on the Internet in the autumn of 2002. The policy was based on two propositions: (1) America's responsibility for homeland security obligated it to take aggressive action, in coalitions with others or alone if necessary, "to create a balance of power that favors human freedom: conditions in which all nations and all societies can choose for themselves the rewards and challenges of political and economic liberty," and (2) America's unmatched military power presented a unique opportunity for the expansion of freedom throughout the world, and therefore, implied an imperative to shape a new American century.

These propositions assumed that threats could not be managed by conventional containment and deterrence, and, further, that the war on terrorism could not be won "on the defensive," but must be taken to those who would attack America, or any other country. This approach reflected the American conclusion that the issue was black and white; that is to say, terrorists needed to be taught a lesson. The concept of deterrence was based on an expanded arsenal of options, which included using preemptive attack as a weapon of defense. Embedded in this policy was the assumption that America's European allies would agree with the conclusions and support the strategy's implementation.

Also contained in this approach, however, were seeds which could divide the Atlantic alliance. The purpose of the strategy was to eliminate terrorism with military force, not to intensify discussions with Europe about the various faces of the threat, many of which Europeans thought were shrouded in different shades of gray. Nor were the recommendations developed by the National Security Council the result of an American-

European agreement on what constituted dangers to freedom and peace, and how to react to them.

Equally serious was that the Europeans faced two dilemmas of their own making. In their effort to stand for peace in a united Europe, they had let their own military capabilities grow weak. Their minimal defense expenditures limited military options, and weakened their ability to provide convincing leadership. As one journalist later put it, Europeans want "to maintain the role they have long enjoyed—leading the world debate. But without the power to back up your perspective, such leadership can prove elusive."[20]

The Europeans thus produced their second dilemma. They did not share a common vision. There were at least three, in Berlin, London, and Paris. Americans saw within the European Union independent and assertive European countries that wanted to be equal partners in consultation and decision, but which did not speak with one voice. The debate among Europeans stood in counterpoint to the American preference to define clear alternatives between what is right and what is wrong, and then to choose one or the other. Failure to act, most Americans believed, was inherently more dangerous than taking a false step—and they saw this view corroborated in the history of war and peace in Europe. The result was not only acrimony within the European house, but a once whole Atlantic alliance was pulled apart as well.

That seeds of discontent sprouted was inevitable. The reaction from Europe's intellectuals was entirely in keeping with their response to the East-West confrontation during the Cold War. Their principal contention, which they considered morally beyond reproach, was that the new threat to peace was not terrorism, but America's response to it. Others in Europe, such as Sir Roy Denman, former ambassador of the European Commission in Washington, D.C., held very different views. In mid-2002 he concluded that "the Europeans have no influence because they have no policy," and suggested that there were three lessons the Europeans had not yet learned:

Unless it gets its act together it will not count. It needs to stop lecturing
Americans on why they should behave like Europeans. And European leaders should spend less time with worldly State Department folk and more
with businessmen, the Congress and grassroots America.[21]

A related consequence was that the most important dysfunctional organization in the world, the United Nations, was locked in disagreement. Still
another was a selective and insulting personalization of differences by Europeans and Americans alike. As the disagreement bore upon relations
between France and America, a British commentator called the disaffection exactly what it was, a tragedy: "If each of the world's two great republics," he wrote, "has come to view the other as not so much misguided as
insane, it is the result of a decade in which the two countries grew more
and more alike, and more and more sympathetic, to the point where
nothing short of mass murder could pull them apart."[22]

The antidialogue—that is to say, Americans and Europeans steadfastly
refusing to listen to each other—continued during 2002 and into 2003.
Americans, to a significant degree, asserted that they understood the real
threat terrorism posed in the post–Cold War world, and that those Europeans who did not agree, failed to understand. When American leaders
discussed the merits of preemptive war the primary issue in the immediate
term was where to use massive military power, not whether it was justified
nor whether a combination of other options should be pursued first.
When some European governments endorsed the approach, and others
rejected it as premature, various European and American leaders began to
draw the disingenuous conclusion that fundamental differences divided
"New Europe" from "Old Europe" and "Old Europe" from America.

   In America there was little room for opposing views in early 2003. In
mid-February the lead editorial in the *Wall Street Journal* summed up the
prevailing mood vis-à-vis the American-European alliance:

If this is what the U.S. gets from NATO, maybe it's time America considered leaving this Cold War institution and reforming an alliance of nations

that understand the new threats to world order. . . . the Cold War is over, and the main threat to the West now is global terrorism employing nuclear and bioweapons. If NATO cannot adapt to this reality by moving its resources to meet that threat, then as currently constructed it has outlived its usefulness. What President Bush calls a "coalition of the willing" will become American's new security alliance.[23]

By the time the war began in Iraq in mid-March 2003 the debate between America and "Old Europe" was far more than just joined.[24] It had moved on to the level of concluding statements. Many Americans, both in and out of government, had decided that an alliance whose members were divided was no longer useful. More important, however, was the reason why it was divided. This was a factor of greater weight which British foreign minister Jack Straw, writing in March 2003, defined as an "indictment of European military capabilities." "For more than a decade," he wrote, "—with the notable exceptions of France and Britain—most European defense budgets have fallen below 2 percent of gross national product. . . . The alliance will flourish only as long as both sides of the Atlantic shoulder the burden."[25]

Straw's "indictment" was the crux of the issue. In 2002 America's defense budget, in dollar terms, was almost double that of the twenty-five other NATO members combined. America had spent 3.5 percent of its gross domestic product on defense, followed by Britain at 2.5 percent and France at 2.4 percent. The defense budgets of the remaining twenty-two members were all below 2.0 percent. In 2006 American defense spending was almost 40 percent of the world's total, seven times larger than that of China.[26]

From the American viewpoint the Europeans did not have the power to deter aggression and preserve peace, and therefore had no choice but to embrace diplomacy and negotiation as the principal tools of national security. The Europeans were lauding one history lesson—that war always produces tragic and unexpected consequences—and ignoring another—that effective diplomacy must be backed up with credible military power and the willingness to use it.

This state of affairs suggested two changing relationships: (1) in the view of many Americans and of some Europeans, Europe could not play a significant role in maintaining peace, either on the continent or elsewhere in the world, and (2) America would be forced by European default to play an ever greater role in the future. Europeans would continue to resent what they were already criticizing as "the American century," and Americans would continue to deride what they saw as arrogance born of European weakness. Some Europeans would find it deceptively tempting to brand America as the legitimate successor to Russian imperialism, while others would unreservedly share American commitment to the defense of freedom.

The result, in turn, would be twofold. Europeans would be divided by opinion rather than by an iron curtain, and America and Europe would be divided by two very different interpretations of the paths that lead to freedom and peace. Some Europeans would eventually call America's leader "the warrior president . . . [resembling] no one more than Kaiser Wilhelm II, the self-described supreme warlord."[27] And some Americans would eventually conclude, "that so long as Europe tries to build itself into a sort of soft superpower, using such things as declarations of principle and diplomacy to exert its influence rather than military might, a lot of Americans are just not going to take it very seriously."[28]

The seesaw of recrimination recalled, for some, Winston Churchill's admonition that "the only thing worse than fights with Allies is fighting without them,"[29] and suggested to others that Americans and Europeans would be wise to spend more time discussing a common vision and less time on divisive rhetoric. But to find a common vision would require agreement on common objectives, if there were any, and the willingness to devote equal attention to their pursuit. It would also require mutual respect for our differences and cultivation of our affinities. The success of such an effort, if it were to be undertaken, would depend on the strength of leadership provided in America and in Europe.

CHAPTER VII

The Force of Things

Aspects of Leadership

IN EARLY 2002, in both America and Europe, leadership appeared ·
on the diplomatic stage in the form of appallingly bad manners. The
display of unbalanced judgment lasted more than three years, as a
healthy segment of European and American media, fed with the observations of patronizing intellectual, educational and government leaders,
successfully personalized transatlantic differences. There were no beneficiaries, but there were many casualties.

Their public statements, phrased in a way which both common sense
and civility would normally preclude as unacceptable, insulted our intelli-
gence and belittled the values we have in common. Possibly these public
figures believed that their tough talk, their telling-it-like-it-is, were aspects
of leadership. But their abrasiveness weakened the merit of their positions,
focused attention where it did not belong, and set a contagious example.
Many Americans and Europeans found the use of invective inexcusable,
but fewer found the courage to condemn publicly behavior which, by any
standard, was childish, irresponsible, and rude.

The period of contention produced, in addition to exasperation and
disappointment, self-serving conclusions that did linguistic violence to
history's lessons. A duplicitous example occurred in the autumn of 2002.
After assuring American president Bush, on two occasions, that he would
not make a German electoral issue of American policy toward Iraq, Chancellor Schröder publicly accused Bush of "adventurism." During the same

campaign Germany's minister of justice, Herta Däubler-Gmelin, asserted that Bush's contemplation of war against Iraq was designed to divert attention from American domestic problems, and compared his leadership to that of Adolf Hitler. The minister was subsequently forced to resign; but the German illustration was not unique in Europe, nor was this practice confined to the continent.

Incredulous Americans also excelled at the use of ridicule. Critics in Belgium, France, and Germany who opposed preemptive war against Iraq were described in America as an "axis of weasels." The countries themselves were described as "EU-nuchs" and the French as "cheese-eating surrender monkeys." To take matters from the ridiculous to the absurd, the name "French fries" on congressional restaurant menus was changed to "Freedom fries," while officials at the French embassy observed that French fries were actually a Belgian invention. Meanwhile, Americans, exhibiting inventive but illogical behavior, purchased French wine and then poured it into the streets in front of French government diplomatic offices.[1]

California congressman Tom Lantos, a Hungarian immigrant and a member of the Democratic Party, declared that French and German failure to "honor their [NATO] commitments is beneath contempt," and accused them of "blind intransigence and utter ingratitude" for their rescue by Americans from Hitler and Stalin. The American secretary of defense, Donald Rumsfeld, in dismissing Belgium, France and Germany as "Old Europe," pronounced the Franco-German position a "disgrace," praised those European countries supporting the American position as members of "New Europe," and compared Germany's stance on Iraq with that of Cuba and Libya. Not to be outdone, Robert Kagan, who had coined the power-versus-weakness comparison, wrote in the autumn of 2002 that France found it "more fun to play Don Quixote, tilting at American windmills."[2] And, to deliver what he undoubtedly thought was the *coup de grâce*, Richard Perle, at the time chairman of the advisory U.S. Defense Policy Board, recommended at a conference in Munich in early February 2003 that America "should come up with an anti-French strategy." His proposal did not contain the disclosure that he owned vacation property in France.[3] Almost four years later, in an article published in a leading French newspaper, Perle wondered why the sentiment expressed in *Le Monde* after September 11—"We are all Americans now"—had disappeared. Answering his own question, in effect, he concluded his article with the insulting and incorrect observation that the Europeans, "in their 'wisdom,' prefer words to action and the status quo to democratic progress."[4]

༺∾⋎∽༻

Americans did not appreciate European comparisons of American leadership with Nazi dictatorship, especially coming from Germany. Nor did they find amusing European claims that American military power posed a greater threat to peace than the tyranny practiced by Saddam Hussein. And they took special offense to the desecration of graves of American and British soldiers buried on French soil, as well as to French public opinion polls which indicated that one-third of the French population hoped Iraq would win the war.

As always, however, the coin had two sides. In this case, the verso was described in a private letter from a longtime French friend of my wife. She was able to keep both her humor and her sense of balance when she wrote in March 2003 from Brussels:

> We admire those French who adopted the attitude of an old dog [France] persecuted by a young puppy [America], jumping around, biting ears-nose-tail, while the old dog patiently accepted those tortures and waited until the young puppy would either fall of exhaustion and things to bite, or reflect on how much biting an old dog could stand. Nevertheless, the war in Iraq has brought out to light hard feelings. No mutual love was wasted. It was a slap in the face for France, who thinks that she's always right in whatever she does, and is thus loved by everyone—*voila, l'exception Française*! [There it is, the French exception!]. Little does she realise that others are not only throwing Beaujolais in the gutter—it was a bad year—but what she represents is sometimes pure *merde* [*shit*]. Sorry! Personally, I think this "happening" did a lot of good for us all. Now everyone knows where they stand, and what mistakes should not be repeated. Chirac went overboard, but Bush worries us here.[5]

In early April 2003 the tone and tenor of the time were summarized well by former German chancellor Helmut Kohl in an interview with the German newspaper *Die Welt*. "Comments out of Washington," he said, "by individual Secretaries, like that of 'Old Europe' are just as foolish as European comments about 'the Texas cowboy who shoots from the hip.' Sometimes the Americans' view of Europe and the Europeans' view of America are really dim-witted."[6]

His point was well taken and was prompted by many strident voices and presumptuous conclusions. Among them, undoubtedly, was Robert Kagan's artful but fatuous observation that on questions of "major strategic and international" importance today, "Americans are from Mars and Europeans are from Venus."[7] The difference in outlook, he wrote, does "not spring naturally from the national characters of Americans and Europeans." Rather, he argued that Europe has a greater tolerance for threat because it is militarily weak, and conversely, America can threaten because it is powerful. Power gives America the ability to lead. Weakness means the Europeans cannot. So Kagan concluded that "if Europe's strategic culture today places less value on power and military strength and more value on such soft-power tools as economics and trade, isn't it partly because Europe is militarily weak and economically strong?"[8]

The unmistakable admonition was that if the Europeans would only "get it," to use the vernacular, everything would be in order. In other words if the Europeans understood the world as it really is, and not as they would like it to be, they would build up their military power to match that of America. But, so argued Kagan, the Europeans did not get it: "Just as Americans have always believed that they had discovered the secret to human happiness and wished to export it to the rest of the world, so the Europeans have a new mission born of their own discovery of perpetual peace."[9]

The frank observation that Americans possess an open "secret" called freedom is well known at home and abroad. Less persuasive, however, is the assertion that the Europeans have a new mission. It sounds clever, but it rings hollow. Europeans are not on a messianic crusade to bring the world perpetual peace any more than Americans are on a perpetual quest for truth. If the Irish, or Spaniards, or those who live in the Balkans, were congratulated by the Secretary General of the United Nations on their new mission, born of their own discovery of perpetual peace, they would respond in disbelief, and say, "What mission? We're still dealing with religious feuds, separatist movements and ethnic cleansing."

The important issue has less to do with missions and more to do with questions. Do Europeans believe that there is no connection between military weakness and strong leadership? With a huge discrepancy in military power separating them can Europeans and Americans continue to lead together, as they have in the past? Do they even want to?

Whether they want to or not is a rhetorical question, because their political and economic strengths thrust responsibilities of leadership upon them, irrespective of whether they are militarily powerful or militarily weak. The real concern is how they want to lead and with what means. Europe and America enjoy a historical regard as imposing figures on the world's stage. They already know that power comes not only from the idea of freedom, but also from the means and the will to protect it. What makes this knowledge valuable for both is that Americans and Europeans acquired it together in the course of the twentieth century. But it is valuable only if they remember it, if they recall that all of history's lessons are important, not just those which support emotional and self-serving judgments.

If Americans and Europeans want to draw on the strengths of their shared historical experiences, they must do so together. They must also agree that the value of military power depends on having it at their disposal, as well as on what they do with it. Then, they must be able to rely on each other. Without that assurance the American-European partnership is made of clay, the friendship is built on sand, and the alliance is not worth the paper it is written on.

Among the greatest possessions belonging to the Old World and to the New World is our common heritage of Western civilization, the majesty of our freedom and the integrity of our trust, affection and respect. It is true that trust, affection, and respect are not weapons in a military arsenal, but without them how effective, in the long term, will be the use of our military power in defense of Western civilization?

As American philosopher Sidney Hook was fond of pointing out, especially to economists, at the heart of policy are values. What we believe determines what we do. If we limit the definition of what unites or divides us to the naive belief that matters of policy are merely a question of who is militarily powerful and who is weak, we will always see the world in black and white. This blind vision limits our choices and weakens our leadership.

The strength of what Americans and Europeans have in common gives both a powerful incentive to renew our concentration on a vision for the future. In doing so we would be well counseled to keep in mind a sense of history. It is not our respective histories that create our difficulties, but our failure to remember the lessons they have taught us. The countries with the richest future of freedom, with peace, and with the means to defend both, are not countries that moralize and then regret. They are the countries whose distinguishing hallmark is great leadership, whose politicians understand that peace alone is not a policy. They are the countries with not only the longest memories, but the countries whose leaders understand that power does not only come out of the barrel of a gun.

This was the distinguishing standard left by then-candidate George W. Bush during the second presidential campaign debate of 2000. He was talking about confronting anti-Americanism: "It really depends on how our nation conducts itself in foreign policy. If we're an arrogant nation, they'll resent us. If we're a humble nation, but strong, they'll welcome us." Two years later, however, in August 2002, a pro-American human rights activist in Sri Lanka made an observation which many of America's friends had come to share in Europe, and elsewhere: "America as an idea, as a source of optimism and as a beacon of liberty is critical to the world— but you Americans seem to have forgotten that since 9/11. You've stopped talking about who you are, and are only talking now about who you're going to invade, oust or sanction."[10]

There is a lesson here, for America. It is about wise leadership so well expressed by an American president Theodore Roosevelt, more than one hundred years ago, and echoed a century later by George W. Bush. Roosevelt's adage is beyond challenge. There is the wisdom of both diplomacy and defense in speaking softly and carrying a big stick. But the advice is only helpful if all of it is followed.[11]

In turn another conclusion also has merit, and provides a lesson as well, for Europe. Classicist and historian Victor Davis Hanson argues that "the U.S. cannot remain a true ally of a militarily weak but shrill Europe should its politics grow even more resentful and neutralist, always nursing old wounds and new conspiracies, amoral in its inability to act, quite ready to preach to those who do."[12] If, indeed, that Europe exists which Hanson describes, there is no hereafter for the American-European alliance. But is this the shape of things to come or is the American-European future still in the making? One answer was given by a member of the French National Assembly following the reelection of America's president in November 2004:

> Our old Europe is no longer sure about its roots or its frontiers. Young America is just as sure of its past as it is of its future. America has managed to preserve its faith while we have consigned much of ours—either faith in God, or in our countries, or in liberty—to history. . . . Much misunderstanding between America and Europe (and especially between America and France) stems from our loss of confidence in ourselves. . . . Americans still have faith in themselves. In order for us to heal the breach with the United States, we must first reconcile with ourselves. We must revive our love for freedom.[13]

No one should be surprised if America and Europe—that is to say, individual European countries—take positions which are not always in concord. In other words, if Americans and Europeans act as though they are independent, it is because they *are*, in spirit and in nature and in fact.

Americans and Europeans are not yet, however, irrevocably embarked on a path leading to separation, although the temptation to take it is becoming stronger and to some, appealing. But if we take that path sooner or later the friendship so carefully built through adversity and strife during the twentieth century will find itself in pieces. Would America and Europe be able to put it back together again?

If the friendship is broken so will be the strength it gives Americans and Europeans as partners in the common enterprise called "dealing with life's challenges and opportunities." We will start to go our own ways. We will, of course, in stentorian voices announce that we are right to march to our own drummer. But eventually we will discover that we need each other's help. It will not be forthcoming, because we will no longer trust each other. Americans and Europeans should be careful what kind of independence they practice.

If we allow ourselves to be divided, it is at our peril. We will become rivals, not competitors. The tremendous difference between the two is that, as rivals, each of us will be alone. The consequences for America and Europe will be many. We will become much more aware, in our splendid isolation, that threats await us everywhere, and that we face them separately. Those who once looked to us—to America and Europe—with admiration and respect, will become our critics, and ultimately our enemies. Only the opportunistic will listen to us, as they wait in the wings to capitalize on our weaknesses.

If our relationship deteriorates to the extent just described the world will become even more unbalanced than it is now. The only element of control will be American military power, but its well-intended and unilateral use will not preserve freedom and maintain peace in the long term. On the contrary, it will call forth violence and counter-violence, as force fails to cure what ails the planet; namely, the absence of American-European leadership in a world badly in need of it.

What Americans and Europeans believe will determine whether we take the same path, jointly, or follow different ones, independently. Americans and Europeans are fortunate to still have the freedom to choose.

New Crossroads

In the late 1930s Europe and America both arrived at crossroads. The paths open to them led to war or peace, to freedom or oppression, to weakness or to courage of conviction. Europeans and Americans made choices about which paths to take. One result was a devastating war of unprecedented nature. Another was the division of Europe for fifty years, until 1989–1990. And for many, both Europeans and Americans, the consequences were a painful reminder of words written by an Englishman, Edmund Burke, toward the end of the eighteenth century, that "the only thing necessary for the triumph of evil is for good men to do nothing."

Now, more than sixty years later, Europeans and Americans have come to new crossroads. This time we will decide whether our "interests" are more important than our friendship, or whether they are in fact the same. The choice we make will affect the quality of the leadership and influence we will bring to bear on shaping affairs in the world.

Some Europeans and Americans believe we continue to have common interests, and that those of lasting value are found precisely in the friendship shaped by our hearts, heritage, and history, and not in short-term coalitions of the willing and opportunistic. This path, preferred by the "Atlanticists," contrasts with that of the "Realists." They argue that it is naive, sentimental and unrealistic to claim that our friendship is more important than our interests, that there is a difference between the two. Still others, known as the "Dreamers," assert that "the American spirit is tiring and languishing in the past," while "a new" European dream is being born.[14]

Do these paths lead to different places, or are they all part of one path leading to the same place? How can we know? How do we choose? Europeans and Americans cannot escape the answers to these questions, because there is no safe place to go. Some recognize that the nature of the relationship may be changing in ways that we can neither predict nor manage. Some know also that an absence of American-European leadership will create a vacuum, and that there are those around the globe who will try to fill it with chaos and terror. And some are aware that Benjamin Franklin, more than two centuries ago, admonished the thirteen American colonies at the time they signed their Declaration of Independence. "We must all hang together," he urged, "or assuredly we shall all hang separately."

That warning, were Franklin to give it today, would surely be directed to Europe and America—and, it might also be accompanied by the suggestion that Americans, who are ignorant of how little they know about Europeans, and Europeans, who presumptuously think they understand Americans, spend more time talking to each other. Should we follow this advice, we may rediscover the responsibility to respect our differences and the obligation to value what we have in common.

If it is the essential difference that separates us, it is the values of Western civilization that unite us. Half a century ago Friedrich Hayek described them as "the sacredness of truth . . . the ordinary rules of moral decency . . . a common belief in the value of human freedom . . . an affirmative action towards democracy," and "opposition to all forms of totalitarianism, whether it be from the Right or from the Left." These convictions were then, and are today, our most important foreign policy asset.

Like any art, that of conversation improves with practice, which bodes well for the future because Americans and Europeans have a great many things to discuss. Among these are the lessons and legacies of history. Irrespective of whether Americans like it or admire it, European history affects how many Europeans think about freedom and order, and about war and peace. In turn, their history colors the eye-glasses through which they see and judge American motives and behavior. Europeans are saddled with a heritage of warfare which they do not want to leave as a legacy in the future. If they often seem to be preoccupied with peace, and with freedom as a second-order effect, it is because they are.

Another subject for discussion is selective European interpretation of American history. Most Europeans critical of America are certain that Americans consider themselves the world's policemen. That is how many interpreted the American initiative in the Middle East in 2003, which is why critics continue to ask, "Who appointed you?" They believe this question is legitimate and accuse America of peremptory behavior on the world's stage. Here Europeans ignore America's historical commitment to freedom, demonstrated in Europe on three different occasions during the twentieth century, and arbitrarily dismiss contradictory historical facts, such as Jean-François Revel's observation that American "unilateralism . . . is the consequence, not the cause, of power failures in the rest of the world."

A third matter of concern is the future of Europe and the European Union. This discussion will take place among Europeans themselves, but Americans must listen to it closely. In June 2005, following French and Dutch rejection of the EU constitution, the prime minister of Luxembourg, Jean-Claude Juncker, defined rival opinions as representing two ideas of Europe: (1) a European market with a big and free trade zone, or (2) an integrated Europe.[15] In his judgment the issue is which view of Europe will prevail.

It would be reassuring for Americans and Europeans if the choice were that simple, but the history of the EU sends another message. Differing views concern many things and represent many struggles, of which the following three are primary: (1) rule from the top down or rule from the bottom up, (2) free and open competition in a single European marketplace or a union dominated by the old *European socioeconomic model,* and (3) strong European leadership in concert with America or a union of Europeans in opposition to America. How these matters are decided will be of vital importance for the health of the Atlantic relationship, just as it will be for the success of the European dream.

Americans and Europeans, of course, have always known that they look at the world through different glasses, and that they are not always aware of what the other sees. An attempt to explain why this is so was made by the British foreign secretary, Jack Straw, during a visit to Washington, D. C., in May 2002:

Americans, correctly and rightly, consider that it is they as Americans who created the modern world's greatest democracy. But Europeans tend to see the U.S. through a different prism. They see a U.S. born out of Europe; born from those with the courage, imagination, iconoclasm to break away from the straitjacket not just of poverty but of institutional and political constraints in Europe to form what has long represented, in an almost idealized form, the best of European values and institutions.[16]

Disputatious Americans may be tempted to respond that Europeans should not take credit for what descendants of European immigrants achieved on their own, but that was not what Straw had in mind. His point was that millions of Americans and Europeans recognize the significance of what unites. At the end of his speech Straw spoke specifically about the alliance, but he could just as well have been speaking about friendship, "founded," as he put it, "not just on interests but on values. . . . Our unshakeable faith in democracy and the rule of law is the foundation not only of our freedom, but also of our security and prosperity. There will be debate, and there will be differences of approach. Yet neither will undermine an enduring alliance of enduring values."[17]

There are millions of Americans and Europeans who believe in these words, and who know they are full of meaning, not devoid of it. Less than one year later Straw's emphasis found its reflection in "a vision of Europe" described by Germany's ambassador to the United States, Wolfgang Ischinger. He spoke of a Europe "that manages to become stronger without making the Atlantic wider, that thinks about the transatlantic relationship in terms of real partnership, not in terms of confrontation."[18]

Ischinger's vision is held by many in America and Europe who believe it is time to give it substance. This is a challenge which cannot be met with the deceptive claim that "Europe's vision of the future is quietly eclipsing the American dream," or with the idea that the purpose of "The United States of Europe" is to contain America.[19] On the contrary, if the Europeans are as confident in their "unshakeable faith in democracy and the rule of law" as Britain's foreign minister argued in May 2002, they must decide what Europe stands *for*, and not just what it stands *against*. Europe's challenge is to earn respect as a union that possesses courage and conviction, that assures security with credible military balance, and that pursues peace and prosperity, in freedom.

Obligations Written in the Heart

Americans and Europeans who know each other well seek a transatlantic relationship defined by faith in freedom and in order, and by the commitment to defend both. They understand that the real choice Europeans and Americans face, together, is not between rule from the top down and rule from the bottom up, not between *the European socioeconomic model* and *the American model*, not between power and weakness, and not between the American who "does" things and the European who "sees" things. It is Franklin's choice. Shall we, Europeans and Americans, decide that our future lies in hanging together, or shall we all hang separately?

The quality of the choice, lest one be deceived by arguments to the contrary, is not measured by degrees of military force. It is self-evident that in the short term the ability to project power is decisive, just as is the willingness to use it. This is why Americans focus so intently on it. If the ability to defend ourselves is not credible and our willingness to do so is in doubt, stronger enemies will rise to challenge the weaker. History teaches both Americans and Europeans that this is a distasteful part of the human condition. That is a lesson which Americans have learned very well from the histories of Europe and America.

The choice, however, will not be made by armed forces, but will be determined by whether Americans and Europeans recognize another history lesson, of greater weight. It is that in the long term our fate rests in the power of our ideas. This is why the cultural, economic, and political ties that bind Europeans and Americans so closely together are invaluable. By themselves they cannot make a friendship. We have to do that deliberately. But if the choice is made, it is the quality of the ties that will form the substance of the relationship, that will endow it with meaning, and that will give it resiliency.

What makes these ties essential in our contemporary world is their historical nature. A perfect description was given more than two hundred years
ago, in the wake of the French revolution, by Edmund Burke in "Letters
from a Regicide Peace." He wrote,

> Nothing is so strong a tie of amity between nation and nation as correspon-
> dence in law, customs, manners and habits of life. They have more than
> the force of treaties in themselves. They are obligations written in the heart.

Symbols of these obligations appear in cities throughout Europe, in the
form of boulevards, streets and squares named after America and Americans. And in America similar symbols, such as the names of towns and
cities in the American Middle West, are found throughout the country
and begin in Washington, D. C. There the streets were laid out by a
Frenchman, l'Enfant, and the public square opposite the White House is
named after Lafayette. During the Revolutionary War he was made a general, and he became the first foreign dignitary to address a joint session of
the Congress. Today the portraits of George Washington and the Marquis
de Lafayette hang on either side of the rostrum in the United States
House of Representatives.

When Lafayette married on his return to France, he and his wife gave
their first son the name of George Washington. He also brought with him
a trunk of earth to be put on his grave, over which the American flag flies
today. But perhaps the most eloquent sign of amity is also the most famous symbol of freedom in the world, the Statue of Liberty. It was a gift
from the people of France. On the bronze plaque at the base of the statue
are words written in 1883 by Emma Lazarus, a member of a fourth-
generation New York Jewish family:

> Give me your tired, your poor,
> Your huddled masses, yearning to breathe free,
> The wretched refuse of your teeming shore,
> Send these, the homeless, tempest-tossed, to me:
> I lift my lamp beside the golden door.

Americans generally prefer freedom to order and Europeans prefer order to freedom. But our views are remarkably similar, even as we consider the world from our different perspectives. The root and branch of what unites us is our shared desire to preserve and advance freedom and order.

This commitment is also one of the unique and precious legacies of Western civilization. The political form is democracy. The social norm is freedom of conscience in the context of the dignity and worth of the individual. Americans and Europeans have a common interest in the survival of both.

The obligation and the interest compel us to forge an indivisible covenant to recall where we have come from, to understand who we are, and to decide together where we want to go. In doing so, it will stand us in good stead to ask each other—"Why is it that I know you?"—and to remember that the answer is important. But should we find one day that we have forgotten why, an old French adage exists to give our ignorance sad and modern meaning . . . *qui s'excuse, s'accuse* !—whoever excuses himself, accuses himself.

If our memories serve us well neither of us will ever become forced to invoke the adage, because we will be able to explain why our most important asset is ourselves. It is with this conviction that these pages have been written, and why they have dealt with our differences and affinities, our interests, and our habits of life. Many of these are complementary, just as many are also contradictory. That is to say, Europeans and Americans, as friends and allies, enjoy an unmatched wealth of both different and shared perspectives. If we make the effort to learn what *the essential difference* teaches us about ourselves, and to draw on the vitality of the affinities we share, we are stronger, not weaker.

Many Europeans and Americans have not given these matters serious thought in a long time. So it may not be easy to begin anew the interrupted conversations of yesterday. But the commanding force of things obligates us to stop dancing in the dark in a world filled with turbulence, and with new threats to freedom and order which we are just beginning to learn about.

This point was reinforced, with unequivocal emphasis, in an essay by the French historian Nicole Bacharan that appeared in the French daily *Le Figaro* in the autumn of 2006. Following the observation that democracies occupy too small and fragile a planet to afford the luxury of being divided among themselves, she concluded,

> There will be no safety and advancement of law and justice without an American engagement that . . . is wise, strong, and durable. In order to convince the next Congress and the next American president [of this point] France and Europe must proclaim clearly their fidelity to common values and alliances and demonstrate their determination to exercise their responsibilities.
>
> A France and a Europe that invents a new Atlanticism, enlightened and balanced. The future [does not lie] in American hegemony, that will surely call forth fanaticism, but in sharing tasks and in a united front of all democracies."[20]

"So, where do we begin?" an American might ask. "Let's start by kissing the lady's hand," a European might answer. In the question, as in the answer, there is also a force. It is made of manners, judgment and leadership, of individualism, liberty and freedom, of power, courage and conviction, and of trust, affection and respect.

A Comparative Chart of European Countries

European Countries	European NATO Member	European Union (EU) Member	European Monetary Union (EMU) Member
Albania	—	—	—
Andorra	—	—	
Armenia	—	—	—
Austria	—	yes	yes
Azerbaijan	—	—	—
Belarus	—	—	—
Belgium	yes	yes	yes
Bosnia-Herzegovina	—	—	—
Bulgaria	yes	yes	—
Croatia	—	—	—
Cyprus	—	yes	—
Czech Republic	yes	yes	—
Denmark	yes	yes	—
Estonia	yes	yes	—
Finland	—	yes	yes
France	yes	yes	yes
Germany	yes	yes	yes
Georgia	—	—	—
Greece	yes	yes	yes

European Countries	European NATO Member	European Union (EU) Member	European Monetary Union (EMU) Member
Hungary	yes	yes	—
Iceland	yes	—	—
Ireland	—	yes	yes
Italy	yes	yes	yes
Latvia	yes	yes	—
Liechtenstein	—	—	—
Lithuania	yes	yes	—
Luxembourg	yes	yes	yes
Macedonia	—	—	—
Malta	—	yes	—
Moldova	—	—	—
Monaco	—	—	—
Netherlands	yes	yes	yes
Norway	yes	—	—
Poland	yes	yes	—
Portugal	yes	yes	yes
Romania	yes	yes	—
Russia	—	—	—
San Marino	—	—	—
Serbia/Montenegro	—	—	—
Slovakia	yes	yes	yes
Slovenia	yes	yes	—
Spain	yes	yes	yes
Sweden	—	yes	—
Switzerland	—	—	—
Turkey	yes	—	—
Ukraine	—	—	—
United Kingdom	yes	yes	—
Vatican City	—	—	—

The newest member of the European Monetary Union (EMU) is Slovenia. In addition, several small European countries, like the Vatican, Monaco, and San Marino—although not members of the European Union or of the EMU—have adopted the euro because of currency unions with EMU member states. The so-called microstates of Andorra, Montenegro, and Kosovo have unilaterally adopted the euro for international financial transactions. The euro also serves as the legal currency of French overseas territories of French Guiana, Réunion, Saint-Pierre et Miquelon, Guadeloupe, Martinique, and Mayotte.

APPENDIX 2

"An American Is . . ."

Original Message
Sent: Thursday, February 27, 2003 12:22 PM
Subject: an American. . . .

Subject: an American. . . .

You probably missed it in the rush of news last week, but there was actually a report that someone in Pakistan had published in a newspaper an offer of a reward to anyone who killed an American, any American.

So an Australian dentist wrote the following to let everyone know what an American is, so they would know when they found one:

An American is English, or French, or Italian, Irish, German, Spanish, Polish, Russian or Greek. An American may also be Canadian, Mexican, African, Indian, Chinese, Japanese, Korean, Australian, Iranian, Asian, or Arab, or Pakistani, or Afghan. An American may also be a Cherokee, Osage, Blackfoot, Navaho, Apache, Seminole or one of the many other tribes known as native Americans.

An American is Christian, or he could be Jewish, or Buddhist, or Muslim. In fact there are more Muslims in America than in Afghanistan. The only difference is that in America they are free to worship as each of them chooses. An American is also free to believe in no religion. For that he will only answer to God, not to the government, or to armed thugs claiming to speak for the government and for God.

An American is from the most prosperous land in the history of the world. The root of that prosperity can be found in the Declaration of

Independence, which recognizes the God-given right of each person to the pursuit of happiness.

An American is generous. Americans have helped out just about every other nation in the world in their time of need. When Afghanistan was overrun by the Soviet army 20 years ago, Americans came with arms and supplies to enable the people to win back their country. As of September 11, Americans had given more than any other nation to the poor in Afghanistan.

Americans welcome the best, the best products, the best books, the best music, the best food, the best athletes. But they also welcome the least.

The national symbol of America, the Statue of Liberty, welcomes your tired and your poor, the wretched refuse of your teeming shores, the homeless, tempest tossed. These in fact are the people who build America. Some of them were working in the twin towers the morning of September 11, 2002 [sic] earning a better life for their families. I have been told that the World Trade Center victims were from at least 30 other countries, cultures, and first languages, including those that aided and abetted the terrorists.

So you can try to kill an American if you must. Hitler did. So did General Tojo, and Stalin, and Mao Tse-Tung, and every bloodthirsty tyrant in the history of the world. But, in doing so you would just be killing yourself. Because Americans are not a particular people from a particular place. They are the embodiment of the human spirit of freedom. Everyone who holds to that spirit, everywhere, is an American.

Pass this around the world.

"The International"

"The International" was written to celebrate the Paris Commune of March–May 1871. The words, as originally written in French, are by Eugene Pottier (Paris 1871); the music was composed by Pierre Degeyter (1888). The original version has six verses. This translation is taken from C. and E. Paul.

The International

Arise! Ye wretched of all regions
Arise! All bound in hunger's chain!
Now reason stirs the worker's legions,
for lo, the end draws on amain!
Away with wreckage of past nations!
Enslaved crowd, rise at the call!
The world shall change from its foundations;
We that are nothing shall be all.

Chorus:

The call to arms has sounded!
Close ranks the foe to face!
The Workers' International
Shall be the human race.

We ask no aid from Gods or Caesars
From haloed saviour or from king;
'Tis we, 'tis we, the world's producers,
Who to our own selves help must bring.

To free the spirit from its prison;
To make the thief his gains disgorge,
With mighty strokes we'll strike the iron
Just taken glowing from our forge. CHORUS

The law supports the state's oppressions,
Whilst endless taxes bleed us white.
An empty word the rich man's duty,
And empty word the poor man's right.
Too long, too long, we've pined in wardship;
Equality seeks other lights,
For duties should attach to lordship,
While duty's odious without rights. CHORUS

How hideous they seem in their splendour,
These barons of mine and rail,
Whose sole art has been but to plunder
The workers who suffer and toil.
What is ours to them we've been handing;
Labour's fruit should to labour accrue;
A full restitution demanding,
The people ask naught, but what's due. CHORUS

With fumes of battle we've been drunken.
Against our brothers we've made war,
In mutual slaughter for our tyrants –
'Down arms!' will take the soldier far!
Perchance they're stubborn, these man-eaters?
Would make us still for 'heros' pass?
We'll find a good use for our bullets
Against th' oppressors of our class! CHORUS

March onward, O, army of the toilers,
Of all who work for daily bread!
We'll give short shrift to the despoilers,
Let them reign in the realm of the dead!
On our flesh have these ever been feeding;
Birds of prey since the dawning of days,
Should they vanish, the sun, all unheeding,
In reckless splendour still will blaze. CHORUS

Notes

Introduction

1. In 1931 an American musical entitled "The Band Wagon" introduced what its writers thought was a "dull" song entitled "Dancing in the Dark." Whatever description is used to refer to American-European undertakings, the themes presented in this book make music that both Europeans and Americans can follow, and produce a tune with a clear message found in the "dull" song's most famous lyric: ". . . we can face the music together," even if we're dancing in the dark.

Chapter I: Differences

1. The "history of winning" and the "history of losing" are descriptions used in a letter to the author by a professor of political science at the University of Bonn, Christian Hacke.

2. A distinctive reference to this subject is found in an article by Tunku Varadarajan, "Right-Wing? Who're You Calling Right-Wing?" *Wall Street Journal*, May 10, 2002.

3. The Magna Carta was signed in Runnymede, in Surrey, not far from London. The Declaration of Arbroath was drawn up in the Abbey of the same name, not far from the city of Dundee in Scotland.

4. Today, according to Father Allen Duston, international director for the Patrons of the Arts office in the Vatican in Rome, "a great deal of the project's success [a reference to the recent restoration of the Sistine Chapel] is due to the 'generous nature' of Americans . . . . Americans have a long tradition of philanthropy." See Sabrina Arena Ferrisi, "Private donors, most of them American, have financed the restoration of Vatican art treasures," *www.catholic.net*, World Watch—Catholic world Report, May 2001.

5. Of the exceptions most are in the United Kingdom.

6. See James Kanter, "EU pushes plans for institute to halt 'brain drain,'" *International Herald Tribune*, February 23, 2006, and also *Wall Street Journal*, August 4, 2006.

7. The term is used here to describe the general juxtaposition between the role of the state and the individual defined by *the essential difference*. It should be carefully noted, however, that there is not one, single European model, embraced by all Europeans. Bel-

gian economist André Sapir, for example, argues in a paper published by the Bruegel Institute in Brussels that one can identify at least four models. All of them, however, to differing degrees, embody the concept and practice of rule from the top down. See André Sapir, "Globalisation and the Reform of European Social Models," Bruegel *Policy Brief*, Issue 2005/01, November 2005. This study is cited in an enlightening paper by Helle C. Dale entitled "Challenges Facing Europe in a World of Globalization" delivered as a lecture at the Heritage Foundation (Washington, D. C.) on November 28, 2005.

8. This phrase comes from former Spanish foreign minister Ana Palacio, who in mid-2005 chaired the Spanish parliament's joint committee on European affairs. See *International Herald Tribune*, June 16, 2005.

9. American author Jeremy Rifkin, for example, does so in his book *The European Dream*, published in 2004.

10. See Nicolas Barotte, "Quand Lionel Jospin regarde le monde . . . ," *Le Figaro*, October 20, 2005, and Lionel Jospin, *Le monde comme je le vois*, Gallimard, Paris, 2005.

11. See Robert Aitken, "James Wilson: A Lost American Founder," *Litigation*, summer 2003 (29, no. 4), pp. 61–66, 74.

12. A fascinating discussion of this subject has been written by David Brooks and is entitled *Bobos in Paradise: The New Upper Class and How They Got There*, Simon & Schuster (New York), 2000, 284 pages.

13. James Fullarton Muirhead, *The Land of Contrasts*, John Lane: Bodley Head, London and New York, 1890, p. 280.

14. Kenneth L. Woodward, "Christianity's Place in Europe," *International Herald Tribune*, June 16, 2003.

15. In German it reads as follows: "Ich glaube an die Unantastbarkeit und an die Würde jedes einzelnen Menschen. Ich glaube, dass allen Menschen vor Gott das gleiche Recht auf Freiheit gegeben wurde. Ich verspreche, jedem Angriff auf die Freiheit und der Tyrannei Widerstand zu leisten, wo auch immer sie auftreten möge."

16. Figures for church attendance are generally higher in the ten countries which joined the EU in May 2004. See Alain Barluet, "Une Europe laïque aux confessions variées," *Le Figaro*, April 28, 2004, Kenneth L. Woodward, "Christianity's place in Europe," *International Herald Tribune*, June 16, 2003, and Niall Ferguson, "Why America Outpaces Europe (Clue: The God Factor)," *New York Times*, June 8, 2003.

17. In 1939 Franklin Roosevelt moved the holiday to the fourth Thursday of November.

18. On this subject see the essay by Samuel P. Huntington, "'Under God,'" *Wall Street Journal*, June 16, 2004, and on the same subject the superb study by Jon Meacham entitled *American Gospel: God, The Founding Fathers, and the Making of a Nation*, Random House, New York City, 2006, 399 pages.

19. According to U.S. Census Bureau statistics for 2005 America's population of almost 295 million was made of approximately 238 million Caucasians, with 42.6 million Latinos representing the largest minority group, followed by 37.9 million African Americans and 12.7 million Asians. Of the total foreign-born population in America at the beginning of 2002—approximately 31 million or 11 percent of total population—51 per-

cent were born in Latin America, 25.5 percent were born in Asia, 15.3 percent were born in Europe, and the remaining 8.2 percent were born in other parts of the world. *San Francisco Chronicle*, June 19, 2003, and Ann Morse, "Demographic and the 2000 Census," *www.stateserv.hpts.org* , January 30, 2002.

20. An e-mail, emphasizing this point in an especially memorable way, was given wide and anonymous circulation in America in January and February 2003. See Appendix Two: "An American Is. . . ." See also the books on life in America by Charles Kuralt, especially *Charles Kuralt's America*, G.P. Putnam's Sons, New York, 1995.

Chapter II: On History, Heritage, and Habits of Life

1. In 2004 the Greek portion of the island became a member of the European Union.

2. See Appendix One: A Comparative Chart of European Countries. The number "50" is a consequence of which criteria are used to define a "country." In this case the total includes Andorra, Liechtenstein and Vatican City, as well as the republics which have emerged following the breakup of the Soviet Union and Yugoslavia.

3. Timothy Egan, "Along full-of-surprises Missouri, a way of life is receding," *International Herald Tribune*, June 2, 2003.

4. This impression of America comes from a series of letters written as e-mail messages during 2002 and 2003 from Burkhard Koch.

5. The impressions of the mountains and the effects of space have also been beautifully described by Irving Stone in a famous book called *Men to Match My Mountains* as well as by Bernard DeVoto in *Across the Wide Missouri*, and more recently by Stephen Ambrose in his history of the Lewis and Clark expedition, entitled *Undaunted Courage*. A book of equal merit, about "a nation heading west," is authored by J. S. Holliday and is entitled *The World Rushed In: The California Gold Rush Experience*.

6. From Ray Allen Billington's foreword to the reedition of Turner's essays entitled *The Frontier in American History*, Holt, Rinehart and Winston, New York, 1962.

7. This phrase, still in use, which dates from the early nineteenth century and possibly earlier, is a condescending French description of the selfish and self-serving conduct of England's foreign affairs. "La perfide Albion" may be a reference to the white cliffs of Dover, but may have earlier origins.

8. Venture capitalist Hermann Hauser of Cambridge, U.K., as quoted in William Drozdiak, "Old World Reinvents Itself as Model for New Economy," *International Herald Tribune*, February 19, 2001.

9. See the editorial "Merry Philanthropy," *Wall Street Journal*, December 24, 2004. See also, as a detailed reference, Robert D. Putnam entitled *Bowling Alone: The Collapse and Revival of American Community*, Simon & Schuster, New York, 2000, page 118. A thorough analysis of American giving is contained in Joel L. Fleishman, *The Foundation: A Great American Secret: How Private Weath Is Changing the World*, Public Affairs, New York, 2007.

10. CARE (Cooperative for American Remittances to Europe) was founded in 1945. The first 20,000 CARE Packages arrived in Le Havre, France on May 11, 1946, and

millions followed. The first packages were U.S. Army surplus "10-in-1" food parcels intended to provide one meal for ten soldiers during the planned invasion of Japan. Following the surrender of Japan the packages, which had never been used, were obtained by CARE which in turn began a service that allowed Americans to send the packages to friends and families in Europe where millions were in danger of starvation. Ten dollars bought a CARE Package and guaranteed that its addressee would receive it within four months.

11. See *Wall Street Journal*, March 9, 2005.

12. See David Brooks, loc. cit.

13. Tod Richissin, "Crying over Gas? Europeans Cope," Alexander's Gas & Oil Connections (News and Trends North America), May 6, 2005. See also "Pursuing Happiness," *The Economist*, July 1, 2006, p. 50, and "Nearly One Car per Two People in EU," www.eubusiness.com (September 19, 2006).

14. The ambassador was Jean-Jules Jusserand who later, in 1917, became the first recipient of the Pulitzer Prize in History for his book *With Americans of Past and Present Days*.

15. James Fullarton Muirhead, op. cit. p. 153.

16. "France Blocks Free Trade," *International Herald Tribune*, September 2, 2003.

17. William Packer, "Untouched Fields of Dreams," *Financial Times*, February 26, 2002.

18. From the obituary for Françoise Giroud, *The Economist*, January 25, 2003.

19. An excellent essay on this subject is by James F. Cooper, "I Found It at the Movies," *American Arts Quarterly*, spring 2006, pp. 2–8.

20. No reference is made to folk music, because few Americans and Europeans are familiar with this genre of their respective musical heritage, a genre rich in history but not illustrative of the contrasts drawn here.

21. The role of the state fair in midwestern American life is still of significance. The best description I have found is by Michael Judge, "Some Pig! A Midwestern Rite of Summer," *Wall Street Journal*, August 16, 2006.

22. Ethan Mordden, "Everything's Up to Date in 'Oklahoma!'" *International Herald Tribune*, February 28, 2002.

23. This statistic applies to the original fifteen members of the European Union. The French and German languages are in second and third place, respectively, spoken by 28 and 24 percent of the population. In Europe foreign-language study is obligatory everywhere except in Ireland and Scotland. See "Languages of Europe" (last update 2/22/05) at http://www.europa.eu.int/comm/education, and Doreen Carvajal, *International Herald Tribune*, February 18, 2004. See also www.eubusiness.com, "Half of All Young Europeans Are Multilingual," February 16, 2005.

24. Observance of this distinction is affected by education and social class, and today, among those in their thirties and younger, it is followed less frequently than it was twenty-five years ago. It is of note that European socialists, committed to the idea of equality, do not make this distinction when speaking among themselves. See an unusual article on contemporary usage by Sebastian Hammelehle, *Welt am Sonntag*, April 10, 2005.

25. The ordinance was known as the *Ordonnance de Villers-Cotterêts*. Until 1606 French dictionaries were French-Latin or other combinations.

26. It is not well known in America, or in Europe, that federal law requires ballots to be printed in non-English languages if 5 percent of the population in a voting jurisdiction, or ten thousand people, speak a language other than English. Ballots and election materials are printed in foreign languages in 375 voting districts in 21 states.

27. A fascinating description of this condition has been written by Sarah Turnbull and is entitled *Almost French*, Gotham Books, New York, 2002.

28. See Peter Schneider, "Conquering Europe, Word for Word," *New York Times*, May 1, 2001. Schneider makes these comparisons and leaves the readers to draw their own conclusions.

29. The International Organization of Francophonie has 51 member states. Of these, 28 countries have French as an official language. French is the only language other than English spoken on five continents. See Richard Shryock, Virginia Polytechnic Institute and State University at http://www.fll.vt.edu/french/whyfrench.html.

30. In Madrid about 600,000 people use a taxi cab every day. See the *International Herald Tribune*, January 26, 2005.

31. As quoted in Simon Schama, "The Unloved American," *New Yorker*, March 10, 2003.

32. Arnold Beichman, *Weekly Standard*, February 28, 2005.

33. In the March 3, 2003, issue of the *New Yorker* Simon Schama's article "The Unloved American" presents a fascinating description of the American manner and character as seen through nineteenth- and twentieth-century European spectacles.

34. Marianne Jacobbi, "The French Know How to Make a Meal of It," *International Herald Tribune*, March 6/7, 2004.

35. Clyde Prestowitz, *International Herald Tribune*, January 27, 2003.

36. The most entertaining and enlightening history of Franklin, France and America I have ever read is entitled *A Great Improvisation: Franklin, France and the Birth of America*, and was written by Stacy Schiff. Henry Holt, New York City, 2005.

37. Oscar Wilde, *A Woman of No Importance*, 1893, Act I.

38. Alan Riding, "EU Cultural Elite Learn to Love the Constitution," *International Herald Tribune*, May 12, 2005, and Neal Gabler, "U.S. Cultural Hegemony Lives on in Movies, not TV," *International Herald Tribune*, January 10, 2003.

39. See Victor Davis Hanson, *A War Like No Other*, Random House, New York, 2005.

40. Peter Schneider, "Separated by Civilization," *International Herald Tribune*, April 7, 2003.

41. Allan E. Goodman (president and CEO, Institute of International Education), from a speech entitled "The Closing of the American Mind: A Progress Report" delivered at Tufts University, November 18, 2004. Goodman writes: "In the sixties . . . almost 90 percent of the 4-year colleges in the United States had a language requirement for graduation. Today the figure is under 60 percent and well under 10 percent for those who actually require the student to take college level courses rather than pass a proficiency exam." See also his address, "It Is not a Pond," delivered to the Tenth Anniversary Conference Academic Cooperation Association held in Ghent, Belgium, May 11, 2003.

42. See the National Geographic–Roper 2002 Global Geographic Literacy Survey, November 2002.

43. Condoleezza Rice, "Campaign 2000: Promoting the National Interest," *Foreign Affairs*, January/February 2000. President Bush appointed Rice secretary of state in January 2005.

44. As quoted from the review of Berns's book *Making Patriots*, by Roger Kimball, "The Reason for All Those Parades and Fireworks," *Wall Street Journal*, July 3, 2001.

Chapter III: Equality, Opportunity, Stability

1. Gregory Viscusi, "French Senators Get Lessons in the Realities of Business," *International Herald Tribune*, October 19, 2006.

2. Wolfgang Munchau, *Financial Times*, January 26, 2004.

3. Dominique Moïsi, *Financial Times*, November 18, 2002.

4. Larry Siedentop, in 2002 a fellow of Keble College at Oxford University, made a similar point in the February 28, 2002, issue of the *Financial Times*: "The instincts of the *énarques* are bureaucratic rather than constitutional—putting a premium on coherence and efficiency rather than [on] the checks and balances of a constitutional order." See his excellent study entitled *Democracy in Europe*, Penguin Press, London, 2000. See also John Carreybon, "Is Elite School France's Failing," *International Herald Tribune*, January 16, 2006, and Katrin Bennhold, "France's Murky Mix of School and Scandal," *International Herald Tribune*, May 15, 2006.

5. An excellent analysis of this subject is by Bruce Bawer, "We're Rich, You're Not. End of Story," *New York Times*, April 17, 2005.

6. Among the most illuminating studies of American life and values are those written by Seymour Martin Lipset and Daniel J. Boorstin. Especially relevant here is Lipset's explanation of why socialism has never taken hold in America, entitled *American Exceptionalism*, published in 1996, and his lengthy article "Still the Exceptional Nation?" published in the *Wilson Quarterly*, Washington, D. C., winter 2000. Boorstin's three-volume work, entitled *The Americans*, was published between 1958 and 1973. See also David Brooks, "The American Way of Equality," *New York Times*, January 14, 2007.

7. Friedrich A. Hayek, *The Intellectual and Socialism*, University of Chicago Press, 1949.

8. See Appendix Three: "The International."

9. A fascinating description of the effect of *socialism* on the individual was written in 1999 by a German woman, born in 1944, who grew up in West Berlin with her grandmother. When the Berlin Wall was built on August 13, 1961, she was on vacation with relatives in East Germany and awoke the next day to discover that she could not return home. She was locked in, and spent the next twenty-eight years in East Berlin. The book, by Rita Kuczynski, is entitled *Mauerblume*. In German the word means *Wall Flower*, but in the context of divided Germany the title can be given several, very different interpretations. Rita Kuczynski's life is a painful and powerful account of one of socialism's twentieth-century legacies.

10. As conveyed in a private conversation with the author in Paris in June 2000.

11. See François d'Orcival, "Le Gros Chèque de Lady Thatcher," *Le Figaro Magazine*, October 29, 2005.

12. Elaine Sciolino, "Outrage at Raffarin," *International Herald Tribune*, July 3, 2003.

13. See the excellent study of the social and political habits of life of twentieth-century America by Robert D. Putnam entitled *Bowling Alone: The Collapse and Revival of American Community*, Simon & Schuster, New York, 2000.

14. In the daily life of postwar Europe CARE packages were so important that Europeans still spoke of them in the late 1960s, and Austrians still spoke of the packages sent by Trapp Family Austrian Relief. It was an effort directed by the same Captain von Trapp and his wife who had left Austria for America in 1938, and whose story was told in the American musical *The Sound of Music*. Between 1947 and 1949, thanks to their efforts, more than 300,000 pounds of goods donated by Americans went to Austria.

15. The 1948 Foreign Assistance Act and consequential legislation provided a total amount of approximately $13 billion for Europe of which about 3.1 billion went to Great Britain, 2.7 to France, 1.5 to Italy, slightly less than 1.5 to West Germany, and the remainder to other western European countries. West Germany, however, received an additional estimated $1.8 billion (via GARIOA—Government and Relief in Occupied Areas) for a total of $3.3 billion, of which $1 billion was repaid to America.

16. A. J. P. Taylor, "The European Revolution," *Listener* (London), November 22, 1945, p. 576.

17. As cited in Dennis L. Bark and David R. Gress, *A History of West Germany. Volume I: From Shadow to Substance, 1945–1963.* Basil Blackwell, Oxford and New York, 1989, pp. 195–96.

18. Ibid., p. 196.

19. Ibid., p. 208.

20. Ibid., p. 209.

21. See Henri Amouroux, "L'histoire à la figure," *Le Figaro Magazine*, March 8, 2003, and *La grande histoire des Français sous l'occupation*, R. Laffont, 1999. See also François-Georges Dreyfus (editor), *Unrecognized Resistance: The Franco-American Experience in World War Two*, Transaction Publishers, 2004.

22. Roger Cohen, "Divided We Grumble: Europe's Loss of Focus," *International Herald Tribune*, June 9, 2004.

23. See Norman Barry, "Germany Must Rediscover the Market," *Financial Times*, January 23, 2003. Barry's citation of the cartel recalls the industrial cartels in Nazi Germany that supported Hitler's rise to power. For this reason one of the four "d's" established by the four powers occupying defeated Germany was decartelization, the others being democratization, denazification, and dismantlement.

In the EU the percentage of unionized workers is at an average 30 percent compared with approximately 12 percent in America. See Thomas Fuller, "Day of French Protests Draws Droves Nationwide," *International Herald Tribune*, October 5, 2005, and "In the East, Many EU Work Rules Don't Apply," *International Herald Tribune*, June 15, 2005.

24. See Jeremy Rifkin, *The European Dream: How Europe's Vision of the Future is Qui-*

etly Eclipsing the American Dream, Jeremy P. Tarcher/Penguin, New York, 2004. See also John Vinocur, "U.S. Model for Europe: Immigrant Work Ethic," *International Herald Tribune*, December 6, 2005, and Edward C. Prescott, "Why Do Americans Work More Than Europeans?" *Wall Street Journal*, October 21, 2004.

25. See *Key Indicators of the Labour Market*, 3rd ed. International Labour Office, Geneva, 2003 and the *Examiner* (San Francisco), June 25–27, 2004. The value of statistics, of course, depends on which studies are used. So, some argue that growth in productivity during the past ten years has been roughly the same in Europe and America. See, for example, *The Economist*, June 9, 2004, pages 65–67.

26. See David Brooks, "A Tale of 2 Systems," *New York Times*, January 4, 2005, Niall Ferguson, "Why America Outpaces Europe (Clue: The God Factor), *New York Times*, June 8, 2003, and "Trichet Urges Action to Buoy 'Mediocre' Growth," *International Herald Tribune*, October 17, 2006.

27. European immigration rates are increasing slowly vis-à-vis America, but successful assimilation of foreigners, especially Muslims, is difficult, slow, and the exception. See the extensive commentary in the European and American press on the reasons for the violence that erupted in the suburbs of numerous French cities in late October 2005. It is interesting also to note Roger Cohen's observations in an article entitled "A European Model for Immigration Falters: Dutch Façade of Tolerance under Strain," *International Herald Tribune*, October 17, 2005. Cohen's article appeared ten days before the first French demonstrations.

28. See ibid. John W. Miller, "Pension Systems Strain Europe," *Wall Street Journal*, June 17, 2004, Niall Ferguson from a speech delivered at the American Enterprise Institute (Washington, D. C.) on March 1, 2004, the editorial entitled "Europe vs. America," *Wall Street Journal*, June 18, 2004, and "EU Versus USA," a report prepared by economists Fredrik Bergström and Robert Gidehag for the Swedish think tank Timbro, Stockholm, 2004. See also Graham Bowley, "Barroso Underscores Pro-Business Reforms" and the article entitled "European Union Is Advised to Free Up Markets," *International Herald Tribune*, March 2, 2005.

29. These statistics apply to the twelve EU members who use a common currency.

30. In March 2004 former Dutch prime minister Wim Kok was appointed by the European Council to review EU progress toward creating a single market. The "Kok Report," presented to the council in early November 2004, concluded in effect that the EU was "steering its economic future dangerously off course," and cited as reasons an overloaded agenda, poor coordination, conflicting priorities, and a lack of political will. See Graham Bowled, "A Grim Report on Future Grabs Europe's Attention," *International Herald Tribune*, November 12, 2004, and www.euractiv.com.

31. T. J. Rodgers as cited in the *American Spectator*, November/December 2001, p. 44.

Chapter IV: Uncommon Marketplaces

1. In 1970, against $11 billion dollars in gold reserves in American, $45 billion dollars were held by foreigners, and the following year President Nixon took America off the

gold standard. See Chris Mayer, "The Poet of Finance," the *Daily Reckoning*, July 27, 2004. The *Daily Reckoning* is a daily online economic newsletter edited by Bill Bonner and Addison Wiggin.

2. See Appendix One: A Comparative Chart of European Countries.

3. The agreement was originally signed in 1985 aboard a ship, *Princesse Marie-Astrid*, on the Moselle River, near the Luxembourg town of Schengen. By 2005 all of the EU's original fifteen members had approved it, with the exception of Ireland and the United Kingdom. Iceland and Norway had endorsed the treaty as well. The EU's ten new members were expected to implement the agreement in 2006 or thereafter, as was Switzerland.

4. See the *Financial Times*, June 5, 2002, and *International Herald Tribune*, June 13, 20, 2002. Jacques Delors served as French minister of finance in the early 1980s, and was president of the European Commission from 1985 to 1994. He is also the father of Martine Aubry, the French minister of labor from 1997 to 2000, who spearheaded the successful effort to create the 35-hour work week in France, a subject treated later in this chapter.

5. Alexei Barrionuevo, "As Europe Seeks A Stronger Voice, Words Get in Way," *Wall Street Journal*, January 5, 2005.

6. In French it reads, "l'Europe se fera par la monnaie ou ne se fera pas." Jacques Rueff, one of the founding members of the Mont Pèlerin Society, served as a judge in the Court of Justice of the European Coal and Steel Community (ECSC), as a judge in the Court of the European Economic Community (EEC) from 1958 to 1962, and later as minister of finance under Charles de Gaulle. See also Carter Dougherty, "A Single Voice for Europe?" *International Herald Tribune*, September 16/17, 2006.

7. Examples of what this can mean in practice were still evident in France at the beginning of 2000. In 1959 one hundred old French francs were exchanged for one new franc. Forty years later many Frenchmen in their seventies and older, particularly in the countryside, still converted new francs into old ones in order to determine if the value being accepted or paid was fair.

8. G. Thomas Sims, "Germans Come Late, but with Enthusiasm, to the Anti-Euro Party," *Wall Street Journal*, May 30, 2002.

9. Martin Feldstein, *Financial Times*, April 22, 2003. Feldstein was chairman of President Ronald Reagan's Council of Economic Advisers from 1982 to 1984.

10. This statistic is for the year 2004, as cited in *Le Figaro* (Paris), October 10, 2005.

11. The Accession Treaty was signed, most symbolically, at the foot of the Acropolis in Athens on April 15, 2003. Bulgaria and Romania joined in 2007. Were Turkey to join as well, altogether another 100 million citizens would be added. It is unclear, however, when and under what circumstances Turkish membership will take place. The subject is a much debated one within the EU. The former president of France, Valéry Giscard d'Estaing, has openly opposed admission and Jacques Chirac has publicly endorsed it. If Turkey were admitted, its population of 68 million would be the second largest in the EU after Germany.

12. See Philip Stephens, "Europe's Nations Are Bound Together Despite Everything," *Financial Times*, February 14, 2003.

13. See Laurent Fabius "A Stronger Europe for a Better World," *Financial Times*,

March 27, 2003; Jack Straw, "Don't Write Off Europe's Global Role," *International Herald Tribune*, March 27, 2003.

14. Neal E. Boudette, "Searching for Solutions, Germany May Tackle Taboo," *Wall Street Journal*, February 28, 2003.

15. Carter Dougherty, "VW Workers Agree to a Longer Week," *International Herald Tribune*, September 30/October 1, 2006

16. Judy Dempsey, "Germany's Social Democrats Campaign against Unbridled Capitalism," *International Herald Tribune*, April 20, 2005, and Mark Landler, "Germany Bristles at Foreign 'Locusts,'" *International Herald Tribune*, May 5, 2005.

17. David Rennie and Toby Helm, "Blair Caves in to Chirac over EU Reform Proposal," *Daily Telegraph* (London), March 23, 2005.

18. Katrin Bennhold, "Lawmakers in France Debate Longer Hours," *International Herald Tribune*, February 3, 2005.

19. Kenneth Maxwell, "France Opts for Job Funds in Lieu of Broad Change," *Wall Street Journal*, June 9, 2005.

20. Bennhold, "Lawmakers in France Debate Longer Hours."

21. By the end of 2006 pressure had mounted within the EU to establish a work week of no more than 48 hours. See Dan Bilefsky, "U.K. Fights to Retain Workweek Exemption," *International Herald Tribune*, October 17, 2006, and Gaëtan de Capèle, "Le poison des 35 heures," *Le Figaro*, October 21/22, 2006.

22. Blair was the first, and thus far the only European socialist leader of major stature to proclaim, in 1995, that the era of big government was over. Two years later, after the British Labour Party renounced its historic devotion to class warfare and loyalty to public ownership, his party won an overwhelming election victory and Blair became prime minister. Ironically, none other than Thatcher proclaimed that "Britain will be safe in the hands of Mr. Blair."

23. See the briefing by David Anderson, solicitor and chartered tax adviser, Sykes Anderson LLP solicitors, December 9, 2004, *Financial Times*, May 27, 2005, and *Le Figaro*, July 11 and 12, September 26 and 29, 2005, and the *International Herald Tribune*, November 12/13, 2005.

24. See Yves de Kerdrel, "L'ISF entre injustice, dogme et inefficacité," *Le Figaro*, and *Le Figaro Magazine*, October 22, 2005, and Philippe Alexandre and Béatrix de l'Aulnoit, *Trop d'Impôts tue l'Emploi*, Robert Laffont, Paris, 2005. See also, for example, BNA, Inc. Daily Report for Executives, March 31, 2003; *French Weekly Economic Report*, April 2, 2003; *Le Figaro*, May 7, September 29, October 21 and 22, 2004; David Anderson, Sykes Anderson LLP solicitors (London), December 9, 2004; "Bercy sous-estime le rendement de l'ISK en 2007," *Le Figaro*, October 4, 2006.

25. Technically the tax is a levy imposed at each addition of "value" in the processing of a raw material, the performance of a service, or the production and distribution of a commodity with each payer, except the consumer, reimbursed from payment at the next stage. Originally introduced in France in 1954, it raises government revenue "invisibly." In effect it is a hidden sales tax ultimately passed on to the consumer at the time a good or service is purchased.

26. "Europe's VAT Crisis," *Financial Times*, August 29, 2006.

27. *Le Figaro*, September 2, 2005.

28. See www.eubusiness.com/Finance (December 13, 2006).

29. In the spring of 2005 German chancellor Gerhard Schröder proposed lowering the base corporate tax rate from 25 to 19 percent, creating an effective rate of a little more than 33 percent (the effective rate is the base rate plus a "trading tax" which makes up the difference). See Daniel Altman, "In EU Tax Race to Bottom, Who Wins?" *International Herald Tribune*, March 26/27, 2005. In November 2006 Germany, in fact, did lower its corporate tax rate from an average of 38.7 percent to 29 percent, to begin on January 1, 2008 (see *International Herald Tribune*, November 3, 2006). See also Thomas L. Friedman's fascinating analysis of the Irish economy in the June 30, 2005, issue of the *International Herald Tribune*, entitled "The End of the Rainbow."

30. From an e-mail to the author from Burkhard Koch, March 30, 2004. Columnist Paul Krugman, who does not know Europe as well as he asserts, makes the opposite argument concerning France. See his article entitled "French Family Values," *New York Times*, July 29, 2005.

31. See Christopher Rhoads, "Europe's Division over Deficit Rules Is Intensifying," *Wall Street Journal*, July 16, 2003.

32. See Lionel Barber, "Crocodile Tears for the Pact's Timely Death," *Financial Times*, December 9, 2003.

33. See *International Herald Tribune*, March 21, 22, 23, and 24, 2005.

34. "Europe's Essentials: Barroso Promises to Focus on Jobs, Growth and Investment," *Financial Times*, February 2, 2005.

35. Guy Sorman, *Wall Street Journal*, January 24, 2003.

36. See Eric Pfanner, "In Slowing Europe, Reforms Easier to Take," *International Herald Tribune*, July 22, 2003.

37. In 2005 statistics were published in *Le Figaro* on October 17 and 28. See also Philip H. Gordon, "Liberté, Fraternité, Anxiety," *Financial Times*, January 19/20, 2002.

38. Katrin Bennhold, "France votes to Overhaul 35-Hour Workweek," *International Herald Tribune*, March 23, 2005. The union is known as the CFDT (Confédération Française Démocratique du Travail).

39. See *Le Figaro*, October 19 and 21/22, 2006.

40. Christopher Rhoads, "In Deep Crisis, Germany Starts to Revamp Vast Welfare State," *Wall Street Journal*, July 10, 2003.

41. See Josef Joffe, *Die Zeit*, April 28, 2004.

42. Michael González, "Being Berlusconi," *Wall Street Journal*, July 16, 2003.

43. See Charlie McCreevy, "The Lisbon Strategy: Why Less Is More," European Policy Forum, January 24, 2005, and also "Europe's Essentials: Barroso Promises to Focus on Jobs, Growth and Investment," *Financial Times*, February 2, 2005.

44. Peter Weinberg, "Europe Is Falling Well Short of Its Potential," *Financial Times*, January 28, 2005.

45. Paul Betts and Bertrand Benoit, "Business Wants Both Drive and Decisions," *Financial Times*, February 2, 2005.

46. See an excellent article on this subject by Martin Wolf, "Europeans Must Agree to Disagree for Unity's Sake," *Financial Times*, February 12, 2003.

47. See Robert C. Toth, "What Makes Americans Different?" *International Herald Tribune*, October 3, 1977.

48. Thomas Fuller, "Schröder Aids Chirac in Push for EU Charter," *International Herald Tribune*, April 27, 2005.

49. Eric Pfanner, *International Herald Tribune*, December 4, 2002.

50. See Alison Beard, "Not Just an Ocean Divides European and US Millionaires," *Financial Times*, June 18, 2002, and Robert D. Putnam, *Bowling Alone: The Collapse and Revival of American Community*, Simon & Schuster, New York, 2000, page 117.

51. Heather Higgins, "Death by Bureaucracy," *Wall Street Journal*, April 4, 2005.

52. See Beard, "Not Just an Ocean Divides European and US Millionaires."

53. Manuel Barroso, "Europe 2010: A European Renewal," a speech delivered in Davos, Switzerland, January 29, 2005.

54. See Jean-Claude Trichet (president of the European Central Bank), "Euro Vision," *Wall Street Journal*, February 24, 2005.

55. Charles A. Kupchan, "The End of the West," *Atlantic Monthly*, November 2002. See also William Pfaff, "Why the U.S. Fears Europe," *International Herald Tribune*, February 11, 2003, and Charles A. Kupchan, *The End of the American Era*, Alfred A. Knopf, New York, 2003.

56. John K. Glenn, "You're OK, but Your President . . . ," *International Herald Tribune*, February 22, 2005.

57. See an interview with Manuel Barroso in the *Financial Times*, February 2, 2005, and Thomas Fuller, "France Deals Blow to EU Services Plan," *International Herald Tribune*, February 3, 2005. See also Manuel Barroso, "Working Together for Growth and Jobs: A New Start for the Lisbon Strategy," Brussels, February 2, 2005.

58. See Richard Bernstein, "Europe's 'Revolt against the Establishment,'" *International Herald Tribune*, June 2, 2005.

59. See Graham Bowley, "Barroso Underscores Pro-Business Reforms," *International Herald Tribune*, March 2, 2005, and "EU Seeks to Cut Red Tape with Services Shake-Up" (March 3, 2005), www.eubusiness.com. In the spring of 2006 there were approximately 150 Polish plumbers in France, and about 6,000 unfilled vacancies in the same profession. See *Europe's World*, spring 2006, p. 100.

60. See Mary Jacoby, "Borderless Flow of EU Services Dealt Big Setback," *Wall Street Journal*, March 4, 2005.

61. "EU Seeks to Cut Red Tape with Services Shake-Up" (March 3, 2005), www.eubusiness.com.

62. Nick Prag, publisher of Eubusiness, www.eubusiness.com/topics/SMEs/EU-News.2004-03-02.1753.

63. See an interview with Manuel Barroso in the *Financial Times*, February 2, 2005.

64. Frits Bolkestein, "France's Verdict Tells Us That Europe Has Been Oversold," *Financial Times*, May 31, 2005.

65. Elaine Sciolino, "EU Leaders Step Up the Sniping over Future," *International Herald Tribune*, June 22, 2005.

Chapter V: Legacies, Ancient and Modern

1. The English translation of the first two stanzas is by Daniel Platt, and the third stanza is the author's. The poem in German follows: "Amerika, du hast es besser als unser Kontinent, der alte, hast keine verfallenen Schlösser und keine Basalte. Dich stört nicht im Innern zu lebendiger Zeit unnützes Erinnern und vergeblicher Streit. Benutzt die Gegenwart mit Glück! Und wenn nun eure Kinder dichten, bewahre sie ein gut Geschick vor Ritter-, Räuber- und Gespenstergeschichten."

2. André Malraux, *New York Times*, July 27, 1974. See as useful, Rodney Stark, *The Victory of Reason: How Christianity Led to Freedom, Capitalism, and Western Success*, Random House, New York, 2005.

3. See Renwick McLean, "Spain Backs EU Charter, but Turnout Stirs Doubts," *International Herald Tribune*, February 21, 2005.

4. See the *International Herald Tribune*, March 16, 2003, and March 1, 2004.

5. *International Herald Tribune*, December 30, 2002.

6. See Heather Grabbe of the Center for European Reform in London, as cited in the *International Herald Tribune*, October 30/31, 2004.

7. Elaine Sciolino, "Giscard Puts Blame on Chirac," *International Herald Tribune*, June 15, 2005.

8. See the *International Herald Tribune*, June 8, 9 and 10, 2005, and the *Wall Street Journal*, May 31, 2005.

9. See Katrin Bennhold, "EU Won't Shy from Wider Competition," *International Herald Tribune*, June 8, 2005.

10. Javier Solana, "Toward a United European Voice," *International Herald Tribune*, October 30/31, 2004. Solana served as secretary general of NATO between 1995 and 1999, and is the grandson of the distinguished Spanish diplomat and writer Salvador de Madariaga.

11. See Edward Rothstein, "Europe's Constitution: All Hail the Bureaucracy," *New York Times*, July 5, 2003. See also Hans Werner Sinn, "There Is No European Right to a Place in the Sun," *Financial Times*, February 13, 2003, Philip Stephens, "Europe's Nations Are Bound Together Despite Everything," *Financial Times*, February 14, 2003, Thomas Fuller, "Too Baffling to Bother: Europe's Disconnect," *International Herald Tribune*, June 16, 2004, and Thomas Fuller and Katrin Bennhold, "EU Leaders Forge Accord on Charter," *International Herald Tribune*, June 19–20, 2004.

12. "Spain All but Begs for Votes on EU Charter," *San Francisco Chronicle*, February 19, 2005.

13. "Social dumping" is a Western European term that refers to the image of "the Polish plumber"; a euphemism for the ten central European countries which joined the EU in 2004 whose citizens are willing to work longer hours, for less money, in more flexible labor environments than their Western European counterparts: "the easterners' creative ways of skirting EU law amount to 'social dumping,' a term used by trade unions and politicians in the West that implies the erosion of social benefits and labor costs through external competition." In other words labor performed at lower wages by those in the new-member countries enjoys a competitive advantage that is condemned by Western

Europeans. See Daniel Vaughan-Whitehead, "Working and Employment Conditions in the New EU Member States: Convergence or Diversity," financed by the European Commission and International Labor Organization and cited in the *International Herald Tribune*, June 15, 2005.

14. From a private conversation conducted by the author in Paris, May 25, 2005.

15. "French Socialists Set to Vote at 'Historical' Point for Their Party," *International Herald Tribune*, December 1, 2004.

16. See the excellent appraisal of the EU in the aftermath of the French election by Paul Johnson, "What Europe Really Needs," *Wall Street Journal*, June 17, 2005.

17. As cited in *The Economist*, June 23, 2003.

18. May 9 was selected in honor of the French founder of the European Coal and Steel Community, Robert Schuman, born on this date.

19. Saint Benoît was born in 480 in the mountains of Umbria in Italy and was the founder of the first monasteries from which Christianity spread throughout western and central Europe.

20. Edward Rothstein, "Europe's Constitution: All Hail the Bureaucracy," *New York Times*, July 5, 2003.

21. See Philip Stephens, "It Is Time for Old Europe to Turn Back towards Liberty," *Financial Times*, February 25, 2005.

22. William Pfaff, "EU's Problem with 'No,'" *International Herald Tribune*, June 23, 2005. On this subject see also George Weigel, *The Cube and the Cathedral: Europe, America, and Politics without God*, Basic Books, New York, 2005.

23. The French diplomat who negotiated the Treaty of Versailles at the end of World War I and who died in 1929.

24. Steven F. Hayward, *The Age of Reagan: The Fall of the Old Liberal Order 1964–1980*, Roseville, California, Prima Publishing, 2001 (member of the Crown Publishing Group, a division of Random House), pp. 429–30.

25. See Christopher Caldwell, *Financial Times*, February 14/15, 2004. See also William I. Hitchcock's study entitled *The Struggle for Europe: The Turbulent History of a Divided Continent 1945 to the Present*, Doubleday, New York, 2003.

26. Christian Hacke, "Deutschland, Europa und der Irakkonflikt," *Aus Politik und Zeitgeschichte*, B 24–25/2003.

27. Henri Astier, *Times Literary Supplement*, January 10, 2003. Revel's book *l'Obsession anti-américaine* was published in Paris in 2002.

28. Dominique Moïsi, "Coming Together in Fear and Trepidation," *International Herald Tribune*, April 30–May 2, 2004.

29. See Richard Bernstein, "A Bridge and a Barrier, and the Chasm Between," *International Herald Tribune*, July 23, 2004.

30. Peter Schneider, "Separated by Civilization," *International Herald Tribune*, April 7, 2004.

31. From a speech delivered to the American Council on Germany in New York City in April 2001, entitled "The Euro and the Enlargement of the European Union: Perspectives for a United Europe."

32. Barry James, "The EU? Poll Finds Public Skeptical and Indifferent," *International Herald Tribune*, July 20, 2001.

33. J. J. Jusserand, *What Me Befell*, Houghton Mifflin Company, Boston and New York, 1933, page xv.

Chapter VI: The Fly in the Soup

1. Marc Dugain, "Humanisme réaliste," *Le Figaro*, Ocober 29, 2006. Compare this observation with Dominique de Villepin's judgment in May 2005 (see chapter five).

2. José Manuel Barroso, "Europe Must Open Up to the Globalized World," *International Herald Tribune*, September 21, 2005.

3. This book, published in October 2000, was entitled *Professor Bark's Amazing Digital Adventure* (Woodford Press, Emeryville, California). I began writing it in 1997 as I was learning how to use a computer, but by the time of publication few people were interested in reading any more about computers and Silicon Valley. The boom was ending and the timing of publication could not have been worse. In addition, the publisher, unbeknownst to me, declared bankruptcy shortly after publication, so the book was never marketed and less than 1,000 copies are in circulation. The book, in which I wrote about "a flat world" (page 78) long before Tom Friedman announced to his readers that the world is no longer round, was originally entitled "Virtual Certainties"—a much better title than that recommended by the publisher.

4. See Dennis L. Bark, *Professor Bark's Amazing Digital Adventure*, pp. 200–201

5. T. R. Reid, *International Herald Tribune*, May 21, 2002.

6. See Allan E. Goodman (president and CEO, Institute of International Education), from a speech entitled "Franklin in Paris: Lessons for International Education Week," delivered to the NAFSA Region VIII Symposium held in Philadelphia, November 19, 2004, and his speech of the previous day entitled "The Closing of the American Mind: A Progress Report," delivered at Tufts University, November 18, 2004.

7. In fact, the total value of investments on both continents is far greater because the figures cited here do not take into account when the investments were made and their appreciated value thereafter. See T. R. Reid, *International Herald Tribune*, May 21, 2002, and Rockwell Schnabel, U.S. ambassador to the EU, from a speech delivered at the Centre for European Policy Studies in Brussels, Belgium, February 21, 2003.

8. See Diane Ravitch, *The Language Police*, Alfred A. Knopf, New York, 2003.

9. Dominique Moïsi, "Veterans, Teenagers and History," *International Herald Tribune*, June 11, 2004.

10. Robert Kagan, "Power and Weakness," *Policy Review*, no. 113, 2002.

11. George W. Bush, June 15, 2001.

12. See Frank Viviano, "Europe Won over by War's Success," *San Francisco Chronicle*, December 16, 2001.

13. Ibid. Viviano quotes in English from the December 7 French edition of *Le Monde*.

14. Steven Erlanger, "Europe Seethes as the U.S. Flies Solo in World Affairs," *New*

York Times, February 23, 2002. See also Chris Patten, "Jaw-Jaw, not War-War," *Financial Times*, February 15, 2002.

15. An interview with Pierre Hassner in *Le Figaro*, October 30, 2003.

16. Nicholas D. Kristof, "U.S. Arrogance Comes Home to Roost," *International Herald Tribune*, February 1–2, 2003.

17. An exception in France is writer Guy Sorman. On September 13, 2001, his superb editorial on the significance of the attack and how America would respond to it was published in *Le Figaro* with the title "l'Amérique va gagner" ("America's going to win").

18. See Elizabeth Pond, *Internationale Politik* (transatlantic edition), Berlin, 1/2003.

19. Kagan, loc. cit.

20. Ethan Bronner, *International Herald Tribune*, February 1–2, 2003.

21. Roy Denman, "How to Make Americans Listen," *International Herald Tribune*, July 16, 2002. Denman served as ambassador between 1982 and 1989.

22. Christopher Caldwell, *Financial Times*, March 19, 2003.

23. The *Wall Street Journal*, February 10, 2003.

24. See Graham E. Fuller, "Old Europe—or Old America?" *International Herald Tribune*, February 12, 2003.

25. Jack Straw, *International Herald Tribune*, March 27, 2003.

26. See www.globalissues.org/Geopolitics/ArmsTrade/Spending.asp

27. As reported by Andrew Bacevich, "The Dark Roots of America's Security Strategy," *Financial Times*, March 2, 2005.

28. Richard Bernstein, "From America, Europe Seems a Long Way Off," *International Herald Tribune*, February 4, 2005.

29. See the testimony by Ambassador R. Nicholas Burns, U.S. permanent representative to NATO, on the future of NATO to the Senate Foreign Relations Committee, Washington, D. C., April 1, 2003.

Chapter VII: The Force of Things

1. Among the many articles during this period—between early 2002 and early 2003—the following are noteworthy: R. James Woolsey, "Where's the Posse?" *Wall Street Journal*, February 25, 2002, Charles Moore, "Our Friends in Europe," *Wall Street Journal*, March 8, 2002, Sebastian Mallaby, "Insults Back and Forth over the Atlantic," *International Herald Tribune*, May 14, 2002, Steven Erlanger, "Protests, and Friends Too, Await Bush in Europe," *International Herald Tribune*, May 22, 2002, Gerard Baker, "European Insults Fall on Deaf Ears in America's Heartland," *Financial Times*, February 6, 2003, Sarah Lyall, "Europe's Intellectuals See Freedom 'Trampled,'" *International Herald Tribune*, February 15/16, 2003, and BBC News, "Analysis: Power Americana," February 26, 2003.

2. As quoted in the *International Herald Tribune*, November 4, 2002.

3. See, for example, *International Herald Tribune*, November 4, 2002; Elizabeth Pond, *Internationale Politik* (transatlantic edition), Berlin, I/2003, and Joseph Fitchett, *International Herald Tribune*, February 12, 2003.

4. Richard Perle, "Le jour où les Européens nous ont lâchés," *Le Figaro*, September 12, 2006.

5. A letter to the author of March 30, 2003, from Marie-Thérèse de Maigret, née Poniatowska.

6. See *Die Welt*, April 2 and 3, 2003.

7. The deliberate reference to two Greek names for planets is an irony that Kagan may have ignored or of which he may have been ignorant. The Roman names for Mars and Venus were Ares and Aphrodite. Mars and Venus had a daughter named Harmonia, whose Roman name was Concordia.

8. Robert Kagan, "Power and Weakness," *Policy Review*, no. 113, 2002.

9. Ibid.

10. Thomas L. Friedman, "Bush's Shame," *New York Times*, August 4, 2002.

11. See H. D. S. Greenway, "American Leadership, or Bullying?" *International Herald Tribune*, October 7, 2005, and Stephen M. Walt, *Taming American Power: The Global Response to U.S. Primacy*, W. W. Norton & Company, New York, 2005.

12. Victor Davis Hanson, "Soft Power, Hard Truths," *Wall Street Journal*, February 22, 2005.

13. Olivier Dassault, "La leçon américaine," *Valeurs Actuelles*, November 5, 2004. See also Dennis L. Bark, "The French Lesson," *Hoover Digest*, no. 2, 2005, pp. 96–99.

14. See Jeremy Rifkin, *The European Dream*, Jeremy P. Tarcher/Penguin, New York, 2004, page 3.

15. Judy Dempsey, "Rival Views on EU Are Out in the Open," *International Herald Tribune*, June 20, 2005.

16. Jack Straw, British foreign secretary, from a speech delivered at the Brookings Institution, Washington, D. C., May 8, 2002, as cited in Todd S. Purdum, "Powell encounters Parallel Universe of Europe," *International Herald Tribune*, May 16, 2002.

17. Ibid.

18. Wolfgang Ischinger, at a forum of the Council on Foreign Relations, March 25, 2003.

19. See Jeremy Rifkin, *The European Dream*, Jeremy P. Tarcher/Penguin, New York, 2004, and T. R. Reid, *The United States of Europe: The New Superpower and the End of American Supremacy*, Penguin Press, 2004. Three other studies also merit attention: Rockwell A. Schnabel, *The Next Superpower?* Rowman & Littlefield Publishers, Inc., New York, 2005, Mark Leonard, *Why Europe Will Run the 21st Century*, PublicAffairs (Perseus Books Group), New York, 2005, and Timothy Garton Ash, *Free World: America, Europe, and the Surprising Future of the West*, Random House, New York, 2004.

20. Nicole Bacharan, "L'Europe doit inventer un nouvel Atlantisme," *Le Figaro*, November 11/12, 2006.

A Selected Bibliography
for Further Reading

It is impossible, and would be tedious in the extreme, to read all that has been written about Americans and Europeans. The books listed below, both old and recent, are well worth the reading. In this selection I have made arbitrary divisions, according to time and place, because they make it easier for the reader to judge their interest and scope.

NINETEENTH CENTURY

Cooke, Alistair, *The Americans: Fifty Talks on Our Life and Times*, Alfred A. Knopf, New York, 1979, 273 pages. Familiar to many as the host of Public Television's Masterpiece Theater, Alistair Cooke was a keen and witty, long-time observer of American life from a British perspective.

de Tocqueville, Alexis, *Democracy in America*, 1833. Available are many excellent, English-language editions. No observer of Americans approaches the masterful insight of this brilliant French aristocrat. His examination of the tensions between Americans' love of liberty and their quest for equality is still relevant today. The accuracy of his predictions regarding America's future rings uncannily true.

Dickens, Charles, *American Notes and Pictures from Italy*, Chapman and Hall, London, 1874, 506 pages. The celebrated novelist remains well loved and widely read, largely because of his brilliant descriptions of the human character. His penetrating and often critical observations of Americans are well worth reading.

Jusserand, J. J., *What Me Befell*. Houghton Mifflin Company, Boston and New York, 1933, 360 pages. Jean-Jules Jusserand was a distinguished diplomat, and an equally erudite student of history, whose commitment to friendship with America lasted his entire life. This is a fascinating memoir by the longest serving French ambassador to the United States during the twentieth century—from 1902 to 1925—who married an American woman, Elise Richards, whose family came from New England. His book—*With Americans of Past and Present Days*—won the first Pulitzer Prize in History in 1917.

Muirhead, James Fullarton, *The Land of Contrasts*, John Lane: The Bodley Head, London and New York, 1902, 282 pages. Muirhead traveled throughout America in 1888 and again between 1890 and 1893. The purpose of his visit was to prepare a handbook on the United States for Karl Baedeker. He did so, but during 1895 and 1896 he also wrote about the contrasts he had seen, drawn from visits "into almost every State and Territory in the Union, and . . . (from) direct contact with representatives of practically every class."

Wilkinson, Walter, *Puppets through America*, Geoffrey Bles, London, 1938, 248 pages. Wilkinson was an English puppeteer whose traveling show toured America in the 1930s. This is a charming travelogue, full of interesting observations about America, some of which still hold true.

TWENTIETH CENTURY—*by Europeans*

Ash, Timothy Garton, *Free World: America, Europe, and the Surprising Future of the West*, Random House, New York, 2004, 286 pages. The director of the European Studies Center at St. Anthony's College Oxford presents a sophisticated soft power–hard power discussion, and argues that European-American cooperation will greatly extend the reach of freedom in the world.

Joffe, Josef, *Überpower: The Imperial Temptation of America*, W. W. Norton & Company, New York and London, 2006, 271 pages. The German publisher-editor of the well-known Hamburg weekly *Die Zeit* was educated in America and has taught there as well. This volume posits the notion that America must return "to an earlier, more generous tradition of its foreign policy" marked by more listening and less confrontation.

Jospin, Lionel, *Le monde comme je le vois*, Gallimard, Paris, 2005, 324 pages. In this book the former French prime minister (1997–2002) analyzes the state of the world as he sees it, and presents his concerns about the future of France and socialism. The volume is full of Jospin's reflections on the force of things political, economic, domestic and foreign.

Leonard, Mark, *Why Europe Will Run the 21st Century*, Public Affairs, New York, 2005, 170 pages. The author, director of foreign policy at the European Center for Reform in London, avers that "Europe's reach is broad and deep based on its cultural and economic influence," and that "America's military influence belongs to another era." He does not address the fact that Americans exert a greater cultural and economic influence on much of the rest of the world than does contemporary Europe.

Levy, Bernard-Henri, trans. Charlotte Mandell, *American Vertigo: Traveling America in the Footsteps of Tocqueville*, Random House Trade Paperbacks. New York, 2007, 320 pages.

Michelin, François, *And Why NOT?* Lexington Books, Lanham, Boulder, New York, and Oxford, 2003, 89 pages. François Michelin, when serving as head of the company founded by his grandfather, was one of the most celebrated chief executives in France; on reading this book the reader discovers why. At the age of 87 he consented to an interview on the radio program *The Entrepreneurial Way* conducted by two French journalists who allowed Michelin to present, in his own words, a thoughtful and perceptive examination of the relationship between business and the individual as both customer and employee. He addresses questions concerning capitalism, socialism, competition, free markets, and sound business practice. In this vein he introduces the

Five-Step Method that his grandfather Edouard Michelin wrote as a memorandum in 1912. Since then the method has become the company's guiding management principle. This unique and tremendously powerful book should be required reading in every introductory course on economics, politics, and European history in U.S. colleges and universities, as well as in every graduate school of business in America and Europe.

Patten, Chris, *Cousins and Strangers: America, Britain and Europe in a New Century*, Henry Holt and Company, New York, 2006, 309 pages. The former European commissioner for external relations contrasts Americans and Europeans as cousins and strangers, and finds particular fault with an asserted American preference for unilateralism. He favors a top-down approach to the management of world affairs, by a multinational government elite.

Revel, Jean-François, *Anti-Americanism*, Encounter Books, San Francisco, 2003, 176 pages. Revel, a rare pro-American French intellectual, who died in 2006, presents a balanced and thought-provoking analysis of "anti-Americanism" that, in tone and argument, is far more critical of European failings than of American influence. Revel focuses, especially, on the forces opposing globalization, and, according to a reviewer from the Claremont Institute, Daniel J. Mahoney, "is particularly effective in exposing the economic illiteracy that informs anti-globalization."

Rosa, Jean-Jacques, *The Second Twentieth Century*, Hoover Institution Press, Stanford, 2006, 390 pages. Rosa, professor of economics at the Institut d'Etudes Politiques de Paris, has written an economic, organizational and technical analysis of the history, politics, and ideology of corporations and states at the beginning of the new millennium. He sheds much light on the objective conditions necessary for the preservation and diffusion of the values of freedom and democracy.

Zöller, Michael, and Kamer, Hansrudolf, editors, *Der Westen—was sonst?* Verlag Neue Zürcher Zeitung, Zürich, 2005, 216 pages. These two distinguished German scholars have assembled a collection of essays by both Europeans and Americans that argue what America and Europe have in common is of much greater importance than what divides them.

TWENTIETH CENTURY—*by Americans*

Blankley, Tony, *The West's Last Chance*, Regnery Publishing Company, Inc., Washington, D. C., 2005, 232 pages. This book, by the editorial page editor for the *Washington Times*, is focused on European and American responses to Islamic terrorism. Blankley offers many insights into the differing ways that Americans and Europeans look at this vexing, contemporary problem. He argues, persuasively, that the West—America and Europe—must act together as "the West" to address the threat of terrorism in defense of our common values.

Kagan, Robert, *Of Paradise and Power: America and Europe in the New World Order*, Alfred A. Knopf, New York, 2003, 103 pages. Kagan's book is the most often read if not necessarily the best of the soft power versus hard power critiques which have been written in the last several years. Kagan is a hard-power advocate who misleads his readers into thinking that Europeans are completely unwilling to consider military action, and concludes, tritely, that "Americans are from Mars and Europeans are from Venus." Because of its popularity and influence this book is worth reading.

Kupchan, Charles A., *The End of the American Era: U. S. Foreign Policy and the Geopolitics of the Twenty-First Century*, Alfred A. Knopf, New York, 2003, 391 pages. Kupchan is a professor of international relations at Georgetown University and a senior fellow at the Council on Foreign Relations. In his view Europe is America's rival and the ascending power. This book is another soft power–hard power tome written by a believer in soft power which, he argues, is better understood and further developed in Europe.

Kuralt, Charles, *Charles Kuralt's America*, G. P. Putnam's Sons, New York, 1978, 279 pages. Kuralt, who was a professional news commentator for thirty-seven years, has been called "the laureate of the common man" by *Time* magazine. His great affection for America and Americans is the hallmark of this book, written on the road while traveling across America from New Orleans, to Alaska, to New York City. His book contains enjoyable and entertaining stories about Americans he meets for the first time.

Lindberg, Tod, editor, *Beyond Paradise and Power: Europe, America and the Future of a Troubled Partnership*, Routledge, New York and London, 2005, 245 pages. This volume, with contributions by Europeans and Americans, contains twelve well-balanced essays on issues affecting transatlantic solidarity.

Meacham, Jon. *American Gospel: God, the Founding Fathers, and the Making of a Nation*, Random House, New York, 2006, 399 pages. Meacham, the managing editor of *Newsweek*, has produced a historical study that is eminently readable. It provides, in the words of historian David McCullough, "a refreshingly clear, balanced, and wise historical portrait of religion and American politics at exactly the moment when such fairness and understanding are much needed. Anyone who doubts the relevance of history to our own time has only to read this exceptional book."

Prestowitz, Clyde, *Rogue Nation: American Unilateralism and the Failure of Good Intentions*, Basic Books, New York, 2003, 328 pages. This author, president of the Economic Strategy Institute in Washington, D.C., focuses on the excesses of American unilateralism in terms of American policies and rhetoric. He forcefully advocates a more restrained American projection of power, and increased use of diplomatic persuasion.

Reid, T. R., *The United States of Europe: The New Superpower and the End of American Supremacy*, the Penguin Press, New York, 2004, 305 pages. Reid, a journalist with the *Washington Post* and a commentator for National Public Radio, believes that the European Union is the emerging United States of Europe. While the EU may not become a rival, he suggests, it will certainly compete earnestly with the United States on matters concerning economics and soft power.

Rifkin, Jeremy, *The European Dream: How Europe's Vision of the Future Is Quietly Eclipsing the American Dream*, the Penguin Group, New York, 2004, 434 pages. Rifkin believes that the European social model is the answer to America's cowboy capitalism. The European model, he argues, is making the American dream passé. Rifkin ignores the fact that many Europeans, even those advocates of the current model, privately acknowledge that the current economic arrangements are unsustainable.

Schnabel, Rockwell A., *The Next Superpower? The Rise of Europe and its Challenge to the United States*, Rowman & Littlefield Publishers, Inc., New York, 2005, 198 pages. Schnabel, born in the Netherlands, served as American ambassador to the European Union in Brussels from 2001 to 2005. He has written a sensitive and thoughtful volume on "the complexity of our relationship, at once bilateral and multilateral . . ." An interesting focus of this book is the growing inter-dependence of the EU and the U.S. economies. His book has been generously praised by Jeffrey Immelt, chairman and CEO of General Electric Company.

Walt, Stephen M., *Taming American Power: The Global Response to U.S. Primacy*, W. W. Norton & Company, New York and London, 2005, 320 pages. Dean of International Affairs at Harvard University's John F. Kennedy School of Government, Walt argues that the United States has, in the conduct of its foreign policy since September 2001, moved from moderation to extremism in both word and deed, thus awakening doubts about the wisdom of U.S. dominance in foreign affairs.

Index

Accession Treaty, 134, 243n11
"Action Plan for Entrepreneurship" (Liikanen), 161
Acton, John, 113–14
Adams, John, 37
Adenauer, Konrad, xiii
affirmative action, xiii, 29, 33, 220
Afghanistan
  European allies in, 90, 202–3, 205–6
  U.S. aid to, 232
  war on terrorism in, 90, 202–6
The Age of Reagan (Hayward), 179
agriculture, state policy for, 21, 106, 128, 165
AIDS, 165–66
ALDE Group, 105
Allais, Maurice, 113–14
America
  American dream for, 30, 32, 35, 37, 42–43, 49, 60, 63–64, 81, 99, 108, 110, 145, 155
  "American spirit" in, 79, 82, 85, 87, 90
  arrogance of, 1, 3, 66, 87, 201
  artists of, 59
  Atlantic Divide for, ix, xiii, 1
  attitudes in, x, 2
  Bill of Rights for, 28, 177
  Bretton Woods agreement by, 124, 242n1
  Christian ethic in, 34, 35–36
  Christianity in, 35, 38
  class distinctions in, 28–29, 31
  communication in, 67–68
  competition between Europe and, 4–5, 155–57
  competition in, xi, xii, 4, 9, 26, 30, 32, 37, 90–91, 92, 94, 96, 121–22, 138, 153–54, 161, 223
  concept of freedom in, xi, 14–15, 23, 28, 44, 79, 82, 83, 91, 95, 170, 185

Constitution for, 28, 52, 107
cultural influences in, 38–39
debt forgiveness by, 110
defense budget for, 209
Democratic Party in, 105
difference between Europe and, xii, 4, 5, 9, 11, 12, 15, 27, 28, 33, 42, 50, 79, 82, 85, 91, 92, 98, 122, 123, 128, 154, 165, 166, 194, 220, 221, 225, 235n7
diplomacy by, x, 165–66
economic model for, xi, xii, 4, 9, 26, 30, 32, 37, 90–91, 92, 94, 96, 121–22
education in, 83–84, 239n41
ethnicity in, 40–43
Europe needed by, 86–87
European commercial relationship with, 197–98, 249n7
European commonalities with, ix
European defense by, xiii, 123–24, 183–84
European division with, ix
European impact on, 38–42, 216
federal role in, 93
flag for, 25–26, 43–44, 82, 89, 169, 188, 204, 224
French aid for, 52
frontiers in, 48, 49, 50, 51, 53, 60
GDP growth rates for, 121, 134, 242nn28–29, 243n10
geographical influences on, 46–48, 50–51, 54–55, 237n5
geographical space in, 48
as global policeman, xiii
governance in, xii, 11, 12
guns in, 52–53
holidays in, 12, 35–36, 39–40, 48, 122, 198–99, 236n17
ignorance of Europe by, xii, 2

America (*continued*)
  individual responsibility in, 13–15, 52, 93,
    97, 108
  isolationism of, 83, 239n41
  jazz in, 39, 59, 61
  labor productivity in, 120, 241n22
  land ownership in, 57–58
  language in, 64–68
  law/order in, 52
  leadership in, xiv, 25, 202, 209, 211–12, 213,
    216, 217, 240n43
  legal system in, 155–56
  loyalty in, 89, 108, 121–22
  merit in, 30
  mobility in, 30
  music of, 59–60, 61, 238n20
  National Security Council for, 206–7
  national security for, 202–3
  as New World, 2, 3, 6, 12, 30, 33, 34, 36, 37,
    41, 43, 48, 52, 67, 76, 165, 166, 198, 216
  patronage in, 30
  population of, 38–39, 56–57, 236n19
  privacy in, 56–57, 71
  profit motive in, 144–45, 162
  racial barriers in, 29, 36, 63
  risktaking in, 121–22, 161
  separation of church/state in, 35–36
  shared values between Europe and, ix, x, xiii,
    33, 181, 200, 201
  slavery in, 36
  social criticism for, 62
  Social Security in, 120
  socialism in, 98–99
  Thanksgiving in, 12, 35, 236n17
  think tanks in, 22
  Treasury bankruptcy in, 124, 242n1
  unilateralism by, 83, 186, 221
  universities in, 20
  urbanization in, 63
  use of names in, 82
  voting ballots in, 67, 239n26
  work ethic in, 119–20, 121–22
  work/retirement in, 120, 241n22, 241n24
  world outlook by, xi
  World War II for, 53, 91–92, 93, 96–97,
    109–10, 115–16, 123, 124, 182–83,
    237n10, 241nn13–14, 242n1
  youthfulness of, 12, 27–28, 53, 78, 79, 83,
    168
American dream, 30, 32, 35, 37, 42–43, 49, 60,
  63–64, 81, 99, 108, 110, 145, 155
"An American is . . .", 231–32

"The American Model," xi, xii, 4, 9, 26, 30, 32,
  37, 90–91, 92, 94, 96, 121–22, 138, 153–
  54, 161, 223
American Revolution, 52
"American spirit," 79, 82, 85, 87, 90
"American Sublime—landscape painting in the
  United States 1820–1880," 59–60
Americans
  analytical/direct approach by, xi, 70–71
  attitude of, x, 2, 79–81
  behavior by, 71–72
  CARE packages by, 53, 237n10, 241n13
  characteristics of, xi, 9, 13, 28–29, 36, 52, 84
  concept of time for, 48, 75–76, 77–78
  conversation by, 69
  cultural deprivation/inferiority of, 62, 66
  dress by, 73–74
  as entrepreneurs, 53
  European familiarity with, 45
  European travel by, 55–56, 72–73, 81
  historical perspective of, 78–79, 88–89, 167,
    189, 199, 215
  individualism of, 13–15, 52, 93, 97
  interdependence of, 51–52
  mentality of bigness in, 58
  mobility by, 75, 76
  "openness" of, 13, 49, 54–55, 237n4
  optimism of, 13, 60, 63, 90, 97–98, 122, 216
  patriotism of, 24–25, 43–44, 82, 89–90
  philanthropy by, 13, 19–20, 31, 53, 156,
    235n4, 237n10
  relationships for, 69–70, 197–98, 218, 249n7
  sensitivity of, to Europeans, 64
  tolerance by, xi
  toughness of, 13
  volunteerism by, 13, 84, 95, 156
anti-Americanism, xi, 186, 216
architecture, patronage for, 17
aristocracy, European
  as historical, 12–13, 14, 15, 17–19, 96, 99,
    103, 240n3
  politically elite as, 30, 92, 96, 103, 104
Aristotle, 78
arts
  American philanthropy for, 31, 235n4
  patronage for, 58–59
Astier, Henri, 186
Atlantic Divide, ix, xiii, 1
Atlantic Monthly, 25
Atlanticism, ix, 201–2, 226
Attlee, Clement, 110

Bacharan, Nicole, 226
Baldwin, James, 90
Bark, William Carroll, 5–6, 34
Barroso, Manuel, 159, 194
Barry, Norman, 119
Saint Benedict, 177
Berlin blockade, 34
Berlin, Irving, 40
Berlin Wall, x, 48, 49, 123–24, 178, 240n8
Berlusconi, Silvio, 151–52
Berns, Walter, 89
Bill of Rights, 28, 177. *See also* America; U.S.
    Constitution
birthrates, 119
black market, 24, 140, 143, 145
Blair, Tony, 138, 141, 194, 244n22
Bolkestein, Frits, 159, 163
Breton, Thierry, 92
Bretton Woods agreement, 124, 242n1. *See also*
    America; World War II
Bundestag, German, 151, 205
Burgess, Elisabeth, 70
Burke, Edmund, xi, 6–7, 219, 224
Bush, George W., 25, 202, 209, 211–12, 213,
    216, 217, 240n43

California Gold Rush, 51
capitalism, evils of, 26, 111
CARE, 53, 237n10, 241n13. *See also* World
    War II
Carmichael, Hoagy, 61
Carroll, Lewis, 1
cartels, European, 119, 241n22
Carter, Jimmy, 30–31
CDU. *See* Christian Democratic Party
CFDT. *See* Confédération Française Démocrat-
    ique du Travail
Charter of Fundamental Rights, 171–72
Chirac, Jacques, xiv, 139, 155, 172, 204–5, 213,
    243n11
Christian Democratic Party (CDU), 111–12,
    115. *See also* Germany
Christianity
    as cultural identity, 34, 169, 198
    decline of, 170
    in EU constitution, 177–78
Christmas, 35–36, 39–40
A Christmas Carol (Dickens), 40
church
    influence of, in Europe, 19
    restoration of art in, 235n4
Churchill, Winston, 110, 125–26, 204, 210

Civil War, 89, 188
Clay, Lucius, 34
Clemenceau, Georges, 179, 248n23
Clinton, William J., 30
Cold War, ix, xii, 2, 31, 86, 87, 123, 124, 125,
    158, 163, 184, 207, 208–9
collective bargaining, 178
Colonial Dames of America, 82
Commissioner for Competition, 161
Common Market, 126, 162. *See also* European
    Economic Community
communism, collapse of, ix, 123–24, 125, 184.
    See also socialism
Communist Party of the Soviet Union, 103
comparisons/contrasts, European/American
    advantages of "soft" *v.* "hard" power, 165–66
    American *v.* European constitutional conven-
        tions, 171
    average *v.* extreme for, 95, 97
    for birthrates, 119
    competition for, 4–5, 155–57, 158
    defense of freedom for, 185, 188
    direct *v.* indirect program implementation as,
        149
    of effects of war, 182–83
    essential difference for, xii, 4, 5, 9, 11, 12, 15,
        27, 28, 33, 42, 50, 79, 82, 85, 91, 92, 98,
        122, 123, 128, 154, 165, 166, 194, 220,
        221, 225, 235n7
    free trade *v.* protectionism, 165
    freedom *v.* equality for, 151, 155
    freedom *v.* order/stability for, 165, 176, 180–
        81, 225
    GDP growth rates for, 121, 134, 242nn28–
        29, 243n10
    globalization for, xi, xii, 165, 172, 174, 193–
        96, 198, 249n3
    historical experience for, 78–79, 88–89, 167,
        189, 199, 215, 220
    identity of place for, 169–70
    for immigration, 119, 242n26
    invulnerability for, 203
    in labor productivity, 119, 120, 137–38, 140,
        148, 150, 153, 174, 176, 241n22, 242n22,
        242n24, 245n38, 247n13
    money/profit in speech *v.* thought for, 144–
        45, 162
    nationalization *v.* privatization as, 149–50,
        152–53, 161, 172
    peace *v.* freedom for, 187–88, 210
    perspectives of viewpoint for, xi, 9, 88, 185,
        188, 200, 204, 206, 207–8, 214, 219–22

comparisons/contrasts (*continued*)
  philanthropy *v.* state benevolence for, 32, 156
  present *v.* future result for, 150, 151, 152
  public good *v.* private interests, 101–2
  regulation/stability *v.* competition/growth as, 92, 93, 108–9, 111, 115–16, 180–81
  risk taking for, 94, 121–22, 161
  social strengths v. weaknesses for, 95–96
  social *v.* individual for, 102, 145
  state *v.* individual responsibilities, 22–23, 24, 28, 97, 108, 145
  sufferance *v.* pursuit of progress for, 155
  values for, ix, x, xiii, 33, 181, 200, 201
  work ethic for, 119–21, 121–22
  work/retirement for, 119–20, 241n22, 241n24
  youthful perspective for, 199
competition
  American model for, xi, xii, 4, 9, 26, 30, 32, 37, 90–91, 92, 94, 96, 121–22, 138, 153–54, 161, 223
  EU rules for, 137, 174
  between Europe/America, 4–5, 155–57
  in marketplace, 110, 111, 114–15, 159
  purpose of, 4
  regulation/stability *v.* growth and, 92, 93, 108–9, 111, 115–16, 180–81
  socialism and, 100, 109, 111
Confédération Française Démocratique du Travail (CFDT), 150, 245n38
constitution
  for America, 28, 52
  Christianity in, for EU, 177–78
  for EU, 116, 136, 171, 173, 177–78
Consul d'Etat, 150
Convention on the Future of Europe, 171
Cooper, Gary, 60
Corriere Della Sera (newspaper), 120
Council of Ministers, 126
criminal court, international, 165–66
Crosby, Bing, 40, 61–62
currency, 115, 118, 127, 129–31, 132–33
Cypress Semiconductor, 122

"Dancing in the Dark" (song), 3, 235n1
Dubler-Gmelin, Herta, 211–12
Daughters of the American Revolution, 82
de Gaulle, Charles, 117, 124, 130
de Jouvenel, Bertrand, 113–14
de Villepin, Dominique, 172
death penalty, 165–66
Declaration of Arbroath, 16, 235n3

Declaration of Independence, 18, 34, 37, 107, 189, 220
Degeyter, Pierre, 233–34
Delors, Jacques, 129, 243n4
democracy, action towards, xiii
Democracy In America (Tocqueville), 25, 37–38, 113, 146
Denman, Roy, 207
depotism, enlightened, 27, 236n8
d'Estaing, Valéry Giscard, 46, 171, 174, 178, 243n11
Deutsche Bank, 143
DeutschlandRadio, 34, 236n15
Dickens, Charles, 40
Die Welt (newspaper), 214
diplomacy
  by America, x, 165–66
  by Europe, 165–66
  freedom and, 185
  as obligatory, 87
  tools of, 165–66, 209
discrimination, racial, 29, 36, 63
Disraeli, Benjamin, 136, 153
diversity, cultural, 165–66
divine right, 14, 38
Donne, John, 86
"Don't Fence Me In" (Porter), 61–62
Dvorak, Anton, 41

e pluribus unum, 43, 44
ECB. *See* European Central Bank
The Economic Miracle, 115
education
  in America, 83–84, 239n41
  French ENA for, 96, 240n3
  of French senators, 92
EEC. *See* European Economic Community
Eisenhower, Dwight D., 117
Eluard, Paul, 148
employee, government
  French ENA for, 96, 240n3
  as new aristocrat, 14, 96, 99, 240n3
  patronage/security for, 21, 118
EMU. *See* European Monetary Union
ENA. *See* School for National Administration
énarques (politically elite graduates), 96, 240n3
The End of Work, 120
Engels, Friedrich, 100
England
  British Labour Party in, 110, 244n22
  differences between, and Europe, 16
  governance in, 16

nationalization of heavy industry in, 110
restructuring after WW II by, 106–7
Thatcher in, xii–xiii, 23, 31, 106–7, 129,
141, 148, 158–59, 244n22
Enlightenment, eighteenth-century, xii
entitlement
retirement as, 119–20
from state, 22, 23, 78, 96
environment, protection of, 21, 165, 176, 178
equality
as economic, 94
freedom v., 151, 155
as government-mandated, xii, 92, 94, 95
of opportunity, 176
as social, 34, 92
under socialism, 96, 100, 101, 238n24
Erhard, Ludwig, xiii, 115, 116
ESDP. See European security and defense policy
ethic
Christian, 34, 35–36
work, 119–22
ethnic cleansing, 186–87
EU. See European Union
Eucken, Walter, 113–14
Euro-bonds, 162
euros
circulation of, 130–31
function of, 127, 162, 177
Maastricht Treaty for, 129, 130, 139, 173
redemption of, 124
value of, 131, 243n7
Europe
affirmative action in, 29
in Afghanistan, 90, 202–3, 205–6
American commercial relationship with, 197–
98, 249n7
American commonalities/divisions with, ix
American dress in, 73–74
anti-Americanism in, xi, 186, 216
aristocracy in, 12–13, 14, 15, 17, 19, 96, 99,
103, 240n3
arrogance of, 1, 3, 201, 210
Atlantic Divide for, ix, xiii, 1
attitudes in, x, 2, 88
budgeting for, 146–47, 157
bureaucracy in, 27, 49, 103
cartels in, 119, 241n22
Christianity in, 34–35, 236n16
class structure in, 13, 29, 30, 32, 71, 99,
101–2
competition between America and, 4–5,
155–57

concept of freedom in, 1, 14–15, 23, 87–88,
95, 170–71
cultural nationalism in, 25
defense of, 134, 184–85
difference between America and, xii, 4, 5, 9,
11, 12, 15, 27, 28, 33, 42, 50, 79, 82, 85,
91, 92, 98, 122, 123, 128, 154, 165, 166,
194, 220, 221, 225, 235n7
differences between, and England, 16
diplomacy by, 165–66
economic freedom in, 115–16
economic security in, 11
economic strength of, xiii
entitlement in, 22, 23, 78, 96
EU countries of, 227–29
"fax revolution" in, 104
GDP for, 121, 134, 242nn28–29, 243n10
geographical influences on, 46, 48, 227–29,
237n2
governance in, xii, 11, 12–13, 19
governmental patronage in, 21
guns in, 52–53
as history of losing, 12, 167, 235n1
identity of, 34, 169–70, 175, 176
ignorance of America by, xii, 2
immigration to, 119, 242n26
independence of, from U.S., 125
individual responsibility in, 14–15
interdependence of, 87, 169
labor productivity in, 119, 120, 137–38, 140,
174, 241n22, 247n13
land ownership in, 57–58
language in, 64–65, 66, 68–69, 238nn23–
24, 239n29
leadership in, xiii–xiv, 174
military power of, xiii, 135, 158, 184, 186,
200, 207, 209, 214–16
music of, 59, 61, 238n20
NATO for defense of, 124, 157–58, 181,
183, 184, 201, 205, 208–9, 212, 247n10
obligatory diplomacy in, 87
as Old World, 3, 6, 12, 32–33, 34, 36, 40,
42, 165, 166, 208–9, 216
patronage in, 12–13, 58–59
peace for, 4, 125, 183, 186, 210
pessimism in, 13, 60, 63, 90, 97–98, 122,
155
philanthropy in, 32, 156
political will of, xiii
politically elite of, 30, 92, 96, 103, 104
population of, 56–57
privacy in, 56–57

Europe (*continued*)
  private *v.* public sector in, 22–23, 57, 71,
    104, 128–29
  profit motive in, 144–45, 162
  provincialism in, 54–55
  racial/ethnic barriers in, 29, 36
  recovery after WW II in, 91–92, 93, 96–97,
    109–10, 115–16, 241nn13–14
  risktaking in, 94, 161
  shared values between America and, ix, x, xiii,
    33, 181, 200, 201
  slavery in, 36, 178
  social contract in, 102, 104, 105, 108–9, 116,
    118, 128, 163
  socialism in, xii, 26, 96, 98–99, 103, 104,
    109, 117–18, 176
  socio-economic model for, xii, xiv, 4, 9, 12–
    14, 16, 19, 22, 23, 26, 27, 84, 91, 92, 94,
    95–96, 107, 121, 235n7
  stability in, 11, 93
  tax fraud in, 24
  universities in, 16–17
  urbanization in, 63
  use of names in, 82–83
  war in, 11 5–117, 88, 91–92, 93, 96–97,
    106–7, 109–10, 123, 181–82,
    241nn13–14
  welfare dependence in, xii, 14, 95, 112–13
  work ethic in, 121
  work/retirement in, 120, 241n22, 241n24
  world outlook by, xi, 88
Europe Day, 177, 248n18
European Central Bank (ECB), 127, 130, 133–
  34. *See also* European Union
European Coal and Steel Community, 126
European Commission, 126, 129–30, 158–59,
  243n4. *See also* European Economic Community
European Economic Community (EEC)
  Common Market for, 126, 128
  Council of Ministers for, 126
  creation of, 117, 125
  European Coal and Steel Community for,
    126European Commission for, 126, 129–
    30, 143n4, 158–59
  Treaty of Rome for, 126. *See also* European
    Union
European Institute of Technology, 20
"The European Model," xii, xiv, 4, 9, 12–14,
  16, 19, 22, 23, 26, 27, 84, 91, 92, 94, 95–
  96, 107, 121, 235n7
European Monetary Union (EMU), 127, 130,

  147, 227–29. *See also* euros; European
    Union
European Parliament, 68, 105, 126, 171
European Rapid Reaction Force (EURRF), 135
European security and defense policy (ESDP),
  134–35
European socioeconomic model, xii, xiv, 4, 9, 12–
  14, 16, 19, 22, 23, 26, 27, 84, 91, 92, 94,
  95–96, 107, 121, 152, 153, 158, 161, 163,
  173, 223, 235n7
European Union (EU)
  anthem for, 177
  Saint Benedict as Father of, 177
  change through, 122
  Christianity in, 25, 236n16
  competition rules for, 137, 174
  constitution for, 116, 136, 171, 173, 177–78
  countries of, 227–29
  creation of, 4, 123, 125, 172
  currency for, 118, 127, 129–31, 132–33
  customs duties for, 127, 159, 161
  defense forces for, 134
  deficit spending for, 133–34, 135, 137, 147
  ECB for, 127, 130, 133–34
  EMU for, 127, 130, 147, 227–29
  ESDP for, 134–35
  ethnic cleansing and, 186–87
  euros for, 124, 127, 129, 130–31, 139, 162,
    173, 177, 243n7
  European socioeconomic model for, xii, xiv,
    4, 9, 12–14, 16, 19, 22, 23, 26, 27, 84, 91,
    92, 94, 95–96, 107, 121, 152, 153, 158,
    161, 163, 173, 223, 235n7
  fiscal discipline *v.* largesse within, 128
  foreign policy for, 134, 135, 179–80
  Growth and Stability Pact for, 133–34, 135,
    137, 146–47, 151, 157
  harmonization for, 127–28, 133, 135–36,
    143–44
  institutions of, 123, 158
  labor practices in, 137–38, 139–40, 148,
    150, 153, 174, 176, 245n38, 247n13
  language in, 64–65, 66, 68–69, 238nn23–
    24, 239n29
  leadership of, xiii–xiv, 174
  liberal parties in, 105
  Lisbon Agenda for, 127, 130, 133, 136, 137,
    144, 146, 148, 149, 152, 153, 154, 158,
    159, 162, 172
  loyalty to, 24
  Maastricht Treaty for, 129, 130, 139, 173
  motto for, 177

MPS discussion for, 114
opportunity within, 176
pensions in, 120
privatization in, 149–50, 152–53, 161, 172
qualities of, xii
Schengen agreement for, 127, 242n3
security of, 174
single market for, 127, 129, 130, 132, 133,
    135, 137, 146, 154, 157, 160–61
size of, 134, 243n11
taxation in, 127, 141–42, 143, 245n29
Turkey for admittance to, 46, 174, 243n11
visa controls by, 161
work week for, 137–38, 139–40, 150
youth perspective of, 162–63
Europeans
American familiarity with, 45
art of living for, 75
attitude/behavior of, x, 2, 15, 71, 74–75,
    79–81
characteristics of, xi, 9, 29, 69
concept of time for, 75–76, 78
criticism of Europe by, 198–99
historical perspective of, 78–79, 88–89, 167,
    189, 199, 215
identity of, 34, 169–70, 175, 176
indirect approach by, 70–71
mobility of, 55
patriotism of, 24
perspective of America by, 79–82, 88–89, 91
relationships for, 69–70, 197–98, 218, 249n7
sense of tragedy for, 90
superiority of, x
tolerance by, xi
volunteerism by, 84
EURRF. See European Rapid Reaction Force

Fabius, Laurent, 175–76
Faulkner, William, 4
"fax revolution," 104
Federal Reserve Bank, 133. See also America
Feldstein, Martin, 133, 243n9
Fifty Years' War. See Cold War
film, American, 59, 60–61, 63
Financial Times, 60, 94, 240n3
Fitzgerald, Ella, 61
flag, American, 25–26, 43–44, 82, 89, 169,
    188, 204, 224
Foster, Stephen, 61
France, 92, 96, 240n3
American aid by, 52
CFDT in, 150, 245n38

Consul d'Etat in, 150
governance in, xii, 11, 17
language in, 64–65, 68, 238nnn23–25,
    239n29
nationalization of business/industry in, 118
patronage in, 17
PCF in, 117
privatization in, 149–50, 152–53, 161, 172
revolution in, 13
Socialist Party in, 104, 117–18
U.S. debt forgiveness for, 110
at war, 116–17
welfare dependence in, xii, 14, 95, 112–13
Franklin, Benjamin, 33, 37, 78, 166, 220, 223
free trade, 165
freedom
American concept of, xi, 14–15, 23, 28, 44,
    79, 82, 83, 91, 95, 170, 185
defense of, 9, 85–86, 183
diplomacy and, 185, 188
as economic, 115–16
equality v., 151, 155
European concept of, 1, 14–15, 23, 87–88,
    95, 170–71
interpretation of, 9, 11–12, 82
order/stability v., 165, 176, 180–81, 225
peace v., 187–88, 210
quality of life and, 4, 80, 82
threats to, 165–66
"Freedom Trains," 64. See also King, Martin Lu-
    ther, Jr.
French Communist Party (PCF), 117
French National Assembly/Senate, 105, 139,
    148, 150, 175, 217
French Revolution, 13, 18–19, 99
French Socialist Party, 109
Fribourg school of economic/social thought, xiii
Friedman, Milton, 113–14
frontiers, American, 48, 49, 50, 51, 53, 60

GDP. See gross domestic product
German Marshall Fund, 158
Germany
Bundestag in, 151, 205
CDU in, 111–12
currency reform in, 115
economic freedom in, 115
free-market economy for, xii–xiii
Fribourg school of economic/social thought
    in, xiii
governance in, xii, 11
Hitler/Nazis in, 21, 103, 241n22

Germany (*continued*)
    language in, 64–65, 238nn23–24
    in NATO, 183
    occupation of, 114
    Party of Democratic Socialism in, 103
    patronage in, 17–18
    rearmament of, 183
    Social Democratic Party in, 103, 111, 114,
        138–39
    social market economy for, 115, 116
    socialism in, 103
    tax avoidance in, 24
    unification of, 54, 129
    welfare dependence in, xii, 14, 95, 112–13
Gettysburg Address (Lincoln), 34
The Girl of the Golden West (Puccini), 63
Giroud, Françoise, 60
global warming, 165–66
globalization, xi, xii, 165, 172, 174, 193–96,
        198, 249n3. *See also* essential difference
Goethe, Johann Wolfgang von, 168, 246n1
Google, 20
Gorbachev, Michael, 31
government
    American model of, xi, xii, 4, 9, 26, 30, 32,
        37, 90–91, 92, 94, 96, 121–22, 138, 153–
        54, 161, 223
    dirigist/statist as, 105, 106, 152, 161
    European model of, xii, xiv, 4, 9, 12–14, 16,
        19, 22, 23, 26, 27, 84, 91, 92, 94, 95–96,
        107, 121, 235n7
    European statism as, 94
    obligations of, 21–22
    role/size of, 106
    trust in, 108
government, dirigist/statist, 105, 106, 152, 161
Great Depression, 111
Great Seal, of the United States, 37
Greenspan, Alan, 133. *See also* Federal Reserve
        Bank
gross domestic product (GDP), 121, 134,
        242nn28–29, 243n10
"ground zero." *See* September 11, 2001
Growth and Stability Pact, 133–34, 135, 137,
        146–47, 151, 157
guns, preoccupation with, 52–53

Hacke, Christian, 185–86
Handel, George Frideric, 40
Hanson, Victor Davis, 217
harmonization, tax, 143–44. *See also* taxation
Harrison, Rex, 64–65

Harvard University, 20
Hayek, Friedrich A., xiii, 21, 33, 100, 113–14,
        220
Hayward, Steven, 179
Hegel, Friedrich, 100
Herold, Sabine, 148
Hitler, Adolf, 21, 103, 241n22. *See also* Ger-
        many
Hoff, T.J.B., 113–14
Hollande, François, 109, 175
"Home on the Range," 61
Hook, Sidney, 216
Hoover Institution, 5, 6, 120

IG Metall, 138, 151
ILO. *See* International Labor Office
IMF. *See* International Monetary Fund
immigration
    to America, 30, 32, 35, 37, 42–43, 49, 60,
        63–64, 81, 99, 108, 110, 145, 155
    cultural influence through, 38–42, 67, 231–
        32, 237n20
    English language for, 39, 42, 64, 67
    to Europe, 119, 242n26
    from Ireland, 43
"In God We Trust," 35
"In the Footsteps of Tocqueville" (Lévy), 25
individual
    respect for, 34, 53
    responsibility of, 13–15, 21–22, 52, 93, 97,
        108
    social equality of, 34, 92
    state *v.,* 22–23, 24, 28, 97, 108, 145
individualism, for Americans, 13–15, 52, 93, 97
industrial revolution, 99–100, 100–101, 102
Information Age, 66
Institut Montaigne, 154
"The International" (Degeyter; Paul; Pottier),
        100, 233–34
International Herald Tribune, 48, 194
International Labor Office (ILO), 120, 241n24
International Monetary Fund (IMF), 106
Internet, 165–66, 169
interventionism, 161, 174
Iraq war, 89, 90, 136, 180, 206, 209, 211–13
Ireland, xii, 43
Iron Curtain, ix, 112. *See also* Cold War
Ischinger, Wolfgang, 222
Islamic Fundamentalism, 193
isolationism, American, 83, 239n41
Issing, Otmar, 132
Italy, patronage in, 17

jazz, 39, 59
Jefferson, Thomas, 37, 86
Jews, murder of, 182
Jospin, Lionel, 27, 109, 138, 139, 149–50
Juncker, Jean-Claude, 221
Jusserand, Jean-Jules, ix, x–xi, 56, 190–99,
    238n14

Kagan, Robert, 200, 201, 205, 212, 214, 250n7
Kennedy, John F., 15, 31
Kertesz, Imre, 170
King, Martin Luther, Jr., 63, 64
Koch, Burkhard, 48–50, 54–55, 80, 145–46,
    237n4
Koestler, Arthur, 72–73
Kohl, Helmut, 214
Korean War, 89
Kroes, Neelie, 161
Kulturstaat (state culture), 15–16, 21

labor
    American productivity by, 120, 241n22
    EU practices by, 137–38, 139–40, 148, 150,
        153, 174, 176, 245n38, 247n13
    European productivity by, 119, 120, 137–38,
        140, 174, 241n22, 247n13
    social dumping of, 160, 174, 247n13
language, English
    domination of, 66, 68–69
    by Europeans, 64–65, 66, 68–69,
        238nnn23–25, 239nn29–30
    by immigrants, 39, 42, 64, 65, 67
    study of, by Americans, 64–68
Lantos, Tom, 212
Lavoisier, Antoine, 99
Lazarus, Emma, 224
le Carré, John, 203, 204
Le Figaro Magazine, 132, 226, 243n10
Le Monde, 203, 213
leadership
    in America, xiv, 25, 202, 209, 211–12, 213,
        216, 217, 240n43
    aspects of, ix, xiii, 106, 107, 211, 216
    by EU, xiii–xiv, 174
Lellouche, Pierre, 105, 106
Lenin, Nikolai, 103
Les Echos (journal), 143
"Letters from a Regicide Peace" (Burke), 224
Lévy, Bernard-Henri, 25
liberalism, classical, xiii, 33, 36
Liberty Oath, 34, 236n15
Liikanen, Erkki, 161

Lincoln, Abraham, 34, 35
Lisbon Agenda, 127, 130, 133, 136, 137, 144,
    146, 148, 149, 152, 153, 154, 158, 159,
    162, 172. *See also* European Union
Lisbon Strategy. *See* Lisbon Agenda
"The Lisbon Strategy: Why Less Is More," 152
Lord of the Rings (Tolkien), 60–61

Maastricht, 127. *See also* European Union
Maastricht Treaty, 129, 130, 139, 173. *See also*
    European Union
Machlup, Fritz, 113–14
Madison, James, 37
Magna Carta, 16, 235n3
Malraux, André, 169
market, common, 4
marketplace
    competition in, 110, 111, 114–15, 159
    deregulation of, 137
    in Europe, 128–29, 154–55
    incentives for, 155
    inequality of, 140
    injustice of, 100
    MPS support of, 113–15
    regulation of, 92, 101, 108–9, 115–16
    under socialism, 109
    support of, xiv, 4, 92, 109, 148
    WW II and, 111, 209
Marshall Plan, 110, 124, 241n14. *See also* World
    War II
Marx, Karl, 100, 102
Massachusetts Institute of Technology (MIT),
    20
Mzenatentum (patronage), 15–16, 21
McCarthy, Mary, 146
McCreevy, Charlie, 160
media, American, European news by, 81
Merkel, Angela, 194
Messiah, 40
Michel, Louis, 189–90
military power, xiii, 135, 158, 184, 186, 200,
    207, 209, 214–16
Mises, Ludwig von, 113–14
MIT. *See* Massachusetts Institute of Technology
Mitterrand, François, 117–18, 175
Mosi, Dominique, 94, 186, 199
monetary system, international
    Bretton Woods agreement as, 124, 242n1. *See*
        also currency
Monnet, Jean, 170
Monroe, James, 86
Mont Pèlerin Society (MPS), 113–15, 159

Mordden, Ethan, 62
MPS. *See* Mont Pèlerin Society
Muir, John, 51
Muirhead, James, 57
Mntefering, Franz, 139, 151
Muslims, in America, 231
My Fair Lady (Shaw), 64–65, 68

National Security Council, 206–7
National Socialist Workers Party, 103
nationalism, cultural, 25
nationalization
    of business/industry, 110, 118
    privatization v., 149–50, 152–53, 161, 172
Native Americans, treatment of, 54
NATO. *See* North Atlantic Treaty Organization
Nazis, 21, 103, 241n22
The New World Symphony (Dvorak), 41
Newsweek, 34
9/11. *See* September 11, 2001
"No Man Is an Island" (Donne), 86
nobility, European. *See* aristocracy, European
noblesse oblige, 22
North Atlantic Treaty Organization (NATO),
    124, 157–58, 181, 183, 201, 205, 208–9,
    212, 227–28, 247n10

painting
    by Americans, 59–60, 63
    by Europeans, 58–59
Party of Democratic Socialism, 103. *See also*
    Germany; socialism
patriotism
    of Americans, 24–25, 43–44, 82, 89–90
    of Europeans, 24
patronage
    in America, 30
    for arts/architecture, 17, 58–59
    beneficiaries of, 17
    dependence upon, 18, 19, 21
    by European aristocracy, 17–18
    legacy of, 18
    Mzenatentum as, 15–16, 21
    practice of, 12–13, 15–16
    transformation of, 19
    for universities, 16–17
Patten, Christopher, 203
Paul, C./E., 233–34
PCF. *See* French Communist Party
peace
    military strength *v.,* xiii, 135, 158, 184, 186,
        200, 207, 209–10, 214–16
    pursuit of, 4, 125, 183, 210

Pearl Harbor, 89, 188, 204
Perle, Richard, 212–13
Pfaff, William, 179
philanthropy
    by Americans, 13, 19–20, 31, 53, 156,
        235n4, 237n10
    CARE packages as, 53, 237n10, 241n13
    in Europe, 32, 156
    for universities, 19–20, 31
Pius XII, 177
Plesu, Andrei, 170
Popper, Karl, 113–14
Porter, Cole, 61
Pottier, Eugene, 233–34
poverty, alleviation of, 165–66
power
    military, of Europe, xiii, 135, 158, 184, 186,
        200, 207, 209, 214–16
    "soft" *v.* "hard," 165–66
"Power and Weakness" (Kagan), 200–201
private sector, public sector *v.,* 22–23, 57, 71,
    104, 128–29
productivity, labor, 119, 120, 137–38, 140,
    174, 241n22, 247n13
prosperity, pursuit of, 4
public sector, private sector *v.,* 22–23, 57, 71,
    101–2, 104, 128–29. *See also* state
Puccini, Giacomo, 63

Al Qaeda, 203, 205–6
Quaero, 20

race
    in America, 29, 36, 63
    in Europe, 29, 36
Raffarin, Jean-Pierre, 109, 150, 159–60
Rasmussen, Anders Fogh, 194
Reagan, Ronald, 30–31, 105–6, 118, 243n9
regulation
    competition/growth *v.* stability and, 92, 93,
        108–9, 111, 115–16, 180–81
    of market by government, 92, 108–9, 115–16
Requiem for a Nun (Faulkner), 4
retirement, 119–20, 120, 241n22, 241n24,
    241n33
Revel, Jean-François, 186, 221
Rice, Condoleezza, 88
risktaking
    in America, 121–22, 161
    in Europe, 94, 161
The Road To Serfdom (Hayek), 21, 113
Robbins, Lionel, 113–14

Rochefoucauld, Duc de La, 193
Rockefeller, John D., 198
Rodgers, T.J., 122
Roosevelt, Franklin D., 61, 109–10
Roosevelt, Theodore, ix, 217, 236n17
Rpke, Wilhelm, 113–14
Rousseau, Henri, 100
Royal Elcano Institute, 169
Rueff, Jacques, 130, 243n4
Rumsfeld, Donald, 212
Russia, socialism in, 103
Rstow, Alexander, 113–14

Saddam Hussein, 213
safety, state control for, xii
Schengen agreement, 127, 242n3. See also European Union
Schneider, Peter, 68, 83, 188
School for National Administration (ENA), 96, 240n3
Schrder, Gerhard, 138, 139, 150, 151, 153, 159–60, 163, 205, 211, 245n29
Schwarzenegger, Arnold, 31
Scotland, governance in, 16
September 11, 2001 (9/11), ix, 2, 43–44, 84, 186, 188, 200, 201, 202–4, 213, 232, 249n17. See also terrorism, war on; World Trade Center
Servan-Schreiber, Jean-Jacques, 155
Shaw, George Bernard, 16, 64–65
"The Significance of the Frontier in American History" (Turner), 50–51
Simonis, Heide, 189, 190, 202
Sinatra, Frank, 61
slavery, 36, 178
social contract
    for European countries, 102, 104, 105, 108–9, 116, 118, 128, 163
    Growth and Stability Pact and, 133–34, 135, 137, 146–47, 151, 157. See also Europe; socialism
Social Democratic Party (Germany), 103, 111, 114, 138–39. See also Germany; socialism
social dumping, 160, 174, 247n13. See also labor
social market economy, 115, 116. See also Germany
Social Security, 120
socialism
    in America, 98–99
    arguments against, 26
    class structure under, 101–2
    collapse of, 98

Communist Party of the Soviet Union under, 103
    competition and, 100, 109, 111
    decline of, 176
    dictators under, 102
    effect of, 105, 240n8
    equality under, 96, 100, 101, 238n24
    in Europe, xii, 26, 96, 98–99, 103, 104, 109, 117–18, 176
    "The European Model" and, xii, xiv, 4, 9, 12–14, 16, 19, 22, 23, 26, 27, 84, 91, 92, 94, 95–96, 107, 121, 235n7
    free market and, 109
    French Socialist Party under, 104, 109
    in Germany, 103, 240n8
    as government from top down, 102
    ideology of, 101
    Industrial Revolution and, 99–100, 100–101, 102
    "The International" for, 100, 233–34
    National Socialist Workers Party under, 103
    origin of, xii, 99–100
    Party of Democratic Socialism under, 103
    in Russia, 103
    social contract under, 102, 104, 105, 108–9, 116, 118, 128, 163
    Social Democratic Party (Germany) under, 103, 111, 114, 138–39
    Socialist Party (France) for, 117–18
    Socialist Unity Party (Germany) under, 103
    taxation under, 19–20, 24, 103–4, 108–9
    after WW II, 111–12
Socialist Party (France), 117–18
Socialist Unity Party (Germany), 103
Solana, Javier, 173, 247n10
Solzhenitsyn, Alexander, 66
Sorman, Guy, 148, 175, 249n17
Soviet Union. See Russia, socialism in
Spain, use of English in, 69, 239n30
stability
    competition/growth v. regulation and, 92, 93, 108–9, 111, 115–16, 180–81
    EU for, 178, 180
    after World War II, 11, 93. See also Growth and Stability Pact
Stalin, Joseph, 103
Stanford University, 20
Star Wars, 60–61
"Stars and Stripes." See flag, American
state
    agricultural policy by, 21, 106, 128, 165
    control by, xii, 27

state (*continued*)
  employee of, 21
  entitlement from, 22, 23, 78, 96
  individual *v.*, 22–23, 24, 28, 97, 108, 145
  largesse of, 19, 23, 24
  philanthropy *v.* benevolence of, 32, 156
  as public sector, 22–23, 57, 71, 104, 128–29
  role of, 14–15, 21
  separation of church and, 35–36
  taxation by, 19–20, 24, 103–4, 108–9, 128
statism, criticism of, 94
Statue of Liberty, 224
Stigler, George, 113–14
Straw, Jack, 209, 221–22
sufferance, 155

Taliban, 203, 205–6
Tate museum, 59–60
taxation
  in EU, 19–20, 24, 103–4, 106, 108–9, 127,
    128, 141–44, 244n25, 245n29
  VAT as, 142–43, 244n25
Taylor, A.J.P., 87, 110–11
terrorism, war on, ix, 2, 43–44, 90, 202–6. *See
  also* World Trade Center
Thanksgiving, 12, 35, 48, 236n17
Thatcher, Margaret, xii–xiii, 23, 31, 106–7,
  129, 141, 148, 158–59, 244n22
theater, musical, 59, 60, 61, 62, 63, 238n21
Theophrastus, 78
think tank, 22
The Times, 203
"To The United States" (von Goethe), 168,
  246n1
Tocqueville, Alexis de, 25, 37–38, 113, 146, 198
Tolkien, J.R.R., 60–61
totalitarianism, xiii
Treaty of Rome, 126. *See also* European Eco-
  nomic Community
Trevoux, F., 113–14
Truman, Harry, 30–31
Turkey, EU membership for, 46, 174, 243n11
Turner, Frederick Jackson, 50–51

UNESCO, 165–66
unilateralism, American, 83, 186, 221. *See also*
  America
United Nations, 165–66, 208, 215
United States. *See* America
universities
  in America, 20
  beneficiaries of, 17

  in Europe *v.* America, 19–20
  patronage for, 16–17
  philanthropy for, 19–20, 31
U.S. Census Bureau, 64
U.S. Constitution, 28, 52, 107. *See also* America
U.S. Defense Policy Board, 212
U.S. Treasury, in bankruptcy, 124, 242n1. *See
  also* America

value-added tax (VAT), 142–43, 244n25
Verheugen, Gnter, 172
Vershbow, Alexander, 201
Vietnam War, 89
volunteerism
  by Americans, 13, 84, 95, 156
  by Europeans, 84
vote, right to, 36

Wall Street Journal, 152, 208
war
  Civil War, 89, 188
  Cold War, ix, xii, 2, 31, 86, 87, 123, 124,
    125, 158, 163, 184, 207, 208–9
  in Europe, 88, 91–92, 93, 96–97, 106–7,
    109–10, 115–17, 123, 181–82, 186–88,
    241nn13–14
  in Iraq, 89, 90, 136, 180, 206, 209, 211–13
  in Korea, 89
  on terrorism, ix, 2, 43–44, 90, 202–6
  in Vietnam, 89
  WW I, 13, 84–85, 89, 90
  WW II, x, 26, 30–31, 53, 84–85, 89, 90,
    109–10, 237n10, 241nn13–14
  WW II for America as, 53, 91–92, 93, 96–97,
    109–10, 115–16, 123, 124, 182–83,
    237n10, 241nn13–14
Washington, George, 28
Wayne, John, 60
welfare dependence, xii, 14, 95, 112–13
White Christmas" (Berlin), 40
Wilde, Oscar, 78, 79
Wilson, John, 28
Wordsworth, William, 76
The World As I See It (Jospin), 27, 109, 138,
  139, 149–50
"The World Is Too Much with Us" (Words-
  worth), 76
World Trade Center, 9/11 attack on, ix, 2, 43–
  44, 84, 186, 188, 200, 201, 202–4, 213,
  232, 249n17
World War I (WW I), 13, 84–85, 89, 90

World War II (WW II), x, 26, 30–31, 53, 84–
85, 89, 90, 109–10, 237n10, 241nn13–
14237n10
for America, 53, 91–92, 93, 96–97, 109–10,
115–16, 123, 124, 182–83, 237n10,
241nn13–14
Bretton Woods agreement following, 124,
242n1
British restructuring after, 106–7
CARE packages after, 53, 237n10, 241n13

European recovery after, 91–92, 93, 96–97,
109–10, 115–16, 241nn13–14
hostilities after, 123
marketplace as responsible for, 111
Marshall Plan after, 110, 124, 241n14
socialism after, 111–12
WW I. *See* World War I
WW II. *See* World War II

Zinneman, Fred, 60